PART
OF THE
CLIMATE

PART
◻ OF THE
CLIMATE

American
Cubist Poetry

Jacqueline Vaught Brogan

University of California Press
Berkeley   Los Angeles   Oxford

University of California Press
Berkeley and Los Angeles, California

University of California Press
Oxford, England

Copyright © 1991 by The Regents of the University of California

Library of Congress Cataloging-in-Publication Data
Brogan, Jacqueline Vaught, 1952–
    Part of the climate : cubism and twentieth-century American
    poetry / Jacqueline Vaught Brogan.
      p.   cm.
    Includes bibliographical references.
    ISBN 0-520-06848-3 (alk. paper)
    1. American poetry—20th century—History and criticism. 2. Art
and literature—United States—History—20th century. 3. Cubism
and literature—United States. I. Title
PS310.A76B7   1990   90-34743
811'.52091—dc20   CIP

Printed in the United States of America

9 8 7 6 5 4 3 2 1

Contents

CONTENTS

CONTENTS

Preface

Because Bob Coady is dead there is nothing to be hoped for of just the unique spirit that made The Soil *so brilliantly provocative of new art forms and of controversial opinions about them.* The Soil *was first cousin to the free-verse movement in America which crystallized in Alfred Kreymborg's group of* Others. *That was a magic moment. No one who was touched by the kindling breath will ever forget the joy of it nor cease to regret that a great fiery wind devoured it. It will be worth while some day to review that frail but vital page in literary history.*

ROBERT ALDEN SANBORN
"A Champion in the Wilderness,"
Broom 3, 3 (Oct. 1922), 174–5

While Robert Sanborn obviously thought the "kindling breath" in modern literary history had been extinguished by 1922, the energy driving the creation and publication of a new kind of poetry — what I am here calling "cubist poetry" — was still extending itself not only in America but throughout Europe as well. Far from being simply a "free verse" movement, cubist poetry, at least in the United States, developed specifically in response to exhibitions and reproductions of various cubist paintings and drawings, as well as through continued interaction with a number of cubist painters. Eventually, this new aesthetic would influence virtually every major American poet in this century, so that this "magic moment" marks not the end but rather the beginning of a critical phase in modernism which indeed proves to be a "vital page in literary history."

While other critics may argue that some other aesthetic movement such as futurism or expressionism best defines the modernist movement or, perhaps, best defines the twentieth-century mentality in general, I agree that cubism is "still today the greatest single aesthetic achievement of the century,"[1] one that revolutionized cinematography, drama, prose, and poetry, as well as painting and sculpture. As Henry Sayre says, cubism is "the movement that began everything in the first place,"[2] a remark that can be extended to the *verbal* arts of this century as well as to the visual. Rather than having ended in 1922, when Sanborn lamented the passing of this phase of literary history, the effect of cubism on twentieth-century poetry spread over the next decade and continues to be felt today, most obviously in the L = A = N = G = U = A = G = E poets, but also in the continued work of such poets as Louis Zukofsky and George Oppen. Nonetheless, cubist poetry may have reached its zenith in the late 1920s and early 1930s in the poetry published in such American journals as *Blues* and *Pagany* and in their European counterparts such as *transition*. In fact, as a specific movement, the force of cubism in poetry appears to have waned dramatically during the Second World War, as many artists, poets, and editors previously interested in cubism responded to the horrors of another global war by turning, in an aesthetic gesture, to surrealism or expressionism. Charles Henri Ford, for example, who had earlier edited *Blues* (a journal prominent here), founded *View* in the early 1940s as yet another avant-garde magazine concerned with modern visual and verbal aesthetics. Rapidly, however, as the Second World War progressed, the magazine became more exclusively surrealistic, then almost sadistic in some respects, when, for example, it introduced a "Children's Page" no child should see.

The cubist moment (if we can call it that) has in its verbal form a particular historical constraint and context—that is, the brackets formed by the two world wars. While it may be purely an accident that Picasso would develop cubist techniques in painting (techniques which were rather quickly recognized as corresponding to the fragmented, postwar mentality) *before* the Great War began, it is historically and even politically no accident that cubism in literature largely falls between the Great War (appropriately renamed, in a kind of cubist twisting of perspective, with a number) and World War II. In literature, and in poetry in particular, the cubist moment epitomizes a political moment which at once represents and ironically critiques the growing sense of discontinuity which seems to have become almost universal during this period. In this regard, it is especially interesting to note that in his 1930 essay, "Picasso's Method," A. Hyatt Mayor simply assumes his readers' recognition of the artist's "uncanny prescience" in developing cubism, which he further describes as having "flaired, in 1907 or so, *the jangled nerves of after the war*" (italics mine). Mayor goes on to observe that

Picasso was abandoning his "post war" mood even before the war had ended. Just as he anticipated that chaos by a number of years, so he anticipated the present reorganization, the new classicism that is now busying the freshest minds.[3]

If there was a sense of "present reorganization" in the first year of that decade, it was almost immediately shattered in America and in Europe by the economic crisis begun on Wall Street the preceding October (a crisis that would continue to be felt, in great extremities, through 1933) and, then, by a growing dis-ease, as the inevitability of another world war began to prey on the modern consciousness. Thus Mayor's description of Picasso's "uncanny prescience" is apropos of the entire interim war period, for cubism—ironically an artistic movement initially concerned with form—rapidly evolved into a movement which characteristically fractured form and, by extension, all traditional ways of ordering and rendering the world as intelligible. And it is precisely this sense of fracturing, fragmentation, even chaos that comes to be expressed in some of the most famous literature written between the wars, such as William Faulkner's *The Sound and the Fury* or T. S. Eliot's *The Waste Land*.

It is not without significance that, however unintentionally, the "uncanny prescience" of cubist techniques had a specific manifestation in the Great War itself. As Stephen Kern has recently pointed out, the man who created camouflage for the French troops during the middle of this war—a creation necessitated by the fact that traditional military dress had become virtually "suicidal," given the new, long-range weaponry—knew of Picasso's work and used cubist techniques in the making of camouflage:[4]

> In order to totally deform objects, I employed the means Cubists used to represent them—later this permitted me, without giving reasons, to hire in my [camouflage] section some painters, who, because of their very special vision, had an aptitude for *denaturing any kind of form whatsoever.* (emphasis added)

Kern has even argued that the Great War itself may be most accurately understood as the Cubist War, one in which the broken trench lines, for example, are metonymous for the inadequacy of older traditions—even the tradition of the heroic front line in battle—in the modern world. It is almost chilling that Gertrude Stein reports that Picasso's response to first seeing a camouflaged truck was to cry out, "yes it is we who made it, that is cubism."[5]

The dramatic change in the world's mentality which this connection between visual cubism and the Great War suggests, however, was not largely expressed — with a few notable exceptions — in American poetry until *after* the war, with the widespread "disillusionment" of the postwar period and a concurrent, impassioned interest in social reform. The force of cubism in American poetry thus does not reach its zenith until the late 1920s and early 1930s, though as a force it may well have its earliest expressions in many of the first works reprinted here. Together, they trace at least in part the critical development of an American cubist poetics. This collection, which is intended to add to our understanding of the poetic climate in which such famous poets as William Carlos Williams, E. E. Cummings, and Wallace Stevens first began practicing their verse, potentially offers new insights into the nature of "modernism" itself by challenging the presumption of a Pounds/Williams tradition from which Stevens, among others, is notably excluded. The various poems collected in this volume suggest a way of "seeing" such diverse poets, at least in the early years, as responding to (and as responsive to) the same climate and, consequently, they suggest the need for further exploration into both why and when such poets eventually diverge.

For example, although in his 1951 essay, "The Relations between Poetry and Painting," Stevens would distinguish between "two classes" of modern poetry — "one that is modern in respect to what it says, the other that is modern in respect to form"[6] — in the early stages of his career, Stevens does experiment with modern "form," at least in a minimal way, precisely when he is producing his own cubist poems. The point at which he rejects cubist experimentation (although, I would argue, he never rejects it entirely) seems, ironically, to correspond with a loss of faith in the power of this new aesthetic to discover an undisclosed order in the chaos of the modern world.[7] As Sayre has argued, cubism (and also expressionism and surrealism in both visual and verbal forms) is informed by the "sense that in the abstract lay a revelation of order which might unify the chaos of modernity."[8] In the verbal realm at least, however, cubism largely fails to create such a new order, and Stevens' subsequent recourse to an inner "resistance" to the increasing violence of reality may have been prompted by far more social awareness (and even purpose) than he is usually credited with having. Conversely, Pound's continued preoccupation with the material *form* of poetry — including the effects of verbal collage in *The Cantos* or "Homage to Sextus Propertius" — signals with even greater irony a particular *idealism,* a more enduring faith in the power of the word to have actual social and political consequences.[9] Yet for all their differences, it is obvious that both Pound and Stevens agree that the "modern stage" has changed utterly in the twentieth century, as they clarify in "Hugh Selwyn Mauberly" and "Of Modern Poetry," respectively.[10]

That the stage—or the climate, as it were—did indeed change around the beginning of the Great War, with ramifications that extend well into poetic expressions, is made painfully clear if we consider the difference between T. S. Eliot's *The Waste Land*, published after the war, and Madison Cawein's far more nostalgic "Waste Land," published in *Poetry*, one year before the Great War began:

Waste Land

Briar and fennel and chincapin,
    And rue and ragweed everywhere;
The field seemed sick as a soul with sin,
    Or dead of an old despair,
    Born of an ancient care.

The cricket's cry and the locust's whirr,
    And the note of a bird's distress,
With the rasping sound of the grasshopper,
    Clung to the loneliness
    Like burrs to a trailing dress.

So sad the field, so waste the ground,
    So curst with an old despair,
A woodchuck's burrow, a blind mole's mound,
    And a chipmunk's stony lair,
    Seemed more than it could bear.

So lonely, too, so more than sad,
    So droning-lone with bees—
I wondered what more could Nature add
    To the sum of its miseries . . .
    And *then*—I saw the trees.

Skeletons gaunt that gnarled the place,
    Twisted and torn they rose—
The tortured bones of a perished race
    Of monsters no mortal knows,
    They startled the mind's repose.

And a man stood there, as still as moss,
    A lichen form that stared;
With an old blind hound that, at a loss,
    Forever around him fared
    With a snarling fang half bared.

I looked at the man; I saw him plain;
 Like a dead weed, gray and wan,
Or a breath of dust. I looked again —
 And man and dog were gone,
 Like wisps of the graying dawn. . . .

Were they a part of the grim death there —
 Ragweed, fennel, and rue?
Or forms of the mind, an old despair,
 That there into semblance grew
 Out of the grief I knew?

MADISON CAWEIN
Poetry 1 (4), 1913

The difference between Cawein's and Eliot's rendering of the modern waste land metrically, logically, and structurally defines a critical change in consciousness, in politics, and in aesthetics, which is radicalized as well as symbolized by the first "Great" war of this century. As Dorothy Norman says in her introduction to the reprinting of *291,* "The creators of *291* were affected by free verse, by Cubism, Futurism and Expressionism; by interest in the unconscious; *above all by the war*"[11] (italics mine). For most of the poets included in this volume, the actual *formal* expression of Cawein's poem (however "modern" it may or may not be in theme) is no longer possible, aesthetically or politically, for the poetry of this century. And while cubism must inevitably prove only a part of the climate, it seems to me that in this aesthetic development — one which intentionally dismantles traditional forms while evoking multiple perspectives — we find a salient metaphor or, perhaps more accurately, a salient metonym, for understanding our changed and changing world.

J. V. B.

Acknowledgments

I am indebted to the late O. B. Hardison, Jr., for the initial and then continued encouragement for this project; to Edward Weismiller, Jr., Louis Mackey, Marsha Stevenson, and Jeffrey Roessner for help in research; and to Linda Taylor for many editorial suggestions. In addition, I must thank the generous librarians at the various libraries in which I worked for their help in locating material, but most particularly, Linda Gregory. I also wish to express my gratitude to the Institute for Study in the Liberal Arts at the University of Notre Dame for the financial support needed to bring this project to completion.

I would especially like to thank first Scott Mahler and then Shirley Warren who, as editors, so skillfully guided this book through production; to Deborah Birns the copyeditor, and to Linda Robertson for carefully designing a difficult manuscript.

Finally, I am indebted to the work of many fine scholars and critics, whose work informs every page of this text, often without specific acknowledgment.

As always, I owe more than I can express to Terry Brogan for both practical and moral support.

ACKNOWLEDGEMENTS

1968 by Marion Morehouse Cummings; "this evangelist" and "now that fierce few" are reprinted from *Is 5* by E. E. Cummings, edited by George James Firmage, by permission of Liveright Publishing Corporation, copyright © 1985 by E. E. Cummings Trust; copyright 1926 by Horace Liveright; copyright © 1954 by E. E. Cummings; copyright © 1985 by George James Firmage; "let's start a magazine" and "ondumonde'" are reprinted from *No Thanks* by E. E. Cummings, edited by George James Firmage, by permission of Liveright Publishing Corporation, copyright 1935 by E. E. Cummings; copyright © 1968 by Marion Morehouse Cummings; copyright © 1972, 1978 by the Trustees for the E. E. Cummings Trust; copyright © 1973, 1978 by George James Firmage; "Buffalo Bill's," "O sweet spontaneous," "stinging," "ta," "the skinny voice," "when the spent day begins to frail," "my smallheaded pearshaped," "the wind is a Lady with," and "as usual i did not find him in cafes, the more dissolute atmosphere" are reprinted from *Tulips & Chimneys* by E. E. Cummings, edited by George James Firmage, by permission of Liveright Publishing Corporation, copyright 1923, 1925 and renewed 1951, 1953 by E. E. Cummings; copyright © 1973, 1976 by the Trustees for the E. E. Cummings Trust; copyright © 1973, 1976 by George James Firmage. "Buffalo Bill's," "O sweet spontaneous," "Sunset" ("stinging"), "'let's start a magazine,'" and "'ondumonde'" are reprinted in this volume as they appeared originally in journals and magazines prior to publication in book volumes of Cummings' poetry.

Selected Poems by E. E. Cummings from *Complete Poems* Vol. I and Vol. II (UK and Commonwealth), Grafton Books, a division of the Collins Publishing Group.

"Drawing," "Off Hours" by George Oppen: *Collected Poems,* copyright © 1934, 1972 by George Oppen, New Directions Publishing Corporation; "The Return," "Villanelle" by Ezra Pound: *Personae,* copyright 1926 by Ezra Pound, New Directions Publishing Corporation and Faber & Faber Ltd. "Canto XXIII" by Ezra Pound: *The Cantos of Ezra Pound,* copyright 1934 by Ezra Pound, New Directions Publishing Corporation and Faber & Faber Ltd. "Into the Shandy Westerness" by Kenneth Rexroth: *Collected Shorter Poems,* copyright 1940 by Kenneth Rexroth, New Directions Publishing Corporation. "The Hothouse Plant," "Four Poems," "The Moon" by William Carlos Williams, copyright 1989 by William Eric Williams and P. H. Williams, New Directions Publishing Corporation Agents; "Metric Figure," "The Descent of Winter," "Rain," "El Hombre," "In the 'Sconset Bus," "The Attic Which is Desire," "Perpetuum Mobile" by William Carlos Williams: *Collected Poems 1909–1939 Volume I,* copyright 1938 by New Directions Publishing Corporation.

"Three Portraits of Painters: Picasso" from *Selected Writings of Gertrude Stein,* edited by Carl Van Vechten, copyright © 1946 by Random House, Inc.

"Bison," "Wild Sunflower," "To the Painter Polelonema," "Snow Ghost" from the *Collected Poems of Ivor Winters,* 1978 Swallow Press. Ohio University Press/ Swallow Press.

Poems by Mina Loy by permission of the Jardon Society, the daughters of Mina Loy (Joella Bayer and Fabienne Benedict), and the editor of her complete writings (Roger L. Conover).

Permission to reprint Gertrude Stein was given by Random House and Levin & Gann; permission to reprint Wallace Stevens was given by Alfred A. Knopf; two poems by Ernest Kroll were used with permission by the poet. The poems of Louis Zukofsky were reprinted with the permission of Paul Zukofsky.

Every attempt was made to locate copyrights for other authors not mentioned above. As far as possible, this volume endeavors to reproduce the material as it first appeared in the small magazines from which it was taken. In the case of E. E. Cummings and Mina Loy, in particular, the original versions of poetry in the small magazines may differ from either changed or corrected versions in subsequent final editions.

PART
☐ OF THE
CLIMATE

Introduction

My purpose here is to trace an important part of a major literary develop-
ment (if not *the* major literary development) in American verse during the
first part of this century by offering a brief discussion and select gathering
of American cubist poetry. Numerous critics such as Henry M. Sayre,
William Marling, Marjorie Perloff, and Glen MacLeod (to mention only a
few) have already demonstrated at length the impact of cubism in the
visual arts on such well-known twentieth-century American poets as
William Carlos Williams, Ezra Pound, and Wallace Stevens, and other
critics have shown the critical influence of cubism on numerous other
American poets as well.[1] My purpose here is not to repeat those argu-
ments, which convincingly show a newly perceived relationship between
visual and verbal texts—a relationship brought to its most extreme ex-
pression in some of the later cubist paintings by the inclusion of words as
signs of themselves—that influenced the developing aesthetics of many of
our best modern poets. Rather, I wish to offer a discussion and presenta-
tion of the poetry which demonstrates in praxis both the development
and the extent of this modern aesthetic in its American context. Yet, even
here, the relationship of the visual and the verbal media during this
period (largely the interim war years) is itself much more complex than
this present volume can suggest. In fact, cubism, (which I regard as the
quintessential twentieth-century form of expression) is only one of the
forces in what we loosely call "modernism," and at least some poets of this
time, including both Williams and Stevens, responded to a wide range of
movements in the visual arts. Thus, I should stress, cubism is finally only
part of the picture.

Before considering the development of American cubist poetry,
however, it is necessary to discuss the fact that *cubist literature* in general
and *cubist poetry* in particular are terms which have been debated since
they were first coined, and have been variously defined, if accepted as

3

valid terms for a verbal medium at all. In part because the French poet Apollinaire (who enthusiastically embraced the cubist aesthetic in his *Les peintres cubistes,* 1913) denied being a cubist poet, and in part because of a theoretical questioning of the validity of transferring a term to describe one artistic medium to another, several critics have denied the existence of cubist literature altogether.[2] Picasso himself implicitly rejects the transference of "cubism" to any literary genre when he complains in 1923 that

> mathematics, trigonometry, chemistry, psychoanalysis, music, and whatnot, have been related to cubism to give it an easier interpretation. All this has been pure literature, not to say nonsense, which has only succeeded in blinding people with theories.

He even says that "Cubism has kept itself within the limits and limitations of painting, never pretending to go beyond it,"[3] a remark which should, if taken literally, preclude the possiblity of cubist sculpture as well.

Yet Picasso's complaint—or apologia for the pictorial domain of cubism—points to the degree to which others, if not Picasso himself, were quickly finding in the cubist art a visual technique, perhaps even an aesthetic metaphor, for a world in transition. This particular context for Picasso's statements is signaled in his own text when he says that "arts of transition do not exist," a remark which is countered by the founding three years later of the journal called *transition* (appropriately, in Paris, where Picasso was residing) with the specific intention of encouraging a transition in the verbal arts. Eventually, the collaborative efforts of a number of writers from several different countries would appear in *transition* in a special issue called—and devoted to—"The Revolution of the Word."[4] With more insight than Picasso himself recognized, in the same article he also says that "Art does not evolve by itself, the ideas of people change and with them their *mode of expression*" (italics mine).[5]

The radical change in the poetry produced in the interim war years does reflect what, in hindsight, appears to be an "uncanny prescience"[6] on Picasso's part: a cultural shift in ideas which would be made manifest in the literary modes of expression (as well as the visual ones), including those of Gertrude Stein, William Faulkner, James Joyce, and T. S. Eliot. In fact, the term *cubist literature* was accepted critically as early as 1941 by Georges Lemaître and has subsequently gained so much acceptance that in addition to Stein, Faulkner, Joyce, and Eliot, Wallace Stevens, E. E. Cummings, Alain Robbe-Grillet, Ford Maddox Ford, and Max Jacob have all been called cubist writers. On the popular level, Dorothy Sayers simply assumes the legitimacy of the term as early as 1928 when she begins one of her mysteries with "On this particular evening, Masterman (*the cubist poet*) had brought a guest with him"[7] [emphasis mine].

Despite its increased acceptance, *cubist poetry* has nonetheless been defined quite differently by different writers and critics. On the one hand, Kenneth Rexroth, a poet who was himself a part of the milieu with which we are here concerned, specifically describes William Carlos Williams as belonging "in the Cubist tradition," a tradition he defines as "Imagism, Objectivism, the dissociation and rearrangement of the elements of concrete reality, rather than rhetoric or free association."[8] On the other hand, cubism has also been defined as a style marked by "new syntax and punctuation, based on typographical dispersion," as a poetic movement between futurism and expressionism, or as a style characterized by an unusual amount of "punning, contradiction, parody, and word play" in order to create the ambiguity characteristic of visual poetry.[9] Cubist poetry has also been confined to the writings concurrent with the cubist school in the visual arts, especially in France between 1912 and 1919; to the poetry printed in *Nord-Sud,* a journal edited by Reverdy; or else extended to works marked by visual fragmentation, such as Cummings'; works obsessed with perception, as in Stevens' "Thirteen Ways of Looking at a Blackbird"; or works constituted by multiple voices and temporal layers, such as Eliot's *The Waste Land* or Pound's *Cantos.*[10]

Given this diversity, it is critical to remember that even within the visual arts, cubism proves to be a highly complex and diffuse movement that changed, rapidly, from what has come to be called "analytic" cubism to "synthetic" cubism. As Edward Fry notes,

> crucial changes, particularly in Picasso, often took place during a period of months or weeks, as opposed to years or decades in older historical styles. This accelerated rate of stylistic change seems to have become the rule in twentieth-century art, and it may well be the effect of increased rates of change in other areas of culture, particularly in the speed of communications.[11]

The cubism of Picasso's "Three Women" (1908–9), for example, is quite different from that of his "Still Life with Chair-caning" (1912) or "The Three Musicians" (1921). Somewhat oversimplified, cubism in the visual arts rapidly changed from an aesthetic designed to reintroduce form, largely as a reaction against the ephemeral quality of Impressionism, to an aesthetic which quite ironically but consistently fractured form. This "fracturing" not only includes the actual forms of objects and the introduction of multiple perspectives, but extends to the fracturing of the boundary between visual and verbal representation, primarily through the use of collage. As a consequence, it is also possible to find in visual cubism an implicit *stasis*, emphasizing form, or an implicit *dynamism*, evoked by the suggestion of "movement in space from the viewer," created by multiple perspectives which dramatically challenge the long-reigning tradition of linear perspective.[12]

It is reasonable to expect that if the visual arts did affect the verbal arts, then such diversity as is witnessed in the visual realm would be reflected in the poetry as well, as various poets appropriated different facets of cubism into their work. Thus, Williams' well-known "The Red Wheelbarrow," with cubelike stanzas that continually alter in perspective, corresponds roughly to analytic cubism (or the "analysis" of form) in the visual arts, as does Stevens' "Thirteen Ways of Looking at a Blackbird." Much of Cummings' work, on the other hand, reflects the analytic phase of cubist poetry precisely as it, like cubist paintings, began to change from a close concern with form to the fracturing of form. In Eliot's *The Waste Land,* however, and equally in Pound's *Cantos* and Williams' *Paterson,* we find a verbal equivalent of synthetic cubism (that is, the "synthesizing" of fragments into new aesthetic objects) — essentially verbal collages, with a heightened sense of multiple perspectives, multiple voices, even multiple layers of temporality, and an implicit but ruthless questioning of the status of representation itself. From this perspective, Stevens' "The Man with a Blue Guitar," which continually revolves around the difficult question of presenting "things as they are," juxtaposes sections of the poem that differ in perspective, and dismantles the fiction of any controlling authorial voice while incorporating fragments (such as words from a popular song), may accurately be described as a synthetic cubist poem.[13]

The very multiplicity of possibly realized forms that characterizes visual cubism thus prevents, in the verbal realm as well, any single or simple definition of poetic cubism. Yet while it is impossible to delineate specific characteristics that identify every cubist poem, it is possible to say that as it ranges between analytic and synthetic interpretation, cubist poetry is likely to be marked by concern with visual form (which itself may range from cube-like stanzas to a radical arrangement of the printed page that far exceeds the experimentation of free verse);[14] by a distortion of normal stanza, line, and word boundaries; by a thematic concern with its own modernism and an intense preoccupation with perception; by narrative and temporal disjunctions that, in a collage-like fashion, employ multiple voices, sections, and textual fragments; and finally by a heightened sense of textuality itself, which questions the very nature of representation in a way that anticipates post-structuralist criticism. In addition, the blurring of boundaries between artistic media that occurs in both cubist paintings and cubist poems encourages the blurring of genres as well, most obviously in the *prose poem* (a relatively new hybrid that developed rapidly during the period with which we are concerned).

Given the vast quantity of material that this definition covers, it should be obvious that no volume could reprint all the cubist poetry, not even all the American cubist poetry, written between the two World Wars. I have included here poems that demonstrate the changing *poetics* of the time, especially in America, but to a large degree continue to remain unknown or inaccessible. The influence of the Alfred Stieglitz and Walter Arensberg circles, where (as several critics have demonstrated) the cubist influence in America most directly began during the "teens" of this century, is certainly critical here. Yet as this volume shows, it was an influence that would manifest itself in widening circles over the next two decades.

I would like to stress that what is included here is a mere sampling of what Robert Sanborn called a "vital page of literary history."[15] In this regard, I have chosen to include a very select number of well-known poems by well-known poets, for it is precisely in their contemporary context that they appear so seminal, so successful, and ironically so original. This volume does not, however, reprint the famous synthetic poems (mentioned above) of this period, primarily because they are so well known and accessible that they would extend the length of this volume unnecessarily. Still, they have an important place in the total context of this poetry, for without their presence, cubist poetry in America would seem to be far more simple and far more narrow in range and form than it actually proves to be. The reprinting of a few excerpts from Pound's *Cantos* and Zukofsky's *"A,"* as well as several other excerpts from less well known synthetic cubist poems, as they were originally published in the small magazines, therefore serves in the text that follows as a specific reminder of this critical facet of cubist poetry.

To the extent to which it is possible, the material included here has been arranged in groups, primarily according to the journals in which the poems first appeared. While the rise and fall of some of these avantgarde journals offers a particulary chronological arrangement—*Others* dissolves, to be followed by *Contact,* or *Blues* folds, to be followed by *View*— there is also considerable temporal overlap. Some of the poems I will include from one journal thus may have been printed *after* the first selections of the following journal included here. I rejected a purely

chronological arrangement of this material, however, for such an arrange-
ment would fail to suggest the collaborative efforts that went into creating
a new poetics and which were a crucial part of the cubist experience.

I should also clarify that the relatively small number of poems in this
volume written by women in no way offers a fair picture of women's poetic
activity during this period. The first part of the twentieth century was, in
fact, an extremely active period for women writers, marked by a "con-
vergence of Modernism and feminism."[16] In addition to the obvious
contributions made by such editors as Harriet Monroe and Margaret
Anderson, women poets such as H. D., Marianne Moore, Helen Hoyt, Amy
Lowell, and Evelyn Scott were not only contributing to but significantly
changing the canon and range of American verse. As a reviewer of *The
Second American Caravan* (1928) notes, over one-third of the poets included
were women, and as early as 1916, *Others* printed a special women's issue
edited by Helen Hoyt.[17]

For reasons which need to be more fully explored, however, most of
the major women writers of this time chose not to write the kind of poetry
included here — despite the fact that Williams (incorrectly, I think) once
described Marianne Moore as a cubist poet.[18] While my own sense is that
Moore's poetry is far more subversive than her early critics assumed, her
particular poetic strategies do not seem to me essentially cubist — nor do
those of H. D. (I offer one exception in the text which follows). It may be
that, as many recent historians and critics have suggested, the experience
of women during this period was so different from that of men that their
particular forms of poetic expression — and of poetic resistance — typ-
ically took a very different aesthetic turn during this time. I would also
speculate that from the point of view of feminist theory, the very "denatur-
ing" or "deforming" of objects that is so characteristic of cubism would
have been psychologically repugnant to the majority of women writers
who were trying to find and create a poetic voice.[19] Certainly we find an
especially heightened consciousness of women's place — or lack of place —
in our social, political, and poetic traditions in the vast majority of the
poems written by women poets during this period. *That* part of the
climate, taken together with the one offered here, suggests a critical
intersection which should itself be the subject of future inquiry.

Despite this disclaimer, one of the most prominent figures during
the times, and one who specifically encouraged the development of cubist
literature, is Gertrude Stein, a woman who may accurately be seen as the
"founding mother" of American cubist poetry. Only now is she beginning
to be appreciated again in the way she clearly was by her artistic peers

during the early part of this century.[20] In addition to encouraging specific writers from both sides of the Atlantic at various stages in their careers, Stein produced a body of literature which proved to be one of the most significant forces in transplanting and translating a visual aesthetic developed in France to a verbal aesthetic (including both poetry and prose) subsequently developed in America.

I should also clarify that this work includes only a few examples of that facet of cubist poetry which borders on *visual poetry* (in which the visual arrangement of the words finally supersedes linguistic representation altogether), primarily because other critics such as Wendy Steiner and Willard Bohn have already provided such excellent treatments of the subject.[21] Nonetheless, it should be clear that the simplest and perhaps most direct verbal interpretation of cubist strategies would realize itself in poetry "meant to be read, with the eye on the page," as Sayre says of Williams' late poetry.[22] Yet this aspect of Williams' later verse, which could potentially develop into either *concrete* or *visual* poetry, has precursors not only in his early work but in that of many other poets as well.

Finally, this volume reproduces in the Appendix a few prose essays that seem especially important in understanding the larger context of cubist poetry (though, once again, such material is in no way comprehensive). What may accurately be called cubist prose, such as Gertrude Stein's "Picasso," appears with the poetry in the regular journal selections. And while primarily concerned with American poets and their verse, I have also selected pieces from a few magazines published concurrently in Europe that suggest something of the unavoidably international essence and interaction of this aesthetic movement. The select bibliography which follows the selections is intended as an extension, including references to representative studies in other languages, genres, and media, as well as references to works specifically focused on American cubist poetry. (It does not, however, contain references to the primary texts, whether critical or poetic, that are mentioned in the course of discussing the development of cubism in "little magazines," nor tangentially related subjects. For that information, see Notes and Index.)

1 The "KINDLING BREATH" of the 1910s

Without question, the Armory Show of 1913, an exhibit shown in New York and later in Chicago and Boston, was America's most famous introduction to the cubist paintings of Picasso, Braque, Gleizes, and Leger (even if the latter is more accurately described as a "tubist," rather than a "cubist"). Cubist paintings immediately began to be reproduced in a number of journals, including *Camera Work*, *291*, and *Soil;* more and more exhibits of cubist work began to be shown in New York over the next few years, despite the difficulties presented by the advent of the Great War; and a new kind of poetry began to emerge from the scene — most notably, perhaps, in Alfred Kreymborg's *Others,* but in a number of other journals as well.

The importance of this period, especially among the writers and painters in New York at the time, has already been explored in depth by a number of notable critics. The impact of cubism was not, however, confined to New York nor to the writers who originally formed such groups as "Others," but rather continued to be felt with increasing intensity over the next two decades. And although cubism appears to have diminished as a force in literature before and during the Second World War, the critical change which took place in modern aesthetics in the early part of this century continues to inform the poetry of the latter half of this century.[1] George Oppen and Louis Zukofsky, in different ways, represent an unbroken continuum of the earliest cubist experiments into contemporary verse, and certainly such poets as John Cage, Ron Silliman, and David Atkin may be rightly seen as extending in other ways the self-consciousness of language as a material medium that is so characteristic of most cubist poetry, as does John Matthias, at least in such early work as *Poem in Three Parts.*[2]

My point of departure for this present study is not, however, 1913 and the various responses to the Armory Show, nor the equally famous Palace Exhibit of 1917 (at which both William Carlos Williams and Mina Loy read their poetry), but rather the first appearance of Picasso in *Camera Work* in 1911 and the subsequent efforts of Alfred Stieglitz to introduce cubism to a relatively hostile American audience. The history of this artistic "introduction" is of critical interest here, for by 1912 Stieglitz had (even if unknowingly) already presented to the American audience — and to the American poet — the possibility of cubism in the *verbal* medium.

The *Camera Work* number for April–July, 1911, reprints the pamphlet written by Marius de Zayas for the Picasso Exhibition at Photo-Secession (April, 1911). Although the pamphlet may finally tell us more about de Zayas than about Picasso, de Zayas' insights into the intention and effect of cubism seem to me especially astute:

> Instead of the physical manifestation he [Picasso] seeks in form the psychic one. . . . When he paints he does not limit himself to taking from an object only those planes which the eye perceives, but deals with all those which, according to him, constitute the individuality of form; and with his peculiar fantasy he develops and transforms them. And this suggests to him new impressions, which he manifests with new forms, because from the idea of representation of a being, a new being is born, perhaps different from the first one, and this becomes the represented being.
>
> *Camera Work*, 34–35 (April–July, 1911), 66

While poststructuralist criticism may encourage us to explore further the essentially deconstructive content and process of the passage above, it is important to note that de Zayas' comments describe a dynamic, creative process (thus implicitly blurring the boundary between futurism and cubism, especially when cubism is presumed, falsely, to be essentially static, precluding both temporal and spatial movement).[3] More important, perhaps, is the fact that the passage above could just as easily describe some of the earliest and most successful cubist *poems*, such as Wallace Stevens' "Thirteen Ways of Looking at a Blackbird" (first published in *Others* in the 1917 issue which bears the inscription, "A number for the Mind's eye / Not to be read aloud").

Yet neither Picasso's work nor de Zayas' analysis of it was so readily accepted as the reference to Stevens' well-known poem might suggest. The very next issue of *Camera Work*, which reproduces one of Picasso's cubist drawings, also prints a number of art critics' reactions to both Picasso's work and de Zayas' pamphlet.[4] Most of them are intensely negative, even if the contempt is somewhat humorously expressed. For example, Arthur

Hoeber writes that "Any sane criticism is entirely out of the question; any serious analysis would be in vain. The results suggest the most violent wards of an asylum for maniacs, the craziest emanations of a disordered mind, the gibberings of a lunatic!" Mr. Tyrrell warns that "Unless you are ready to receive the artistic jolt of your young life, don't go to Mr. Stieglitz's Photo-Secession Gallery," and after quoting de Zayas on Picasso's interest in "psychic form" noted above, interjects "Now will you be good!" However, Mr. Tyrrell also, perhaps unintentionally, makes an especially astute observation that portends the impact on cubism over the years to come:

> [W]hen an artist who can draw and paint with the consummately beautiful mastery of a Millet or a Degas—and Picasso unquestionably can... — when such an artist deliberately throws off this traditional technique as a worn-out garment... then there must surely be something doing of large import for the future.
>
> *Camera Work,* 36 (October 1911), 49

Considering the subsequent development of dada, Edgar Chamberlin proves less prophetic when he describes cubism as a "force of anti-traditionalism" which "can surely go no further." Mr. Harrington finds cubism similarly "disquieting," yet Elizabeth Luther Carey (who also dislikes the cubist paintings) again predicts that Picasso's "discordant sound" is "quite apt to precede revolution of one kind or another." Of the numerous critics quoted in this issue, only Israel White appears to have any genuine appreciation of Picasso's "experiments." James Huneker, who implies that Picasso may speak for a new "generation," concludes that "his is not the cult of the ugly for the sake of ugliness, but the search after the expressive in the heart of ugliness. A new aesthetic? No, a very old one revivified, and perhaps because of its modern rebirth all the uglier, and as yet a mere diabolic, not divine, stammering."[5]

Stieglitz's immediate response to this rejection of cubism is, to my mind, not only witty but ingenious. The next issue of *Camera Work,* a special number (1912), prints two articles by Gertrude Stein, one on Matisse, the other on Picasso, along with "representative paintings and sculptures by these artists." Stieglitz nevertheless insists that

> the fact is that these articles themselves, and not either the subject with which they deal or the illustrations that accompany them, are the true *raison d'être* of this special issue.
>
> *Camera Work,* Special No. (1912), editorial

While the entire issue is clearly a modern "apology" for what the editor labels "Post-Impressionism," the critical point here is the emphasis on Stein's ability to convey "through the art of literature, *whose raw material is words*," the same "spirit" as that conveyed in the visual medium: "it is precisely because, in these articles by Miss Stein, the *Post-Impressionist spirit is found expressing itself in literary form* that we thus lay them before the readers of CAMERA WORK" (italics mine). The editorial goes on to stress, again, Stein's "medium" of words, concluding that her articles provide a "decipherable clew to that intellectual and esthetic attitude which underlies and inspires the movement upon one phase of which they are comments and of the extending development of which they are themselves an integral part." Thus, with the publication of Stein's "Pablo Picasso," we find the possibility of what we may call, in retrospect, *cubist literature* (rather than "Post-Impressionist" literature) self-consciously introduced *as such* into the American scene.

Such was the climate — and the interest, both positive and negative, in cubism — *before* the famous Armory Show of 1913. In that year, *Camera Work* published two articles, "Insincerity: A New Vice" and "Cosmism or Amorphism," both of which denigrate cubism for being too abstract, too intellectual, even too mathematical.[6] The assumption in both articles is that cubism is devoid of any genuine artistic *spirit*. However, *Camera Work* then issued another special number (still in 1913) which again attempted to introduce cubist paintings and literature.

This issue too begins with Gertrude Stein, specifically with her "Portrait of Mabel Dodge at the Villa Curona," the title of which heightens our awareness of language as an artistic medium and complicates any naive understanding of artistic *representation*, as does both the style and the content of the "portrait" itself:

> There is not all that filling. There is the climate that is not existing. There is that plainer. There is the likeliness lying in liking likely likeliness. There is that dispensation. There is the paling that is not reddening, there is that protection, there is that destruction, there is not the present lessening there is the argument of increasing. . . . Looking is not vanishing. Laughing is not evaporating. There can be an old dress. There can be the way there is that way there is that which is not that charging what is a regular way of paying. . . . There is not the print. There is that smiling. There is the season.
>
> *Camera Work*, Special No. (June 1913), 4

The issue also reproduces Picasso's portrait of Gertrude Stein — thus doubling the complexity created by Stein's verbal portrait — as well as his "Woman with Mandolin," the same cubist drawing reproduced in 1911, a new Picabia, and an extended defense of the new art movement in Maurice Aisen's "The Latest in Art and Picabia."[7]

One immediate effect of this concern with the relation of visual and verbal representation may be seen in Mina Loy's "Aphorisms on Futurism," published the following year in *Camera Work*. Despite its title, which points to futurism, the list of aphorisms experiments, at least minimally, in a cubist fashion with the texture and typography of words through the use of unexpected capitals and italics (cited in part below):

OPEN your arms to the delapidated, to rehabilitate them.

YOU prefer to observe the past on which your eyes are already opened.

BUT the Future is only dark from outside.
Leap into it — and it EXPLODES with *Light*.

FORGET that you live in houses, that you may live in yourself —

....

CONSCIOUSNESS has no climax.

LET the Universe flow into your consciousness, there is no limit to its capacity, nothing that it shall not re-create.

UNSCREW your capability of absorption and grasp the elements of Life —
Whole.

Camera Work, 45 (June 1914), 13, 14

Although several critics regard Loy specifically, if not exclusively, as a futurist, we should note (for reasons intimated above) that the dividing line between cubism and futurism has always been troublesome — Duchamp said that not even Picasso was cubist.[8] Loy's experiments with the *materiality* of language and her subsequent use of white space as part of the text (a technique ultimately derived from Cézanne) are essentially cubist.[9] And although futurists would indeed adapt such techniques to their concern with motion and dynamism, the possibility of dynamic, temporal motion is (as noted above) implicit in cubism itself. As John Golding remarks of the culmination of the first phase of cubism developed by Braque and Picasso, the paintings suggest that the artist "has felt his way visually around each object and examined its relationships with other objects around it from several viewpoints," with the result that objects and space are fused in a "spatial continuum" — which, inevitably, implies temporal conflation and continuum.[10]

The issues of *Camera Work* during the three years before the outbreak of the Great War thus mark the emergence of a cubist aesthetic in the United States not only in the visual arts but in the verbal arts as well —

though certainly not every painting reproduced or poem published in subsequent issues could be said to extend this aesthetic. Mina Loy's next work, a poem published in the next issue of this journal, is surprisingly old-fashioned in form, despite its theme:

> There is no Life or Death,
> Only activity
> And in the absolute
> Is no declivity.
> ·················
> There is no Space or Time
> Only intensity,
> And tame things
> Have no immensity.

> *Camera Work,* 46 (October 1914), 18

In addition to the regular rhyme and rhythm, this poem uses capitals, for example, in a perfectly traditional way, with none of the typographical experimentation — the sense of the materiality of language — found in her aphorisms.

More concerned with the relationship between verbal and visual media is the collage-like series of responses of various artists to "What 291 Means to Me," a series which anticipates the founding of *291* and the specific concern with experiments in typesetting and printing.[11] Of the numerous testimonies given by a wide range of artists, those of Kreymborg, Djuna Barnes, Charles Demuth, Man Ray, Picabia, de Zayas, and John Marin border on being, or are, recognizably poetry. I include in the text that follows Marin's response, which has visual interest as well, with its concern for empty space — a "passage," as it were — the use of which goes far beyond "free verse" and which was already being fully exploited both in the visual and verbal arts in Europe.[12] In addition, Marin's poem makes a playful allusion to Huneker's "diabolical" assessment of modern art mentioned above.

*****

[Note: throughout, the row of asterisks indicates that a selection of works (which should be read before continuing) from the particular journal being discussed is included in the literary examples of this volume.]

To see the relatively rapid development of a new kind of poetry, however, it is necessary to turn to other avant-garde journals, such as *291* and *Others* (both of which are direct descendants of the people and interests informing *Camera Work*) and to a lesser degree to other contemporary journals such as *Glebe, Rogue,* and *The Trend*.

Glebe, itself, is not especially important for the kind of poetry included in this volume, but it does register the "spirit" of the times, specifically in Adolf Wolff's inscription on the first issue 1913, which points again to the impact of the visual arts on the verbal arts during this period:

To Alfred Stieglitz
The Spirit of "291" Adolf Wolff
O ∂. 1913
Songs, Sighs and Curses

By

A d o l f   W o l f f

(Held at the HRHRC, Austin, Texas)

Also, in its third issue, *Glebe* ran Charles Demuth's one-act comedy, "The Azure Adder" (*Glebe*, 1, 3 [1913], 5–31). Like many other artists of this period, including Kandinsky, Picabia, and Cummings, Demuth worked in more than one medium. The possible intersection of one medium with another is humorously evoked in the stage directions of the comedy when the furniture is described as being the color of "Vivian's gray — really white." It is not without significance that the setting is also given as *The ultra-present,* emphasizing the new and increasingly disturbing self-consciousness of being "modern."

However, *Glebe* is best-known for its special issue of 1914, the anthology of "Des Imagistes." While the poems published in this issue may have seemed, at the time, radically different from such poems as Cawein's "Waste Land" (or Thomas Hardy's poetry, which Pound disliked and which may be the most immediate precursor to Cawein's verse), from a cubist perspective, they seem surprisingly traditional, as for example H. D.'s "Sitalkas":

Thou art come at length
More beautiful

17

Than any cool god
In a chamber under
Lycia's far coast,
Than any high god
Who touches us not
Here in the seeded grass.
Aye, than Argestes
Scattering the broken leaves.

Glebe 1, 5 (1914), 20

Similarly, William Carlos Williams' "Postlude" has, with its Greek gods and goddesses, a distinctly classical and somewhat archaic quality. Even James Joyce's "I Hear an Army" seems to be closer to a mere revision of Matthew Arnold's "Dover Beach" than to an examplar of a new verbal aesthetics. Only Pound's "The Return" (cited in part below) anticipates the visual play noted in Mina Loy and John Marin (in the same year) that would be so successfully exploited in American verse over the next twenty years:

See, they return, one, and by one,
With fear, as half-awakened;
As if the snow should hesitate
And murmur in the wind
                and half turn back;
These were the "Wing'd-with-Awe,"
            Inviolable.

Gods of the winged shoe!
With them the silver hounds
                sniffing the trace of air!
Haie! Haie!
                These were the swift to harry;
These the keen-scented;
These were the souls of blood.

Slow on the leash,
                pallid the leash-men!

Glebe 1, 5 (1914), 42

In *Rogue*, which Marling describes as *Glebe's* chief rival, we find more specific instances of the impact of cubism in the verbal realm.[13] Once again Gertrude Stein is a seminal figure. Her "Aux Galeries Lafayette," published in 1915 (see p. 36), breaks the boundary between poetry and prose, and the theme — "Each one is one. There are many of them" — is, itself, cubist in perspective, prefiguring a similar play in Stevens' "Metaphors of a Magnifico" (1918).

18

Another issue of *Rogue* prints Charles Demuth's "Filling a Page," subtitled, "A Pantomime with Words" (April 1, 1915). The verbal irony of the subtitle points to the extreme self-consciousness of the materiality of language and, appropriately the "directions" are "After Miss Gertrude Stein." The piece is also "decorated" with drawings of miming clowns, thus confusing the boundary between the visual and verbal pantomime. Another issue of *Rogue* (August 1, 1915) contains Carl Van Vechten's "An Interrupted Conversation," a prose piece which is not only full of intrusions within the narrative line, but which is also specifically "interrupted" in the actual printing. Significantly, the piece mentions both Picasso and Mina Loy (as well as Yeats and Lady Gregory).

Nonetheless, most of the poetry published in this journal is largely conventional: the poems published by Allen Norton, Kreymborg, and Walter Arensberg are all relatively traditional. Norton publishes a poem, for instance, that both begins and ends with the couplet, "You are the loveliest of all, / As lovely as Spring-days in Fall" (*Rogue* [April 1, 1915], 6). Similarly, Arensberg's "Human," published one month later, is a regular sonnet, beginning with this quatrain:

> In a cathedral that aspires in thought
> I am, and I perhaps am not alone.
> I am an altar to a God Unknown,
> And with the candles I am clear and hot.
>
> *Rogue* (May 1, 1915), 6

Only Mina Loy's "Three Moments in Paris," both in its title and in its interest in typography, and her "Virgins Plus Curtains Minus Dots" approach anything like cubist poetry. (Both are also especially interesting feminist poems.) Clara Tice's following drawing, "Virgin Minus Verse," makes a witty intersection of the verbal and visual media (even if not a cubist one), by depicting a woman clad only in undergarments (with a line of dots). (Something of the generalized feminist humor of this journal might be indicated as well by the drawing "Prudes Descending a Staircase" (*Rogue* [May 15, 1915], 3), which alludes to Duchamp's "Nude Descending a Staircase," painted the year before.)

*****

In contrast to either *Glebe* or *Rogue, The Trend* (founded in 1911) appears to be a much more traditional magazine in its inception, deliberately wide-ranging in appeal and certainly not an exclusively "artistic" journal. Yet in its own way, *The Trend* proves to be an accurate barometer of the American climate, publishing articles on education, child labor, and the women's suffrage movement, as well as being concerned in a significant way with the arts. It is here that we find, following the Armory Show, Joseph Stella's essay, "The New Art" (1913). Stella anticipates R. J. Coady's rejection of any "-ism" or "school" (in his own essay, "American Art"), a rejection which is characteristic of the inherent multiplicity in cubism itself, while calling attention to the self-conscious modernism and shocking "revelation" of the "unofficial," non-traditional art:

> I tried to forget all schooling of any sort, and see if I could reveal something that belonged to me and to me only. But in spite of my efforts, prejudices and conventions would tie me down. I felt then all the antagonism that anyone should have against the schools.
>
> A dear friend of mine a fine artist and a true, sincere man, Mr. Pach, urged me to go to Paris to renew myself. In need of help, I soon went to the real realm of modern art.
>
> For the first time, I realized that there was such a thing as modern art (not the "official") and as true and great as the old one. It was for me the revelation of truth and gave me a great shock.
>
> *The Trend* 5, 3 (June 1913), 393–94

Nonetheless, once again most of the actual poetry published in this journal reflects very little of a new aesthetic. Walter Arensberg's "An Old Game," for example, seems surprisingly traditional, especially given his involvement with Stieglitz and Kreymborg (cited in part below):

> Is it heavenly *Hide and seek,*
> Playmate, that you have to play?
> — When I closed my eyes to pray
> You were breathless where you lay
> On the bed, and you were weak.
> When I opened them at length
> It was you who had the strength,
> You, the earthly runaway!
>
> *The Trend* 7, 2 (May 1914), 172

This is significantly different both in theme and in form from such poems as "Ing" or "Arithmetical Progression of the Verb 'To Be,'" that he would eventually publish elsewhere.[14]

A 1914 issue of *The Trend*, however, prints Carl Van Vechten's essay "How to Read Gertrude Stein," which stresses the fact that she reports that her "art was for the printed page only," thereby anticipating the special 1917 issue of *Others* for the "Mind's Eye" (already mentioned). This essay testifies again to the extensive influence Stein had in America (as well as in Europe) during this period—as do many subsequent essays, including William Carlos Williams' "The Work of Gertrude Stein," first published in *Pagany* in 1930. Van Vechten also notes that

> everyone tries to make sense out of Miss Stein just as everyone insists on making photographs out of drawings by Picabia, when the essential of his art is that he is getting away from the photographic.
>
> *The Trend* 7, 5 (August 1914), 556

Finally, in 1914 *The Trend* also published Wallace Stevens' "Carnet de Voyage," a series of poems which is, admittedly, far more influenced by Imagism and even visual Impressionism than by cubism (as the following excerpt suggests):

> The green goes from the corn,
> The blue from all the lakes,
> And the shadows of the mountains mingle in the sky.
>
> *The Trend* 7, 6 (September 1914), 743

Nonetheless, the sectional numbering Stevens employs in this sequence (which begins with "An odor from a star" and concludes with "On an Old Guitar") anticipates a poetic strategy that he will exploit much more successfully three years later in "Thirteen Ways of Looking at a Blackbird," possibly the best-known early American cubist poem.

Of far more relevance here are *291* and *Others,* both founded in 1915 and "first cousins" in their concerns. Much has already been written about *291*—Willard Bohn in particular has given a very thorough analysis of the visual and verbal complexities of Marius de Zayas' reorganization of a poem by Agnes Ernst Meyer, "Mental Reactions," in the second issue of this journal.[15] While de Zayas' visual art in this piece may correctly be described as abstract (rather than as cubist), the fragmenting of his own visual forms (which Bohn convincingly demonstrates) and certainly the collage-effect of incorporating and fracturing Meyer's poem are *essentially* cubist strategies.

Notably, the first issue of *291* reproduces one of Picasso's cubist drawings, "Oil and Vinegar Caster," as well as Apollinaire's "Ideogramme." But of particular interest is the brief paragraph and example directly below Picasso's drawing, "Simultanism," which specifically describes the possibility (as well as the problem) of creating verbally the kind of simultaneity being created visually by Picasso and Braque:

> The idea of Simultanism is expressed in painting by the simultaneous representation of the different figures of a form seen from different points

of view, as Picasso and Braque did some time ago; or by the simultaneous representation of the figure of several forms as the futurists are doing.

In literature the idea is expressed by the polyphony of simultaneous voices which say different things. Of course, printing is not an adequate medium, for succession in this medium is unavoidable and a phonograph is more suitable.

291, No. 1 (March 1915)

Although Carolyn Burke has argued that Mina Loy, in anticipation of Apollinaire's *Calligrammes,* may have written one of the "first English poems to employ simultaneity and juxtaposition as formal principles" as early as 1913 (with "Costa San Giorgio"),[16] in general verbal simultaneity — with its obvious relation to cubist simultaneity in the visual arts — was only a possibility just being introduced to the American audience at this point, and accounts, in part, for a number of the more energetic poems to appear in the near future in such journals as *Others.*

The third issue of *291*, which creates a visually interesting collage of Katharine N. Rhoades' prose poem "I Walked into a Moment of Great-ness . . . ," Meyer's poem "Woman," and an abstract drawing by de Zayas, also includes J. B. Kerfoot's "A Bunch of Keys," a visual poem that arranges the words as a ring of keys. However, Rhoades' "Flip-Flap," published in the fourth issue, explores the visual possibilities of verbal texts in a much more cubist fashion (see p. 44), as does her "Narcosis" (p. 46), which appeared in the twelfth and last issue, February 1916. Of all the issues of this short-lived journal, the ninth through eleventh (November 1915 and the double issue, December 1915–January 1916) are the most strictly cubist. The ninth issue includes drawings by Braque, Picabia, and Picasso, as well as de Zayas' "FEMME!" — a concrete poem which makes use of collage. The special double issue features a circular collage by Picasso.

There were only twelve issues of *291* (most of which were only three or four pages in length), it ran for only slightly more than a year, and the number of subscribers was never high. Still, the acute awareness of the interaction and even interconnectedness of visual and verbal "texts" in the emerging aesthetic development that so consistently informs this journal marks a particular and critical step in the development of American cubist poetry. As Dorothy Norman rightly concludes in her introduction to the facsimile edition of this journal, when it closed, "*291* had made an important, incalculable contribution, despite its limited circulation and brief duration,"[17] a contribution which includes the evocation of a new sense of the possibilities in the *poetic* as well as in the pictorial realm.

*****

In 1915, the same year that *291* was founded and *Rogue* printed Stein's "Aux Galeries Lafayette" and Loy's "Three Moments in Paris," *Others* issued its first number. In fact, Kreymborg published "Overheard in an Asylum" not only in the first issue of *Others,* but also the same year in *Rogue,* where he advertises himself as "one of Others." Admittedly, "Overheard in an Asylum" is not an especially cubist poem, even if it is thematically a modern poem in its concern with the psychological effect of war. The first issue of *Others,* however, also contains his "Variations," which marks an increased sophistication in his own verse. Of more interest in the first issue, however, is Mina Loy's "Love Songs," the first of which is included below. Here we find increased attention to the visual impact of the verse, most notably in the first section:

Spawn of fantasies
Sitting the appraisable
Pig Cupid   his rosy snout
Rotting erotic garbage
"Once upon a time"
Pulls a weed   white star-topped
Among wild oats sown in mucous membrane
I would   an eye in a Bengal light
Eternity in a sky-rocket
Constellations in an ocean
Whose rivers run no fresher
Than a trickle of saliva
There are suspect places

I must live in my lantern
Trimming subliminal flicker
Virginal   to the bellows
Of experience
                Colored glass.

Others 1, 1 (July 1915), 6

It is within the total "context" of this very new, but rapidly expanding aesthetic that the sudden appearance of Stevens' famous "Peter Quince at the Clavier" in the second issue of *Others* takes on a special significance not usually noted in Stevens criticism.[18] The sectional breaks, which also amount to multiple perspectives within the poem itself, the allusions to other texts (here, Shakespeare's play and a biblical story), even the attempt at across-media representation (musical, visual, and verbal) mark Stevens' first experiment with the elements of cubist poetry. The next issue of *Others* includes Eliot's "Portrait of a Lady," the title of which once again raises questions about the nature of representation itself. Like "The Love

Song of J. Alfred Prufrock" (published the same year in *Poetry*), this poem
has certain cubist qualities — though not nearly as obviously as Prufrock
does. And in the fifth issue, we find Sanborn's "Soul of Lotus," which forms
a particular bridge between the interest in imagism and new, cubist
aesthetic. (I have included one of the more "cubist" sections ["Lento"]
here — see p. 48).

While I could continue to mention individually the particular
poems which evince a changing poetics, by 1916 the development of cubist
poetry, especially as it was encouraged in *Others,* begins to occur so
rapidly that the verse alone provides ample commentary. Among the
many cubist works that appeared in this journal are Vail de Lencour's
"Poem," which is specifically a prose poem (thus breaking genre bound-
aries, as did many other works, particularly those of Max Jacob, during
this period), Williams' "Metric Fugue," one of his earliest and most suc-
cessful cubist poems, Stevens' "Six Significant Landscapes," and Mary
Carolyn Davies' "Later Songs," which explores the possibilities of num-
bered sections in a much more sophisticated way than Stevens had yet
perceived.

Williams' "Spring Strains" and "El Hombre" also appeared in *Others*
(1916), the latter being a poem which Stevens would incorporate in a
collage-like fashion (in fact, in a very similar way to that in which Coady
"incorporated" Picasso on the cover illustration) in his own "Nuances of a
Theme by Williams." The interaction between verbal and visual texts in
this instance is particularly complex: as Marling has already pointed out,
"El Hombre" also has a specific connection to Duchamp's "Encore à cette
astre" which, in turn, illustrates a poem by Jules La Forgue of the same
name.[19] Edward Ramos' "Rapière à Deux Points," which violates the
imagistic dictum to "use no unnecessary word" with the phrase "are like,"
raises the combined question of similitude and reflection through an
image (a carved gem) Stevens would exploit more successfully in a some-
what cubist fashion years later in "Description Without Place."[20] Among
the other poems reprinted in this volume are Stevens' "Thirteen Ways of
Looking at a Blackbird," sections of Mina Loy's triumph, *Songs to Joannes,*
and one of Demuth's paintings, "New England Houses," which is cubist in
technique. Of these, *Songs to Joannes* deserves special note.

The *Songs* appeared as an entire issue (or "pamphlet," as it was
called) of *Others* in 1917. They begin, in their own collage-like fashion, by
repeating the "Love Songs" that had appeared in the first issue of *Others*
two years before. However, the "songs" demonstrate not only an addition
in content and length, but a particular development in technique. By

song VII, for instance, Loy has introduced a series of dashes as signs for missing words, thereby inverting the cubist play in the visual medium when words are pasted or painted onto canvases as signs of themselves:

VII

My pair of feet
Smack the flag-stones
That are something left over from your walking
The wind stuffs the scum of the white street
Into my lungs and my nostrils
Exhilarated birds
Prolonging flight into the night
Never reaching — — — — — —

Others 3, 6 (April 1917), 6

In Song XIII, Loy explores the possibilities of "simultanism" with a double column of voices that merge into "Something that you must not hear":

It is ambient   And it is in your eyes
Something shiny   Something only for you
                          Something that I must not see

It is in my ears   Something very resonant
Something that you must not hear
                          Something only for me

(p. 9)

In the last sections (see pp. 52–54), Loy plays with a string of dashes as if they were signs of missing metrical feet — or part of a predictable visual figure — only to dissolve the space that they ironically represent into the concomitant mystery of "Love" and the "preeminent literateur." Though too long to be reprinted here in full, this issue of *Others* represents the first sustained American cubist poem to move beyond the relatively simple analysis of form to something more on the order of synthetic reintegration.

*****

Thus in *Others,* the publication of which coincides almost exactly with the years of the Great War, we find the first sustained expressions of cubist verse in America. In *Soil,* however, we find a much briefer, yet still critical, expression of modern American aesthetics — most notably for our purposes in R. J. Coady's essay, "American Art" (see Appendix). In its own cubist verbal collage, this essay mentions specifically *Others, Poetry,* and Gertrude Stein, capturing in a creative way the spirit of the time. (It also bears, as Harold Loeb would later note, a striking resemblance to his own essay in *Broom*.) Of particular significance, however, is Coady's conclusion that American Art

> is not a refined granulation nor a delicate disease — it is not an ism. It is not an illustration to a theory, it is an expression of life — a complicated life — American life.
>
> The isms have crowded it out of "the art world" and it has grown naturally, healthfully, beautifully. It has grown out of the soil and through the race and will continue to grow. It will grow and mature and add a new unit to Art.
>
> *Soil* 1, 1 (December 1916), 4

While the concern with American tradition — the "soil" of *Soil* — would obviously appeal to many poets (including Williams, who would found *Contact* in 1920 precisely for "contact" with that soil), the joint rejection of any "ism" and the insistence that the new art is an "expression of life" anticipates one of Picasso's rare discussions of cubism (in 1923, cited above). Yet it seems precisely to the point that cubism, even if recognizable as a distinct "school" in the visual arts, never had a "manifesto," in contrast to many of the verbal and visual aesthetic movements of the time. Something so obviously concerned with a "complicated life," with breaking down outdated forms and modes of expression, with the multiplicity of perspectives and with the multiplicity of modernity itself, would be inherently resistant in both its verbal and visual manifestations to defining itself as an "ism." This very resistance may account for the initial rejection of the term by several poets accused of writing cubist poetry, as well as the increasing acceptance of the term today, as this period has become somewhat clearer through temporal distance.

Coady's "Cosmopsychographical Organization," chosen for the jacket, is especially significant. By "repeating" one of Picasso's paintings in his own (as well as incorporating many other visual texts, among them a Matisse), Coady makes a collage of the "master of collage" and, simultaneously, announces the indebtedness of contemporary American art to French cubism. (In fact, Coady reproduces Picasso's "Violin" in the same issue, so the visual allusion is impossible to miss.) Even Coady's comments below the reproduction seem appropriately cubist, especially the self-conscious allusion to *Camera Work* and *291* with "'What does 291 mean to you.'" As a strategy, both the visual and verbal allusions are strikingly similar to Stevens' incorporation of Williams' "El Hombre" as a fragment of his own "Nuances of a Theme by Williams," published only three years later. Notably, it was in *Soil* that Stevens' "Primordia" appeared (see pp. 58–60), a group of poems which announces in the title a certain coherence or ordering that is then, somewhat surprisingly, disrupted by the unusual disjunctions between several of the sections. *Soil* also reproduces one of Marsden Hartley's paintings, "Motion," which reminds us of the impact of cubism on American painters, many of whom (including Hartley) were part of the Arensberg and Stieglitz circles mentioned above.

Coady's critical review of the Society of Independent Artists appears in a 1917 issue of this journal, reproducing several paintings, many of them cubist, as well as including a brief assessment of the various artists. Of these, Coady's description of Picasso's "Portrait" provides an interesting parallel to "Architecture," a verbal portrait published the following year in *The New Republic* by Kreymborg. In his summary of Picasso, Coady calls attention to the "vertical line" between the head and edge of the canvas, the "plane in back of the shoulder and in front of the background," concluding — although not entirely favorably — that "this portrait, with its simple and refined color, worked out in simple planes distributed in a series of lighted spaces, develops a grace, a breadth, and almost a stillness (*Soil* 1, 5 [March 5, 1917], 209). Whether as a response to this description (or other similar ones),[21] or simply as a verbal response to the various cubist "portraits" reproduced in various journals and exhibited in numerous galleries, Kreymborg's poem (cited in part below) marks a particular self-conscious response to this aesthetic environment:

> Make of your lips
> a hard straight line;
> parallel with them
> your eyes;
> make of your cheeks and chin
> two strict right angles,
> and of your ears and nose
> two more. . . .
>
> *The New Republic* 15, 183 (May 4, 1918), 23

*****

Yet just how really remarkable in their time the various poems discussed so far really were can perhaps be better clarified by considering the kind of poetry published in another famous journal, *Poetry*, edited by Harriet Monroe, with Ezra Pound as the foreign correspondent for its first five years. Madison Cawein's "Waste Land" (included above), published in *Poetry* the first year it was founded, serves as an indicator of the difference between more traditionally realized poetry and that with which we are concerned here. In general, despite Monroe's intelligence and keen judgment, and despite the rather dramatic appearance of Pound's "A Few Don'ts by an Imagiste" (which also appeared in *Poetry* in 1913), the actual verse published in this long-lived journal tended to be extremely traditional, even old-fashioned, in comparison to most of the work included in this volume. In issue after issue, the majority of the poems printed have normal stanzaic patterns and regular rhyme—even if *Poetry* was the "prime mover of the new foreign forms" before promoting more vigorous verse forms "made of American clay"—or are "free verse" poems that have the kind of traditional (even classical) metrical appeal that Monroe describes so consistently in her own analyses of modern metrical form.[22] The only really remarkable poems to appear in the early period just predating and then concurrent with the World War are T. S. Eliot's "The Love Song of J. Alfred Prufrock," published in 1915, and Pound's "Villanelle: The Psychological Hour" (1915), a poem which appropriately shatters the expectation of that particular *form* (cited in part below):

I

. . . .
Their little cosmos is shaken—
            the air is alive with that fact.
In their parts of the city
            they are played on by diverse forces;

    I had over-prepared the event.
    Beauty is so rare a thing . . .
    So few drink at my fountain.

Two friends: a breath of the forest . . .
Friends? Are people less friends
            because one has just, at last, found them?
Twice they promised to come.
            "Between the night and morning?"

Beauty would drink of my mind.
Youth would awhile forget
            my youth is gone from me.
Youth would hear speech of beauty.

II

("Speak up! You have danced so stiffly?
  Someone admired your works,
  And said so frankly.

"Did you talk like a fool,
  The first night?
  The second evening?"

"*But* they promised again:
               'Tomorrow at tea-time.'")

III

Now the third day is here—
               no word from either;
No word from her nor him,
Only another man's note:
          "Dear Pound, I am leaving England."
                     Poetry 7, 3 (December 1915), 120–21

The concern with time, the unexpected fracturing of such a particular poetic form, the intrusive quotations, and finally the sectional breaks in the poem all signal a major rupture with the prevailing poetics and verse of this journal, a rupture specifically explored by *Others*.

In fact, Harriet Monroe makes her implicit dislike of certain aspects of modern poetry quite clear in her 1920 review, "'Others' Again," which begins by noting sarcastically that *Poetry* had "published all but four of the twenty-six poets represented [in *Others*, 1919] before they became 'others.'" The review gives Wallace Stevens the most extended praise and is supportive of Williams as well. Mina Loy, however, is dismissed as "An extreme otherist, as innocent of all innocences as of commas, periods, sentences. A knowing one. [*sic*] but we would rather have some other other's eyelashes polish our stars" (*Poetry* 17, 3 [December 1920], 153–54). The rivalry between *Poetry* and *Others*—or, more accurately, the kind of aesthetics typified by these two journals—becomes even more intense the following year when Monroe cites the advertisement in *The Dial* for the new journal *Broom* to be edited by Harold Loeb and Alfred Kreymborg. Monroe concludes:

> Some people are born lucky! Nobody ever offered POETRY an hundred thousand, whether in pounds, dollars, or lire! And POETRY has been a conspicuous target for such windfalls these ten years—nearly—whereas Mr. Kreymborg carried *Others* scarcely more than a year.
>   "Kreymborg's Millions," *Poetry* 18, 3 (June 1921), 175

It is precisely to the point that when Monroe does subsequently publish Kreymborg in 1923—and later Louis Zukofsky in 1924—the poems she prints are sonnets.[23]

While it may seem surprising to find either poet writing sonnets in the early 1920s, especially considering the very different kind of poetry each was publishing and. encouraging elsewhere, the sonnets of both Kreymborg and Zukofsky signal and even instantiate the more conservative poetic tradition that *Poetry* ultimately supported—despite its early

29

alliance with Imagism — and which continued to inform the verse of modern poets, at least as a palimpsest (most obviously in Cummings who successfully uses traditional form as a creative "trace"), despite their self-conscious desire to create a new aesthetic.

As Reed Whittemore notes, Harriet Monroe's consistent editorial principle was to "'keep free of entangling alliances with any single class or school,'" a principle he describes as "a curiously unsocial and unhistorical view of the nature of poetry, or of art and literature as a whole."[24] Yet, although *Poetry* (which began with Pound's collaboration) published very little of the kind of poetry included in the present volume, we should be careful to note that *not* adopting the more radical politics and aesthetic expressions of the time is not necessarily equivalent to having an apolitical or even a socially irrelevant response. A conservative stand *is* a political stand, one which may be viewed sympathetically (as with Pound's own ironic attempts to "Make It New") as an attempt at conservation.[25]

Certainly, *Poetry* proves both more socially aware and more "modern" than its rejection of cubist experimentation (and dada as well) might first suggest, when considering the kind of work published in one other journal, *Contemporary Verse*. In 1919, for example, the year both *Others* and the Great War came to a close, *Contemporary Verse* regularly published poems such as John Galsworthy's "At Sunset" (quoted in part below):

> I've seen the moon, with lifted wing —
>   A white hawk — over a cypress tree;
> The lover's star, the bloom of Spring,
>   And evening folded on Tennessee.
>
> *Contemporary Verse* 7, 6 (June 1919), 83

Even more nostalgic in tone is William Alexander Percy's "Three Spirituals" (published in 1921, the same year that Williams published "I Saw a Figure Five in Gold"), the first of which concludes with these lines:

> The peace of God, it is no peace
> But strife closed in the sod.
> Yet, brothers, pray for but one thing,
> The marvellous peace of God.
>
> *Contemporary Verse* 12, 1 (July 1921)

The difference between these particular poems and the poems we have been considering here — a difference which extends to larger aesthetic, political, and metaphysical differences — seems at first almost remarkable given the relatively late date of these poems. Cawein's "Waste Land," for example, which was written before the Great War began, seems in contrast to these understandably nostalgic. However, this "traditional" force in poetry, actually concurrent with the development of cubist poetry and other avant-garde poetry during the time, contextualizes the epigram chosen for *Others*: "The old expressions are always with us but there are always others."

Despite the large number of cubist poems discussed in this volume, it is thus essential to note that in the early part of this century the new cubist aesthetic in poetry was not appreciated in America any more significantly than was cubism in the visual arts. One of the more amusing and specific denouncements of the new kind of poetry that was beginning to appear in *Others* or *291* or *Soil* is Leslie N. Jennings' "An Unrepentant Victorian":

Communications.

AN UNREPENTANT VICTORIAN.
(To the Editor of THE DIAL.)

I am convalescing from a rather serious illness — a complaint which seems to have been epidemic in many communities, particularly among the groups of "serious thinkers." My own experience, while unpleasant, was instructive: maladies may have morals. May I present my own as a case in point? Perhaps there will be other sufferers who will find virtue in a like

CORRECTIVE.

I had been inoculated with the "New."
Everything must have a strong, acrid, unfamiliar taste —
"Reality," I called it.

Kreymborg, you became an apostle
Of the Emancipate!
I absorbed you, sure that I had dropped
My servility and my shackles.

"Mushrooms" were my diet exclusively —
Pearly and pink!
I turned gourmet,
Saucing the most impossible things
With "Others."

One day I was taken ill.
My physician, who is a learned, if old-fashioned,
Gentleman of the Victorian tradition,
Examined me carefully.

"My dear man," he said,
"You have been poisoned!"
He probed and pumped . . .
"I prescribe for you a Tennysonian Tonic."

And when he left I heard him say in passing:
"No wonder! He had gorged himself on —
Toadstools!"

LESLIE N. JENNINGS
Rutherford, Cal., March 15, 1917
The Dial 62, 739 (April 5, 1917), 298–99

Only three years later, it would be *The Dial* which would publish E. E. Cummings' strikingly "New" poetry—with a change in editors and a corresponding change in format and aesthetic policy.

Yet, in spite of the more traditional poetry being published during this period, the concluding issue of *Others* claims that "Everything we have ever done or can do . . . is being done now by any number of other MAGAZINES OF POETRY" (*Others* 5, 6 [July 1919], 3). In the "Supplement" to that issue, Williams specifically praises Margaret Anderson's *The Little Review* and goes on to explain why the "new form" in poetry is

> the ONLY form that CAN CARRY THE NEW MEANING that is imperatively required today. It is the ONE verse form that embodies the quality of thought which can be designated as modern. And it is only the modern which is worth expressing. The denotations, the connotations of all this, the sidelight it casts on religion on philosophy on abstract thought — these things exist and they are important and no poet has the time or ability to go into them.
>
> *Others*, Supplement (1919), 32

The closing of *Others* and the end of the Great War thus mark the end of the first exciting phase in the development of cubist poetry in America. In the following decade, this aesthetic would be more thoroughly disseminated (and more readily accepted) in America, as well as in Europe.

CAMERA WORK

Pablo Picasso

One whom some were certainly following was one who was completely charming. One whom some were certainly following was one who was charming. One whom some were following was one who was completely charming. One whom some were following was one who was certainly completely charming.

Some were certainly following and were certain that the one they were then following was one working and was one bringing out of himself then something. Some were certainly following and were certain that the one they were then following was one bringing out of himself then something that was coming to be a heavy thing, a solid thing and a complete thing.

One whom some were certainly following was one working and certainly was one bringing something out of himself then and was one who had been all his living had been one having something coming out of him.

Something had been coming out of him, certainly it had been coming out of him, certainly it was something, certainly it had been coming out of him and it had meaning, a charming meaning, a solid meaning, a struggling meaning, a clear meaning.

One whom some were certainly following and some were certainly following him, one whom some were certainly following was one certainly working.

One whom some were certainly following was one having something coming out of him something having meaning, and this one was certainly working then.

This one was working and something was coming then, something was coming out of this one then. This one was one and always there was something coming out of this one and always there had been something coming out of this one. This one had never been one not having something coming out of this one. This one was one having something coming out of this one. This one had been one whom some were following. This one was one whom some were following. This one was being one whom some were following. This one was one who was working.

33

This one was one who was working. This one was one being one having something being coming out of him. This one was one going on having something come out of him. This one was one going on working. This one was one whom some were following. This one was one who was working.

This one always had something being coming out of this one. This one was working. This one always had been working. This one was always having something that was coming out of this one that was a solid thing, a charming thing, a lovely thing, a perplexing thing, a disconcerting thing, a simple thing, a clear thing, a complicated thing, an interesting thing, a disturbing thing, a repellant thing, a very pretty thing. This one was one certainly being one having something coming out of him. This one was one whom some were following. This one was one who was working.

This one was one who was working and certainly this one was needing to be working so as to be one being working. This one was one having something coming out of him. This one would be one all his living having something coming out of him. This one was working and then this one was working and this one was needing to be working, not to be one having something coming out of him something having meaning, but was needing to be working so as to be one working.

This one was certainly working and working was something this one was certain this one would be doing and this one was doing that thing, this one was working. This one was not one completely working. This one was not ever completely working. This one certainly was not completely working.

This one was one having always something being coming out of him, something having completely a real meaning. This one was one whom some were following. This one was one who was working. This one was one who was working and he was one needing this thing needing to be working so as to be one having some way of being one having some way of working. This one was one who was working. This one was one having something come out of him something having meaning. This one was one always having something come out of him and this thing the thing coming out of him always had real meaning. This one was one who was working. This one was one who was almost always working. This one was not one completely working. This one was one not ever completely working. This one was not one working to have anything come out of him. This one did have something having meaning that did come out of him. He always did have something come out of him. He was working, he was not ever completely working. He did have some following. They were always following him. Some were certainly following him. He was one who was working.

He was one having something coming out of him something having meaning. He was not ever completely working.

GERTRUDE STEIN
(*Camera Work*, 1912)

(Untitled)

I know a place
        where reason halts
   in season and out of season
  where something takes the place
     in place of reason
  a spirit there hovers   roundabout
a something felt   by those who feel it
  here together   and to those who come
    a place of comfort
  a place electric a place alive
       a place magnetic
     since it started it existed
  for   those sincere: those thirsty ones
   to live their lives
     to do their do
 who feel they have
      yet cannot show.
The place is guarded,
  well guarded it
by He —— who jealously guards
  its innocence, purity, sincerity
 subtly guarded   it
so that — it seems — not guarded at all
     no tyrant he — yet tyrant of tyranny
  so shout — we who have felt it
  we who are of it
its past —— its future
  this place
  what place?
  Oh Hell   291

JOHN MARIN
(*Camera Work*, January 1915)

35

ROGUE

Aux Galeries Lafayette

One, one, one, one, there are many of them. There are very many of them. There are many of them. Each one of them is one. Each one is one, there are many of them. Each one is one, there are many of them, there are very many of them. Each one is one, there are many of them.

Each one is one. Each one is one, there are many of them. Each one is one. Each one has come to be accustomed to that thing. Each one is one. There are many of them.

Each one is one, each one is accustomed to it then. Each one is one. Each one is one, there are many of them. Each one is accustomed to it. Each one is one. There are many of them. Each one is one, each one is used to being that one. Each one is one. There are many of them. Each one is one, each one is quite used to being that one. Each one is one. There are many of them. Each one is one, each one is quite used to being one. Each one is quite used to being that one. Each one is one. Each one is quite used to being that one. Each one is one. There are many of them.

Each one is one. Each one is that one. There are many of them. Each one is one. Each one is that one. There are many of them. Each one is one.

Each one is one. There are many of them. Each one is that one. There are many of them. Each one is one. There are many of them. Each one is one. Each one is accustomed to that thing. Each one is one. There are many of them.

Each one is accustomed to being one. Each one is accustomed to being that one. There are many of them. Each one is accustomed to that thing.

Each one is one. Each one is that one. Each one is any one of them. There are many of them. Each one is one. Each one is that one. There are many of them. Each one is one. Each one is any one of them. Each one is one. Each one is accustomed to being that one. Each one is accustomed to being any one of them.

There are many of them. Each one is one. Each one is accustomed to be that one. Each one is quite accustomed to be that one. Each one is one. Each one is the one that one is being in being that one. There are many of them. Each one is one that is being one being one of them. There are many of them. Each one is one. Each one is one.

Each one is one. Each one is accustomed to being that one. Each one is one. Some one is accustomed to that one being that one. Some are accustomed to that one being that one. Some are sometimes accustomed to that one being that one. That one is accustomed to that one being that one. There are many of them. Each one is one. Each one is that one. Each one is quite accustomed to each one being that one. Each one is one. Each one is quite accustomed to being that one. Each one is one. Each one is that one. Each one is accustomed to being one. Each one is one. Each one is one.

Each one is one. Each one is being the one that one is being. Each one is one. Each one is being one. Each one is one. Each one is being the one that one is being. Each one is one. Each one is being the one each one is being. Each one is being one. Each one is being the one that one is being. Each one is being one. Each one is one.

Each one is one. Each one is very well accustomed to be one. Each one is very well accustomed to be that one. Each one is one. Each one is one. Each one is very well accustomed to be that one, to be the one that one is being. Each one is one. Each one is very well accustomed to be that one. Each one is very well accustomed to be that one. Each one is very well accustomed to be one that one is being. Each one is one. Each one is very well accustomed to be the one each one is being. Each one is one. Each one is one. Each one is being the one that one is being.

There are many of them. Each one is one being that one. Each one is one. There are many of them. Each one is one. Each one is any one, any one is each one. Each one is one. Each one is one and each one is the one each one is being in being that one. Each one in being one is one being one being especially that one. Each one in being one is one being that one, is one being one especially being that one. Each one is one. There are many of them. Each one is one and is being that one, is being that especial one, is especially being that one. There are many of them. Each one is one being especially that one, especially the one that one is being.

Each one is one and is that one and is especially that one and is that especial one and is accustomed to being that one, is used to being that one, is quite used to being that one, is very well accustomed to be that one, is certainly very well accustomed to be that especial one, is very well accustomed to be especially that one, is very well accustomed to be the one that one is being, is one that is being one and each one is one and there are many of them and each one is any one and any one is one, is an especial one, and each one is one, and there are many of them and each one is any one of them and any one of them is an especial one, and each one is one, each one is the one that is being that one, and each one is one, and each one is being the one each one is being, and each one is one, and each one is being each one, and each one is being the one each one is being, and each one is one is the one that one is being, each one is being one is one being the one that one is being. Each one is one. There are many of them. Each one is one. Each one is one being the especial one that one is being.

GERTRUDE STEIN
(*Rogue*, March 15, 1915)

Three Moments in Paris

I.

ONE O'CLOCK AT NIGHT

Though you had never possessed me
I had belonged to you since the beginning
   of time
And sleepily I sat on your chair beside you
Leaning against your shoulder
And your careless arm across my back
   gesticulated
As your indisputable male voice   roared
Through my brain and my body
Arguing dynamic decomposition
Of which I was understanding nothing
Sleepily
And the only less male voice of your brother
   pugilist of the intellect
Boomed   as it seemed to me   so sleepy
Across an interval of a thousand miles
An interim of a thousand years
But you who make more noise than any man
   in the world when you clear your throat
Deafening   woke me
And I caught the thread of the argument
Immediately assuming my personal mental
   attitude
And ceased to be a woman

Beautiful half-hour of being a mere woman
The animal woman

38

Understanding nothing of man
But mastery   and the security of im-
   parted physical heat
Indifferent to cerebral gymnastics
Or regarding them as the self-indulgent
   play of children
Or the thunder of alien gods
But you woke me up
Anyhow   who am I that I should criti-
   cize your theories of plastic velocity

"Let us go home   she is tired   and
   wants to go to bed."

II.
CAFÉ DU NÉANT

Little tapers leaning   lighted diagon-
   ally
Stuck in the coffin tables of the Café du Néant
Leaning to the breath of baited bodies
Like young poplars fringing the Loire

Eyes that are full of love
And eyes that are full of kohl
Projecting light across the fulsome am-
   biente
Trailing the rest of the animal behind them
Telling of tales without words
And lies of no consequence
One way or another

The young lovers hermetically buttoned up
   in black
To black cravat
To the blue powder edge dusting the yellow
   throat
What color could have been your bodies
When last you put them away

Nostalgic youth
Holding your mistress's pricked finger
In the indifferent flame of the taper
Synthetic symbol of   LIFE

In this factitious chamber of   DEATH
The woman
As usual
Is smiling   as bravely
As it is given to her to be   brave
While the brandy cherries
In winking glasses
Are decomposing
Harmoniously
With the flesh of spectators
And at a given spot
There is one
Who
Having the concentric lighting focussed
    precisely upon her
Prophetically blossoms in perfect putre-
    faction
Yet   there are cabs outside the door.

III.

MAGASINS DU LOUVRE

All the virgin eyes in the world are made
    of glass

Long lines of boxes
Of dolls
Propped against banisters
Walls and pillars
Huddled on shelves
And composite babies with arms extended
Hang from the ceiling
Beckoning
Smiling
In a profound silence
Which the shop walker left trailing behind
    him
When he ambled to the further end of the
    gallery
To annoy the shop-girl
All the virgin eyes in the world are made of
    glass
They alone have the effrontery to

Stare through the human soul
Seeing nothing
Between parted fringes

One cocotte wears a bowler hat and a sham
    camelia
And one an irridescent boa
For there are two of them
Passing
And the solicitous mouth of one is straight
The other curved to a static smile
They see the dolls
And for a moment their eyes relax
To a flicker of elements unconditionally
    primeval
And now averted
Seek each other's   surreptitiously
To know if the other has seen
While mine are inextricably entangled with
    the pattern of the carpet
As eyes are apt to be
In their shame
Having surprising a gesture that is ulti-
    mately intimate

All the virgin eyes in the world are made of
    glass.

MINA LOY
(*Rogue*, May 1, 1915)

Virgins Plus Curtains Minus Dots

Latin Borghese

Houses hold virgins
The doors on the chain

'Plumb streets with hearts'
'Bore curtains with eyes'

Virgins   without dots*

---

*Marriage Portions

Stare   beyond probability

See the men pass
Their hats are not ours
We   take a walk
They are going somewhere
And they   may look everywhere
Men's eyes   look into things
Our eyes   look out

A great deal of ourselves
We offer to the mirror
Something less to the confessional
The rest   to Time
There is so much   Time
Everything is full of it
                  Such a long time

Virgins may whisper
'Transparent nightdresses made all of lace'
Virgins may squeak
'My dear   I should faint!'
Flutter . . . . . flutter . . . . flutter . . . .
. . . . 'And then   the man—'
Wasting our giggles
For we have no dots

We have been taught
Love is a god

White   with soft wings
                  Nobody shouts
            Virgins for sale
Yet where are our coins
For buying a purchaser
Love is a god
                  Marriage expensive
A secret well kept
Makes the noise of the world
Nature's arms spread wide
Making room for us
                  Room for all of us
Somebody who was never

          a virgin
Has bolted the door
Put curtains at our windows
See the men pass
They   are going somewhere

Fleshes like weeds
Sprout in the light
So much flesh in the world
        Wanders at will

Some   behind curtains
Throbs to the night
Bait   to the stars

Spread it with gold
And you carry it home
Against your shirt front
To   a shaded light
With the door locked
Against virgins who
Might   scratch

MINA LOY
(*Rogue*, Aug. 15, 1915)

291

Flip-Flap

A man at a piano — thousands assembled, close, elbows touching,
        Waiting,
                Manufactured Soul-Stuff for those who
                    dare not create —
                Come and have your emotions played
                    upon!
                You like to suffer — so?
        Hush . . . . . .
        A Sound!
        Ah!
        He plays — you hear?
        Flip-flap . . . .
        All's forgotten —
                Emotions gyrate in the heavy air,
                  keeping time with the
                whirl and swirl of perfectly poised
                  tones.

        Sound and sound and sound . . . .
        Rippling —
        Flip-flap.

An instrument making sounds, and we the sounding boards!
Laugh loud — Soul — if you have content.

Why this devastating repression?   Can't you laugh? — This noise
    is terrific —
He is thundering out that bass — doing his best —
And the others?
All intently listening . . . . to their own feelings!
                (We are great! we men of inner response)

But you—Soul—could you laugh, yours would be the miracle—
Chopin and Schumann against your laugh!
                    Why don't you?
Can't you see yourself standing here looking down upon these
      cringing, countless,
round heads, and shapeless—and hair upon hair—and hats—and
      heads again—?
All these million eyes would look—
Every living man, even he who plays—would listen—and
      marvel—
                    Where's that laugh?
                    The music fills the house!
                    Louder! louder!
                    He pounds at the climax!
                    C sharp—he slipped—I cannot breathe—
                    Even the air has turned to sound!
                    They are applauding!   Soul!!
Because he finished—because you did not stop him—
He smiles—he almost laughs!
                    Endless noise and hands clapping—
                    A buzz of words—
                    I'm stifled—done for—

He seems quite calm himself—
He has gone beyond his finger-tips to feed these heads with his
      inner dartings—
He doesn't look much of a man—yet all these souls are flapping
      and turning
and beating and yearning—
                    No laugh yet?   Soul of me—why not?
                    To break into this orgie—into this maze of
                        sound and tensity—
                    —where tuned-up Beauty flatters some few
                        hundred humans, and
                    lends them a vitality for this infected Now.

                    Why mock the Artist? the Art that does the
                        trick? the thing
                    that stirs and sighs?
                                    What's a laugh to that?

45

A Laugh! such as this would be—could I laugh now!
Out into this sea of dreadful stutterings I'd throw an invasion—a
   revision—
Fool!
      A Whole Self—laughing—
      Yes, all—only my body dead—left here—
         Flip-flap—
         But the laugh?
Suppose they didn't feel a life float there before them—
   laughing—
Didn't know just what a soul sounds like—
         Could I ever stop?

                                Who's laughing?

                      KATHARINE N. RHOADES
                         (*291*, June 1915)

Narcosis

Black spots
               moving
                      walking
                                   scattering
A million insistent centres at conflict
Countless forces and counter forces
         walking. .
         walking. .
         endlessly walking. .
Interminably dull yet irresistibly hypnotic
         a narcotic
Dull monotonous thuds and endless motion of men.

      Within—without—
      Whirling antagonisms

                              dissipating
                              destroying

Perpetual motion
             Light
             Bulk
             Lesion
             Need
Cohesion?

                                  KATHARINE N. RHOADES
                                      (*291*, Feb. 1916)

OTHERS

Lento

Two children   walking.

So slow their walk,
So like a sleepy wind their talk—

Arm sagging at the other's waist,
Close as leaves fallen on wet grass—

Their slippers follow oily waves of heat,
Lazy as gorged fishes,
Lazy as minutes
Swimming in the silence of an empty house
In midsummer—

The drifting yellow ashes of the sun
cover their hair—

So slow they are,
The drowsy seconds settle on their shoulders
and fold wings—

And one small footstep   sings
To the next one
A lullaby—

The hours wait them   at the gate,
Sighing,
As the little feet   tick by.

ROBERT ALDEN SANBORN
(*Others*, Nov. 1915)

Metric Figure

Veils of clarity
have succeeded
veils of color

that wove
as the sea
sliding above
submerged whiteness

Veils of clarity
reveal sand
glistening—
falling away
to an edge—
sliding
beneath the advancing ripples.

WILLIAM CARLOS WILLIAMS
(*Others*, Feb. 1916)

Rapière à Deux Points

(To G. K.)

Your eyes
are like two flames
dancing
on the carved surface
of a gem.

EDWARD RAMOS
(*Others*, March 1916)

Later Songs

I

The one who gives them out is short of dreams,
With jealous husbandry
He deals them carefully,
One dream to every two people.
"You must share it,
We're short of dreams," he says.
But they
Are only glad of the excuse of sitting down
To the same dream—

II

Perhaps,
God, planting Eden,
Dropped, by mistake, a seed
In Time's neighbor-plot,
That grew to be
This hour?

III

You and I picked up Life and looked at it curiously;
We did not know whether to keep it for a plaything
        or not.
It was beautiful to see, like a red firecracker,
And we knew, too, that it was lighted.
We dropped it while the fuse was still burning—

IV

The careful ocean sews
Pools, like round blue buttons
On the gray coat of the sand.

V

The sun is dying
Alone
On an island
In the bay.
Close your eyes, poppies!
—I would not have you see death,
You are so young—

VI

The sun falls
Like a drop of blood
From some hero.

We,
Who love pain,
Delight in this.

VII

A woman stepped up behind me and spoke confidentially,
"You forgot to put on convention," she said, "and your
        soul shows through."

50

VIII

I waited upon a hill for the sunrise.
(It was a very little hill.)
I waited for the sunrise.
In the chill dark I waited.

And in the cool gray before any dawn.
I waited for the sunrise,
With lips apart to praise.

But when it came it was a very old sunrise,
And I went away weeping.

IX

You are calling upon me,
Fashionably clothed,
Properly prepared with small talk.
I sit sedately and help build up
The stone wall between us, with my little bricks of yes
    and no.

There are hothouse flowers on the table,
New York is outside the window — and inside —

The housemaid has set the chairs as carefully in their
    spheres as God could ever have placed the stars.

Within the grate
There is a fire burning,

It has nearly gone out.
It is only a smouldering red thing now.

But as we look at it
Suddenly ages crumple,
The room vanishes,
You and I are a man and woman in a cave
With fire —

X

Take what the gods give.
Tomorrow may be Monday on Olympus

MARY CAROLYN DAVIES
(*Others,* April 1916)

Excerpts from **Songs to Joannes**

Unnatural selection
Breed such sons and daughters
As shall jibber at each other
Uninterpretable cryptonyms
Under the moon

Give them some way of braying brassily
For carressive calling
Or to homophonous hiccoughs
Transpose the laugh
Let them suppose that tears
Are snowdrops or molasses
Or anything
Than human insufficiencies
Begging dorsal vertebrae

Let meeting be the turning
To the antipodean
And Form   a blurr
Anything
Than seduce them
To the one
As simple satisfaction
For the other

Let them clash together
From their incognitoes
In seismic orgasm
For far further
Differentiation
Rather than watch
Own-self distortion
Wince in the alien ego

XXX

In some
Prenatal plagiarism
Foetal buffoons
Caught tricks
— — — — —

From architypal pantomime

Stringing emotions
Looped aloft
— — — —

For the blind eyes
That Nature knows us with
And the most of Nature   is green
— — — — — — — — —

What guaranty
For the proto-form
We fumble
Our souvenir ethics to
— — — — — —

XXXI

Crucifixion
Of a busy-body
Longing to interfere so
With the intimacies
Of your insolent isolation

Crucifixion
Of an illegal ego's
Eclosion
On your equilibrium
Caryatid   of an idea

Crucifixion
Wracked arms
Index extremities
In vacuum
To the unbroken fall

XXXII

The moon is cold
Joannes
Where the Mediterranean — — — — —

XXXIII

The prig of passion — — — —
To your professorial paucity

Proto-plasm was raving mad
Evolving us — — —

XXXIV

Love — — — the preeminent literateur

MINA LOY
(*Others,* April 1917)

Thirteen Ways of Looking at a Blackbird

I

Among twenty snowy mountains,
The only moving thing
Was the eye of the blackbird.

II

I was of three minds,
Like a tree
In which there are three blackbirds.

III

The blackbird whirled in the autumn winds,
It was a small part of the pantomime.

IV

A man and a woman
Are one.
A man and a woman and a blackbird
Are one.

V

I do not know which to prefer—
The beauty of inflections
Or the beauty of innuendoes,
The blackbird whistling
Or just after.

VI

Icicles filled the long window
With barbaric glass.
The shadow of the blackbird
Crossed it, to and fro.

The mood
Traced in the shadow
An indecipherable cause.

VII

O thin men of Haddam,
Why do you imagine golden birds?
Do you not see how the blackbird
Walks around the feet
Of the women about you?

VIII

I know noble accents
And lucid, inescapable rhythms;
But I know, too,
That the blackbird is involved
In what I know.

IX

When the blackbird flew out of sight,
It marked the edge
Of one of many circles.

X

At the sight of blackbirds
Flying in a green light,
Even the bawds of euphony
Would cry out sharply.

XI

He rode over Connecticut
In a glass coach.
Once, a fear pierced him,
In that he mistook
The shadow of his equipage
For blackbirds.

XII

The river is moving.
The blackbird must be flying.

XIII

It was evening all afternoon.
It was snowing
And it was going to snow.
The blackbird sat
In the cedar-limbs.

WALLACE STEVENS
(*Others*, Dec. 1917)

Steel Town

       Gray
       as with time
       and austere
       as the colonnades of a ruined temple
       stand the steel-mill chimneys
       at sundown.
       Curved
       knotted
       stems of fleurs de lys
       rise the gray smoke columns
       to blossom in blackening mist,

While the trams course along the dull streets
Flashing at intervals with bill-boards,
While sooty Jews sell second-hand furniture
And ladies go on buying laces,
Till the little shop-girls flitter home
Shivering under their cat-furs.

       Then
       red
       as Aurora,
       unchanging,
       glow the furnaces
       all night,
       and the clouds are like meadows of poppies
       the wind waves over and flickers:

Trip hammers thud
in regular fall
streams of white iron flow surely,
While the good folk sleep in their beds,
And the young folk kiss between dances,
While newsies doze on cold doorways,
Till the cinema screens cease to flicker,
Till milkmen scuff on back porches.

Then
gray
as with time
and austere
as the colonades of a ruined temple
stand the steel-mill chimneys
at sunrise,
and curved
like pale
stems of iris
rise the smoke-columns
to blossom
in soot-dripping
mist.

DAPHNE CARR
(*Others*, April–May, 1919)

SOIL

Primordia

1.

All over Minnesota,
Cerise sopranos,
Walking in the snow,
Answer, humming,
The male voice of the wind in the dry leaves
Of the lake hollows.
For one,
The syllables of the gulls and of the crows
And of the blue-bird
Meet in the name
Of Jalmar Lillygreen.
There is his motion
In the flowing of black water.

2.

The child's hair is of the color of the hay in the haystack, around
which the four black horses stand.
There is the same color in the bellies of frogs, in clays, withered
reeds, skins, wood, sunlight.

3.

The blunt ice flows down the Mississippi,
At night.
In the morning, the clear river
Is full of reflections,
Beautiful alliterations of shadows and of things shadowed.

4.

The horses gnaw the bark from the trees.
The horses are hollow,
The trunks of the trees are hollow.
Why do the horses have eyes and ears?
The trees do not.

Why can the horses move about on the ground?
The trees cannot.
The horses weary themselves hunting for green grass.
The trees stand still,
The trees drink.
The water runs away from the horses.
La, la, la, la, la, la, la, la,
Dee, dum, diddle, dee, dee, diddle, dee, da.

5.

The birch trees draw up whiteness from the ground.
In the swamps, bushes draw up dark red,
Or yellow.
O, boatman,
What are you drawing from the rain-pointed water?
O, boatman,
What are you drawing from the rain-pointed water?
Are you two boatmen
Different from each other?

In the South.

6.

Unctuous furrows,
The ploughman portrays in you
The spring about him:
Compilation of the effects
Of magenta blooming in the Judas-tree
And of purple blooming in the eucalyptus—
Map of yesterday's earth
And of to-morrow's heaven.

7.

The lilacs wither in the Carolinas.
Already the butterflies flutter above the cabins.
Already the new-born children interpret love
In the voices of mothers.
Timeless mother,
How is it that your aspic nipples
For once vent honey?

The pine-tree sweetens my body.
The white iris beautifies me.

8.

The black mother of eleven children
Hangs her quilt under the pine-trees.
There is a connection between the colors,
The shapes of the patches,
And the eleven children . . .
Frail princes of distant Monaco,
That paragon of a parasol
Discloses
At least one baby in you.

9.

The trade-wind jingles the rings in the nets around the racks by the
[docks on Indian River.
It is the same jingle of the water among the roots under the banks of
[the palmettoes,
It is the same jingle of the red-bird breasting the orange-trees out of
[the cedars.
Yet there is no spring in Florida, neither in boskage perdu, nor on
[the nunnery beaches.

To the Roaring Wind.

What syllable are you seeking,
Vocalissimus,
In the distances of sleep?
Speak it.

WALLACE STEVENS
(*Soil*, Jan. 1917)

2 The "REVOLUTION"
of the Early 1920s

Despite the dissolution of *291* in 1916, of *Soil* in 1917, and of *Others* in 1919, this "vital page in literary history" did not end, as Sanborn obviously feared it had when he elegized R. J. Coady in "A Champion in the Wilderness" (1922).[1] Rapidly, the new kind of poetry encouraged by these ventures spread to other magazines already established or to new magazines which, alternately, either floundered or survived with at least some short-lived success. In 1920, for example, one year after the closing of *Others*, Williams began the first of his two journals called *Contact*.[2] In the same year, *The Dial* changed its format entirely (under new editorship) and became much more strictly a journal concerned with the arts, including visual art as well as poetry.[3] At the same time, *The Little Review*, which had advertised wittily for "art" in 1917 with a "want ad" of ten blank pages, suddenly surfaced with the kind of work which subsequently made it so famous. *Broom*, a direct descendant of this entire movement (originally begun with the collaborative editing of Harold Loeb and Alfred Kreymborg) printed its first issue in Italy in 1921. Thereafter followed *Secession*, *Blues*, *Pagany*, a second *Contact*, as well as *The Exile* in Italy, *transition* in Paris, and other avant-garde journals in America such as *Furioso* and *View*.

As the allusion to Margaret Anderson's journal in the closing supplement of *Others* suggests, *The Little Review* was one of the earlier (and most long-lived) of the various journals which self-consciously promoted modern aesthetic developments. Despite the praise, however, *The Little Review* was not of real significance to the development of cubist poetry during its first few years. Although Margaret Anderson had specifically called for "revolution" in a 1915 editorial—in the name of a "Spirit" that should revolt against institutions in which no one any longer believed

("Toward Revolution," 1915) — this particular "spirit" was not really pro-
moted until Pound became the foreign editor for the journal in 1917,
ceasing, almost immediately thereafter, to serve as foreign correspondent
for *Poetry*. It was then that what Williams (curiously) calls "Free verse" in
the "Supplement" above became more clearly cubist in the poetry pub-
lished in *The Little Review*.[4] In this second phase of *The Little Review* we also
find a more consistently thematized concern with the correspondence of
aesthetic "revolution" and the socio-political realities of the time.

The role that Ezra Pound played in increasing a certain critical
divisiveness in American poetics is particularly clear in this instance.
Although in his accepting editorial in *The Little Review* he first announced
his continued connection with *Poetry,* Pound criticized Harriet Monroe's
choice of poetry in that same editorial, and it was not long before Pound
broke with *Poetry* altogether. Given Monroe's disparagement of *Others*
(noted in Chapter One), the emergent strife that began between these two
major publishers of American poetry is not altogether humorously sig-
naled by the subtitle *The Little Review* chose in 1918 — "The Magazine That
Is Read By Those Who Write the Others." The friction was to become
more intense, even bitter, as seen in an editorial of the special Picabia
number of 1922, in which Jane Heap vehemently attacked Monroe's criti-
cism of the modernist poetry (particularly that of Else von Freytag-
Loringhoven) which *The Little Review* was publishing:

Dada—

"The trouble is *The Little Review* never knows when to stop. Just now it is
headed straight for Dada; but we could forgive even that if it would drop
Else von Freytag-Loringhoven on the way." — From an article by Harriet
Monroe in *Poetry*.

Any one may say anything he pleases as long as he is willing to stand
by what he says.

I don't think Harriet Monroe knew when to stop. But then we're
different: we don't feel that we have ever suggested we were going to stop,
not even at or in jail.

(Spring 1922), 46

What was at stake was no less than a political stance — one which was
figured in aesthetic "revolution," but extended to actual social revolution
against traditional institutions. As Margaret Anderson had noted as early
as 1916, "There are 'revolutions' going on in all the arts. The revolution in
poetry is coming in for a lot of discussion, so that even the layman is
conscious of it" ("A Deeper Music," *The Little Review* 2, 10 [1916], 3). As her
early editorial "Toward Revolution" had also intimated, such aesthetic
revolutions (and most certainly a lay knowledge of such revolutions) are
deeply aligned with socio-political revolutions as well.

Yet, while many of these writers (including, most notably, Pound himself) had an intensely idealistic, rather than anarchistic, conception of such "revolutions," the aesthetic revolution "going on in all the arts" mirrored for many other people the threat of total social chaos—a chaos which was made manifest in the Great War and which, as most people immediately recognized, had not been resolved by that war. It is with as much fear (and a subsequent kind of isolationist reactionism) as with scientific curiosity that Williams asserts in the 1919 "Supplement" to *Others*, "I am not one damned bit interested in socialism or anarchy but I am interested and deeply interested in the brain that requires socialism and anarchy and brings it on." Whether intentionally or not, this remark clearly points to the more radical interpretation of both political and aesthetic developments that many people had suspected was true of cubism (and would become convinced was true of dada). The divergence we begin to see during this period between various artists, poets, and editors who had been working together is not apolitically motivated on any side, but reflects, instead, very different interpretations of aesthetic *intent* as well as content. (It may go without saying that similar aesthetic/political lines were drawn by rock 'n roll in the fifties, hard rock in the sixties, new wave in the seventies—and, ironically, even by post-structuralist criticism in the eighties.)

Despite Picasso's dismissal of "transitional arts," the arts were thus very much in transition at the time—with increasing visibility and increasing political consequence. Most of these writers seem to have been fully aware of their function and power as "tradition-makers" (to borrow Frank Lentricchia's term), who were necessarily and "profoundly implicated in the enforcement of a politics of sociocultural conservation and continuity."[5] Since this function seems almost unavoidable (although the impulse behind dada may have been to escape if not destroy it), the question was, and remains, which values are to be conserved and which are to be changed. Not surprisingly, perhaps, Nietzsche figured as a major influence during this time, for both painters and poets as well.

Just as *The Little Review* was evolving from a *relatively* tame journal into a more aggressively avant-garde one—that is, in 1918—Williams' "Improvisations" and Stevens' "Anecdote of Men by the Thousand" and "Nuances of a Theme by Williams" appeared in this journal.[6] After that year, however, Stevens ceased to publish in *The Little Review*, appearing with increasing frequency in *Poetry*. This fact marks not only an aesthetic but a political divergence for which several critics have taken Stevens to task.[7] If, however, we remember that the most acute prompting for a kind of aesthetic reactionism was that of dada—and if we have any sympathy for the desire to resist what might seem consciously destructive and essentially anarchistic, given the actual political context of the time—then both Stevens and Pound seem not only sympathetic, but ironically similar in their own idealistic responses to their time.[8] While Pound tried to dismantle the very structures that would lead to another world war—an attempt reflected in the kind of literature he chose to write and to promote—Stevens began to fear and perhaps ultimately to accept the inevitability of the coming global violence, rejecting forms of writing which seemed to him to mirror (rather than resist) that chaos. Increasingly, especially in the late 1930s, he turned his own verse toward a specific "resistance" to that violence.[9] Stevens' break with the "New Poetry Movement," particularly with that facet of the movement which took the form of expatriatism, however, occurred well before then—sometime around the very early 1920s. Not only did he cease to publish in *The Little Review*, aligning himself more solidly with *Poetry*, but by 1922 he had rejected what he seems to have regarded as a new artistic mafia in the form of the "Independents," and to have deliberately moved himself outside of the inner aesthetic circle we have been examining.[10] Yet what is ultimately more important is that from the distance which time now allows, we can see both a certain blindness in the more conservative attitudes of some of these writers and editors and also the potentially painful fanaticism of some of the more liberal attitudes. Both are understandable, if not condonable. In this regard, Pound's subsequent imprisonment at the end of World War II in what amounts to a wire cage may be seen as the realized consequence of a battle being fought on aesthetic and political battle "lines"—with, I should add, some obvious and deeply painful ironies and fanaticisms on both sides.

In terms of this volume, however, it is important to stress that only with the nearly simultaneous closing of *Others* and the end of the first World War, and with the introduction of Pound as foreign editor, did *The Little Review* become increasingly avant-garde, generating a great deal of controversy (as, for example, when it serialized Joyce's *Ulysses*) over the next decade. As with most of the journals discussed so far, the impact of many disparate artistic movements—including futurism, surrealism, constructivism, expressionism—can be seen in the range and variety of works chosen for publication in *The Little Review*. More and more European artists and poets began to appear in the journal, including Brancusi, Else von Freytag-Loringhoven, Jean Cocteau, Apollinaire, and Braque. By 1922 or so, *The Little Review* was virtually indistinguishable from *Broom*, which was founded the previous year and in which, ironically, Stevens frequently appeared, despite his disparagement of "nativist expatriation" at its inception.[11] Before it folded, *The Little Review* had increasingly aligned itself with surrealism. The special issue of Spring 1926, for instance, is devoted to surrealism and dada and bears the subtitle of a "Collection of Some Young Americans — In Contrast with the Work of Some Young Europeans: Mostly French-Surrealistes."

Among the aesthetic movements promoted by *The Little Review,* however, cubism remained prominent. The November issue of 1917, for instance, reproduced Max Weber's drawing of Gaudier-Brzeska and Wyndham Lewis' "The Starry Sky," both of which derive from cubism. As late as 1922 and 1924, special issues were devoted to Picabia, Sheeler, and Juan Gris, respectively, which reproduced several cubist paintings and drawings, as well as critical discussions of cubism. Included in the special Picabia number and the Winter issue of 1922, for example, is Apollinaire's "Aesthetic Meditations," which considers cubism at length. And in addition to serializing *Ulysses, The Little Review* also printed sections of Pound's *Cantos;* both of these works have subsequently been described as cubist literature.[12]

In fact, most of the cubist poems published in this journal are, generally speaking, now so accessible as to preclude their being reproduced in this volume. For instance, Williams' "Improvisations," two sections of which appear below, appeared in the issue that advertised itself as "The Magazine That Is Read By Those Who Write the Others":

1

So far away August green as it yet is. They say the sun still comes up o'mornings and it's harvest moon now. Always one leaf at the peak-twig swirling, swirling and apples rotting in the ditch.

2

My wife's uncle went to school with Amundsen. After he Amundsen returned from the South Pole there was a Scandinavian dinner, which bored him Amundsen like a boyhood friend. There was a young woman at his table, silent and aloof from the rest. She left early and he restless at some impalpable delay apologised suddenly and went off with two friends, his great, lean bulk twitching agilely. One knew why the poles attracted him. Then my wife's mother told us the same old thing, of how a girl in their village jilted him years back. But the girl at the supper! Ah — that comes later when we are wiser and older!

The Little Review 5, 9 (January 1918), 3

Stevens' "Metaphors of a Magnifico" appeared in June, 1918, in an issue that notably includes Williams, Djuna Barnes, and Kreymborg. As noted in the previous chapter, this poems bears a distinct affinity to Stein's "Aux Galeries Lafayette" in which Stein manipulates the possibilities of perspective through verbal repetition of (and substitution in) the line "Each one is one. There are many of them." In Stevens' poem, which extends this visual and verbal manipulation to the realm of philosophical enquiry, "Twenty men crossing a bridge/ Into a village" may be twenty men "Crossing twenty bridges/ Into twenty villages" or simply "one man/ Crossing a single bridge into a village." Furthermore, four separate times a thought ends, or rather begins, only to be left as an ellipsis marks simultaneously the evocation and the absence of the idea. This Cézannean touch (most notable in "The first white wall of the village") calls attention to the material nature of the poem itself, ironically announcing that the meditation it evokes "will not declare itself/ Yet is as certain as meaning. . . ." (ellipsis Stevens').

Of special interest is the American number of December, 1918, (which includes Barnes, Anderson, Marianne Moore, Hartley, and Williams, among others), for the two poems by Stevens which appeared there variously confirm his interest in cubist strategies and prefigure his subsequent rejection of the cubist aesthetic. As previously noted, "Nuances of a Theme by Williams" (see p. 78) is self-consciously a collage in which Williams' text is pasted, as it were, onto Stevens', and thereby transformed from a text of independent status (and, presumably, of independent "theme") into a fragment, the meaning of which is irrevocably altered by the ironic play on mirroring as subversive "reflecting" in the poem's next two sections. Somewhat surprisingly, then, the other poem by Stevens included in this special issue, that is, "Architecture for the Adoration of Beauty," appears to challenge the cubist aesthetic, especially the potential for, if not propensity for, reduction and destruction. It is, perhaps, with a rather playful gesture toward constructivism as well that Stevens asks, "What manner of building shall we build for/ The adoration of beauty?" Yet the seriousness of this seemingly sentimental question is made clear in the fifth section, which challenges cubist fragmentation:

> How shall we hew the sun,
> Split it and make blocks,
> To build a ruddy palace?
> How carve the violet moon
> To set in nicks?

> *The Little Review* (December 1918), 11

The conservative attitude implied by this poem accounts for his never appearing in this journal again, despite its relative longevity.

Of the more radical poets to appear subsequently in *The Little Review*, Else von Freytag-Loringhoven proves especially interesting not only because her poetry prompted the controversy between this journal and *Poetry*, but also because her work shows the specific influence of Mina Loy's cubist strategies. For instance, in her "Buddha" (see p. 78), the use of dashes for "marking" full lines of poetry as well as for signaling incomplete thoughts continues Loy's technique developed in *Songs to Joannes*. In fact, the special Exiles number of *The Little Review* (which includes Hemingway, H. D., Stein, and Cummings, among others) also includes the first part of Loy's remarkable "Anglo-Mongrels and the Rose" (part of which is included here), a poem which has been described as "one of the lost master-poems of the twentieth century."[13]

Finally, I have included here Robert McAlmon's "The black cat loops," which appeared in the special Juan Gris issue (August–Winter, 1924–25). In this particular poem, which humorously contrasts an older black cat with a Siamese kitten, the white space and unusual line breaks succeed in creating the sensation of movement and agility rather than emphasizing the materiality of the text. In this sense, McAlmon's verse demonstrates the dynamic possibilities of developing verbal techniques just as Duchamp demonstrates the dynamic possibilities of cubist forms in such works as "Nude Descending a Staircase."

Despite its diversity, then, and despite its particular alliance with dada and surrealism, *The Little Review* proves to be critical to the development of American cubist poetry and to its increasing influence.

*****

Just as *The Little Review* was changing both in tone and content at the end of the War, *The Dial* also changed in format and focus as it became, essentially, the *fourth* magazine of that name. In 1920 the new editors chose to include for the first time reproductions of visual art and to print the first of E. E. Cummings' remarkable "experiments," a group of seven poems. Of these, the third one most clearly points to a strategy that Cummings would explore with so much success and with such rapidity in the next few years. In particular, the violation of word boundaries, such as "onetwothreefourfive," quickly becomes inverted in subsequent poems so that words are broken, rather than fused, with parts of the same word (even monosyllabic words) appearing on different lines. This strategy is then further complicated, so that parts of words intrude between parts of other words — largely a synthetic cubist strategy. It is not surprising, then, that Cummings would write in his review of Eliot, that by

> technique we do mean one thing: the alert hatred of normality which, through the lips of a tactile and cohesive adventure, asserts that nobody in general and some in particular is incorrigibly and actually alive.
>
> *The Dial* 68 (1920), 783

In the same year that it introduced Cummings into the American scene, *The Dial* also published Pound's fourth "Canto," one of Demuth's cubist pieces, "A Box of Tricks," as well as Cummings' review of Eliot mentioned above. Soon followed Pound's now famous "Hugh Selwyn Mauberly," accompanied by a sketch of Pound done by Wyndham Lewis, and several other poems by Cummings. The fourth *Dial*, then, was clearly committed to promoting the cubist aesthetic in American verse.

The difference between the kind of cubist poetry with which we are concerned here and what might be termed more generally "free verse" (however modern in theme) can be seen in the work of Evelyn Scott and Alfred Kreymborg printed in *The Dial* at approximately the same time. Scott's "Designs," for example, printed in the same issue which first included Cummings, is indebted to imagism, as the following example shows:

Night

Fields of black tulips,
And swarms of gold bees
Drinking their bitter honey.

> *The Dial* 68 (1920), 71

In fact, none of her nine poems published in this issue in any way explores the possibilities of *form* suggested by Cummings' unusual typography — or that of Mina Loy, for that matter — even if such lines as Scott's "Washed by the light/ My sharp breasts silvered" do reflect the growing feminist interest in sexual liberation so typical of Loy's verse.[14] Similarly, Kreymborg's "Dorothy," also included in the same issue, appears relatively traditional in technique when compared to most of the poems collected here, despite his own obvious interest in and promotion of the more experimental poetry. Nonetheless, the breaking of the female body into disconnected parts, with alternately violent and sentimental moods, repeats on the thematic level a strategy employed in cubist paintings, from Picasso's "Girl with a Mandolin" (1910) to "The Dream" (1932).

The few examples of cubist poetry from this journal reprinted here signal the degree to which this new aesthetic was increasing in power and influence in America at the beginning of the twenties. It was an influence which would expand somewhat erratically but tenaciously over the next three years.

*****

Of the "other" magazines to follow rapidly on the American scene after the close of *Others,* William Carlos Williams' *Contact,* first issued in December of 1920, was among the least successful of these—even though Mina Loy, Marsden Hartley, and Wallace Stevens all appeared on its pages. Nonetheless, Ezra Pound's parenthetical conclusion to his review of *Credit Power and Democracy,* which also appeared in this journal, is worth citing as one of many instances of political and aesthetic convergence:

> Don't imagine that I think economics interesting—not as Botticelli or Picasso is interesting. But at present they, as the reality under *political camouflage,* are interesting as a gun muzzle aimed at one's own head is "interesting," when one can hardly see the face of the gun holder and is wholly uncertain as to his temperament and intentions. [italics mine]

A twentieth-century military term, "camouflage" had particular visual and cubist connotations lent by Picasso via Stein, as we have seen immediately after the Great War, as well as the obvious military ones usually associated with the word now.

The Measure, founded in 1921, seems curiously untouched by the force of cubism, given the date of its first issue. While the poems published are not nearly so nostalgic or traditional as those which appeared in such journals as *Contemporary Verse,* the more acutely experimental poems we have been considering are not typical of this more traditional journal. Among the few exceptions are Stevens' 1923 "New England Verses" and Wyndham Lewis' "Notes for an Epilogue," as well as an especially astute review of Cummings written by Robert L. Wolf ("On The Right, Ladies and Gentlemen...," *The Measure,* 41 [July 1924], 14–18), which is included in the Appendix.

The review, written by a former classmate of Cummings, ultimately proves to be quite favorable, but begins with the complaint that when Cummings published "Orientale" in the *Harvard Monthly* (described as "that fertile organ which has given birth successively to the *New Republic* and *The Dial*"),

> the poem was printed like any other poem, reading from left to right, from the top of the page to the bottom, and with scansion, spelling, punctuation, and grammar quite according to the rules of the English Department.

Then, Wolf says, after a "war and a few other things intervened," Cummings remained obscure "until one day he broke out like a new kind of typographical measles in *The Dial*":

> The effect, of course, was to set everyone talking of the new poet—those who dislike eccentricity for its own sake with irritation, and the Others with admiration and delight.

As witty as these remarks may be, Wolf's most important contribution is the observation that Cummings "has invented a new form of entertainment—he is a linotype-sketcher, possibly, or a draughtsman in printer's ink," that he has succeeded "for the first time in history, in freezing the gesture onto the printed page," and that he has abandoned "voice, with its single dimension, for the surface, which has length and breadth." Although Wolf credits his friend with more initiative than he perhaps deserves, his description of Cummings' poetry could, with very little adjustment, quite accurately describe a number of the poems discussed so far.

As a reminder of other parts of the climate, *The Measure* also proves interesting for suggesting something of the growing preoccupation with the younger "generation" that was so universal after the war: the cover of the second issue reads, "Nineteen Poems by Americans of the Younger Generation." And a 1925 issue, which announces, "Two Girl Poets Reviewed," reminds us of the difficulty women were still having in being taken *seriously* (even though, as we know, a large number of women were publishing at the time), a difficulty which is made quite specific in Maxwell Anderson's review of Amy Lowell, "A Prejudiced Word on Amy Lowell," and in Rolfe Humphries' review of Marianne Moore, "Precieuse, Model 1924."[15]

*****

All of the journals mentioned so far were published on American soil, even if particular individuals, such as Pound, were "exiled" in Europe. With *Broom*, however (a journal in which Cummings regularly appeared), we see a specific example of the truly international and intercontinental intersection of the modernist movement in general and of cubism in particular. Founded by Americans Loeb and Kreymborg in 1921, but first published in Italy, ironically for economic reasons, the first issue reproduces Stella's "Brooklyn Bridge" and a cubist still life by Gris. This issue also contains Conrad Aiken's powerful essay, "The Function of Criticism," which (possibly as a reaction to growing Marxist thought) argues that when aesthetic values have been lost, "criticism" rather than the arts becomes "the debate," while intimating that as the "tyranny of religious ethics" is vanishing, a new tyranny of "utilitarian ethics" may be taking its place (*Broom* 1, 1 [November 1921], 33–38). Although not the most important essay published in the journal, "The Function of Criticism" simultaneously points to the growing divisiveness among those who thought of themselves as "modernists" and anticipates something of the growing importance of—and conflict within—criticism today.

As is true of *The Little Review,* on the pages of *Broom* many different strands of the modern art movement come together. Perhaps because of the hostility Harriet Monroe felt toward the founding and funding of this journal, Stevens seems to have been contemptuous of the journal as well. Yet even though he wrote in 1921 that "Kreymborg, his ox, his ass, his maid-servant, and so on, are going to Italy in June to publish a magazine which they intend shall be something a good deal more portentous than the *Dial*," he still appears to have arranged for John Rodker to join the project.[16] Certainly, he published in the journal quite regularly (though not always with cubist or cubist-influenced verse)—as did Williams, who shared Stevens' attitude toward the inherent contradiction of expatriated Americanism. Curiously, then, Else von Freytag-Loringhoven, whose alliance with dada provoked the heated argument between Harriet Monroe and Jane Heap and the schism between *Poetry* and *The Little Review,* also published in *Broom.* Her "Circle," while not included here, calls attention to typography in a way that is similar to that of Apollinaire, while espousing a dadaist theme, and thereby suggests one way in which the simplest interpretation of verbal cubism as a visual phenomenon verges on another aesthetic development.

In general, the pieces included here from *Broom* reflect the impact of an American cubist aesthetic on that of Europe, as well as the continued impact of European art on the American. Many of the artists and poets now seem quite familiar. In addition to Stevens, Williams, and Cummings, Man Ray, Sanborn, Marianne Moore, Yvor Winters, Paul Klee, Jean Cocteau, Papini, and Virginia Woolf (to name only a few) all published in this journal. And although *Broom* embraced many different artistic movements (especially surrealism), cubism is clearly identifiable. Stein's "If You Had Three Husbands" appears in this journal, as does Cummings' "Sunset" and "Three Portraits." Malcolm Cowley's "Portrait by Leyendecker" (not included) is an especially witty conflation and collage of prose, poetry, and the particular visual use of language beginning to be found prominently on billboards. The force of cubism is especially clear in the

71

August issue of 1923, which includes Harold Loeb's "A Note on Juan Gris and Cubism," illustrated by several of Gris' cubist drawings, and to a lesser degree in the October issue, which reproduces three different versions of Sheeler's "Bucks County Barn."

Of particular interest here is the November issue of 1923, which prints Stevens, Cummings, and Williams together, as if in a group. In this context, Stevens' "Discourse in a Cantina at Havana" (which would be reprinted in *Hound & Horn* in 1929 as "Academic Discourse at Havana"), with its peculiar line- and section-breaks, appears to be far more influenced by cubism than it is in his *Collected Poems*. There are notably more line-breaks in the *Broom* version than in the later reprinting, perhaps indicating a greater willingness on Stevens' part to experiment with form during this relatively early stage of his career, or illustrating the (understandable) assumption of the type-setter, given the other poetry being published at the time, that the line-breaks and spacing were significant.[17] Cummings' following four poems are numbered I–IV, just as the sections of Stevens' poem are, and Williams' four poems are also numbered 1–4. Taken together, it is difficult to decide if Cummings' and Williams' poems are more responsibly read as different sections of the same poem, as in "Discourse in a Cantina," or if Stevens' poem would be more accurately interpreted if regarded as four poems merely "set" in the same place. Also of interest is another "Four Poems" (not included here) Cummings published in *Broom* the following year, three of which explore typographical effects, while the last explores the possibilities of the prose poem.

Finally, in "Toward a Professional Prose" (1923), Matthew Josephson ironically calls for experiments in prose similar to those found in poetry—something of a curiosity given the obviously successful experiments in prose by contemporary authors such as Stein and Joyce. Nonetheless, he argues that

> American literature within recent years has been sufficiently experimental and enterprising to justify terming the present period *one of transition* toward resolved forms. Poetry, especially, has been profitably exploited; an astonishing variety of genres has been essayed and the *medium has been enriched.* (italics mine)
>
> *Broom* 5, 1 (August 1923), 59

Of prose, he says, "American writers have shown less impulse to explore and plunder." Yet in spite of this distinction, his summary of the ways in which a writer can "revolt against traditional style" describes many of the strategies we have seen in the poetry (as well as the prose) discussed so far:

[O]ne writer employs violent thought-dissociations; another ripe collo-
quialisms, and the terminology of our popular magazines, newspapers,
advertisements; others, again, employ the most shocking opposition in
word-relationships, distort syntax, and punctuation and typography. Even
at this, modern writers of English scarcely exceed the violent figures of
speech and the vigorous profanity which were seemly to the courtliest ears
of earlier centuries.

The various selections from this journal included in this volume
illustrate, at least in part, the extended influence of these "others," who
had gained far more acceptance and importance by the time *Broom*
ceased to publish in 1924 than when *Others* had folded only five years
before. Certain essays published in this journal, such as Loeb's "Foreign
Exchange" or "Mysticism of Money," seem seminal for a full understand-
ing of the changing American climate. Despite Pound's efforts to the
contrary, for example, Loeb argues in "The Mysticism of Money" that
money has (already) become a "religion in America," and he calls, as a
consequence, for a new literature that corresponds to the new religion
(while noting the basic immorality of this structure). In this regard, Scott
Fitzgerald's *The Great Gatsby,* published only three years after Loeb's essay,
takes on a very specific aesthetic context. In the same year that "Mysticism
of Money" was published (1922), *Broom* also printed Matthew Josephson's
"After and Beyond Dada"; Jean Epstein's "New Conditions of Literary
Phenomena"; Jean Cocteau's description of cubism and his bust; Jacques
Rivière's "French Letters and the War"; De Fayet's "Painting, Past and
Present" (which specifically focuses on cubism); and Sanborn's "A Cham-
pion in the Wilderness," which laments the passing of the "vital page" with
Soil and *Others*. All of these essays are intimately involved with the rapidly
changing times—as is Eliot's *The Waste Land,* published elsewhere the
same year. The total context of the force of cubism, then, must be recog-
nized in what is itself an increasingly cubist collage of modern concerns
and perspectives, one which ultimately defies national boundaries as
much as it does the traditions that had supported "traditional" versifica-
tion. Thus, while published in Europe (first in Italy and later in Germany),
Broom proves to be a significant factor in the development and dissemina-
tion of American cubist poetry.

*****

One year after *Broom* began publishing, and the same year in which
The Waste Land appeared, Gorham B. Munson founded *Secession,* issuing
its first number in the spring of 1922. With a "temporary editorial office" in

Austria and a permanent business office in New York, this journal demonstrates again the specific international exchange which is so characteristic of all the modernist movements. Although more narrow in aesthetic range (that is, more specifically committed to dada and surrealism), *Secession* must be regarded as a near relative of *Broom* and ultimately, like *Broom,* as a direct descendant of the aesthetic movement begun at the Photo Secession Gallery a decade before. In addition, the relationship between the two journals is signaled by the fact that Munson specifically mentions *Broom* in his review of Cummings and by the fact that Malcolm Cowley's "Old Melodies" (printed in the fifth number of *Secession*) appears again in *Broom* as "Memphis Johnny."

Even though much of this journal is specifically aligned with dada — Tristan Tzara, in fact, appears in the first issue with the "Unpublished Fragment from Mr. AA the Antiphilosopher," a piece with a decidedly Nietzschean flavor — in the context of its own contemporary literature, the acute fragmentation and the ambiguous line between the creative and destructive that characterize this more extreme avant-garde movement are the logical extensions of the very fragmentation and creative "deforming" of forms which characterized even the first cubist paintings. There is an uncanny similarity between Picasso's remark that, for most, "un tableau était une somme d'additions," but that for him "un tableau est une somme de déstructions" (translated it seems by Stevens as a "horde of destructions"), Cummings' remark that "to create is first of all to destroy" (a line cited in Munson's review of Cummings in *Secession*), and the following lines from Tzara's supposedly more radical "fragment":[18]

> The finale of symphony is hard the music cannot end without cutting up the fragments of beauty into yet smaller pieces and beginning over again.
>
> *Secession* 1 (1922), 20

A similar concern with fragmentation is also apparent in Cowley's "Poem" (actually a prose poem), stylistically and thematically: "I have watched crumbs of brick descend like *fragments of untidy*" (emphasis added).

Cowley also wrote "Day Coach," which conveys the new sense of time and space that rapid locomotive transportation had recently made possible and which was equally part of the climate, as Jean Epstein makes clear in "The New Conditions of Literary Phenomena," published in *Broom* the same year:

> The speed realized by man has given a new character to civilized life, spatial speed first of all. . . . At certain moments. . . machines become part of ourselves, interposing themselves between the world and us, filter-

ing reality as the screen filters radium emanations. Thanks to them, we have no longer a simple, clear, continuous, constant notion of an object. Man has seen a landscape not only with his naked eyes while walking, but blurred by speed through the window of a train, with eyes bitten by wind and dust from the front seat of an automobile, from the height of an aeroplane. . . . The world for man today is like descriptive geometry, with its infinite planes of projection.

Broom 2, 1 (April 1922), 3, 6–7

Whether consciously intended or not, the experience conveyed above and in Cowley's similar poem seem to be quintessentially cubist expressions.

In addition, Gorham Munson's critique of Cummings[19] (see Appendix) is of particular significance, for it makes the point that "cummings *sees* words" and goes on to give a very sophisticated analysis of his use of *"punctuation and typography"* as *"active instruments for literary expression."* More provocatively, Munson writes that

Here his painter's skill in composition aids him. Yet, in no case, does he leave the frontiers of literature for the plastic arts as did Apollinaire in *Calligrammes*. His typographical design in every example reinforces his literary content. He has perceived that the printing-press has made poetry something to be seen as well as heard. . . .

"Syrinx," *Secession* 5 (July 1923), 2–11

Curiously, the poems by Cummings printed in the same issue are far less "visual" — or visually interesting and experimental — than those discussed by Munson. (I have included only the last one, "this evangelist," here.)

Finally, I should note that other famous American poets, including Stevens, Marianne Moore, Hart Crane, and Williams, all published in this short-lived journal, though I have chosen only Williams' "The Hothouse Plant" (1923) for this volume. While perhaps less cubist and more "sentimental" than many of the poems included here, the dedication to Charles Demuth (with, presumably, a reference to Demuth's own "sentimental" phase) points to the very complex intersection of the visual and verbal arts during this period.[20] In addition, Williams' use of white space in this poem creates the sensation of movement rather than stasis in a way that anticipates McAlmon's "The black cat loops" (published in *The Little Review* the following year).

*****

As the various poems from the various journals of the early 1920s amply show, the "kindling breath" of a new American poetics was far from being extinguished in 1922, as Sanborn had prematurely and incorrectly announced in "A Champion in the Wilderness." Rather than having killed poetic development and experimentation, the "great fiery wind" of the Great War (which Sanborn felt had consumed *Others* and the aesthetic movement typified by it) seems to have fueled the aesthetic. Ironically, however, Sanborn's false conclusion was to have its own "uncanny prescience," for it appears that the greater fiery wind of the Second World War did virtually extinguish the force of cubist poetry. Still, for our purposes, what is important is to recognize the degree to which cubism had transformed — and was continuing to transform — the best of modern poetry in the years just after the end of the Great War.

In 1921, for example, Williams published his famous poem, "The Great Figure," (a poem which may have its source in Kandinsky's "Klange"):[21]

The Great Figure

Among the rain
and lights
I saw the figure 5
in gold
on a red
firetruck
moving
tense
unheeded
to gong clangs
siren howls
and wheels rumbling
through the dark city.

Although it would not be until "This Florida: 1924," a poem written after having read Juan Gris' "Possibilities of Painting," that Williams would specifically acknowledge what Henry Sayre has called "his debt to cubist painting,"[22] many of Williams' now best-known poems amply demonstrate this debt. In addition, the particular poem cited above inspired an equally famous cubist expression in Demuth's 1928 painting, "I Saw the Figure 5 in Gold."

More important, at least for this generation of writers and readers, in 1922 T. S. Eliot's *The Waste Land* appeared (part of which is cited below):

Your shadow at morning striding behind you
Or your shadow at evening rising to meet you;
I will show you fear in a handful of dust.

> *Frisch weht der Wind*
> *Der Heimat zu.*
> *Mein irisch Kind,*
> *Wo weilest du?*
> 'You gave me hyacinths first a year ago;
> 'They called me the hyacinth girl.'
> — Yet when we came back, late, from the Hyacinth garden,
> Your arms full, and your hair wet, I could not
> Speak, and my eyes failed, I was neither
> Living nor dead, and I knew nothing,
> Looking into the heart of light, the silence.
> *Öd' und leer das Meer.*

Although Eliot denied that he had a "generation in mind" (and although Stevens immediately derided the poem as a "bore," the "supreme cry" of Eliot's despair and "not his generation's"),[23] the multiple voices and perspectives of the poem's first section and the collage-effect of different languages and the numerous allusions to other texts not only capture the disoriented experience of the post-war mentality, but also instantiate an entire aesthetic experience (and experiment). While far more sophisticated than most of the poems included here, *The Waste Land,* regarded within this aesthetic context, stands clearly as a synthetic cubist poem which, well in advance of most of the other poems mentioned so far, extends the possibilities and ramifications of a new "mode of expression" beyond experimentation and well into great literature. At approximately the same time, Mina Loy was producing "Anglo-Mongrels and the Rose" and, if we can momentarily widen the critical lens beyond American cubist poetry to cubist literature in general, Joyce was completing *Ulysses* while Faulkner was beginning the kind of verbal experimentation that would produce the best American novels of this century.

As this flurry of artistic creativity might suggest, the early 1920s do not mark the end of this "vital page in literary history" any more than did the closing of *Others* in 1919. The next chapter, which concentrates on the poetry of the late 1920s and early 1930s, traces in part the continuing growth and importance of cubism in American verse before its rather dramatic decline in the latter part of the interim war period.

THE LITTLE REVIEW

Nuances of a Theme by Williams

It's a strange courage
you give me, ancient star:

Shine alone in the sunrise
toward which you lend no part!

I

Shine alone, shine nakedly, shine like bronze,
that reflects neither my face nor any inner part
of my being, shine like fire, that mirrors nothing.

II

Lend no part to any humanity that suffuses
you in its own light.
Be not chimera of morning,
half-man, half-star.
Be not an intelligence,
Like a widow's bird
Or an old horse.

WALLACE STEVENS
(*The Little Review*, Dec. 1918)

Buddha

Ah—the sun—a scarlet balloon
Ah—the sun—
—scarlet baloon
giant balloon
touching spires and steeples
down the misty grey—late
afternoon—
crystalline—late—
afternoon — — —
— — — —

vanishing
immense—
immune — —
God:
scarlet balloon—
Everything simple!

Giant balloon—
God—!
vanishing—
immense—
immune—
eye on us—!
on *Himself!*
Circle!
Sufficient
Most importantly round!
Withal: space!
Fact.
Gay God—scarlet balloon.

Gay God—scarlet baloon.

Round!
Deed—joy:
Round!

Perfection!
Who is he—
crowds *thee*
with responsibility!
Gay God—scarlet balloon?

Whirring God—immense in sky

Lightness—
emptiness—
out of
heaviness!
material to
immaterial!
Ether—soul—
fliest:

touching spires and steeples —
down a misty grey —
— late afternoon —
crystalline — late —
afternoon — — —
—   —   —   —

vanishing
obscure
immune —
Essence!
Whirring God — immense in sky.

Ah — soul — scarlet balloon —
Ah — soul —
Soul — scarlet balloon —
giant balloon —
touching spires and steeples —
down thy misty grey —
afternoon —
crystalline —
afternoon — — —
—   —   —   —

balancing —
immense —
immune —
soul — scarlet balloon —

Everything simple!
Ah — Mustir — scarlet balloon —
giant balloon —
Ah — Mustir — simple!
Touching spires and steeples
down thy misty — grey — dim
afternoon —
crystalline — dim —
after — —
noon —

ELSE VON FREYTAG-LORINGHOVEN
(*The Little Review,* Jan. 1920)

Excerpt from **Anglo-Mongrels and the Rose**

Exodus lay under an oak-tree
Bordering on Buda Pest   he had lain
him down   to over-night   under the lofty rain
of starlight
having leapt from the womb
eighteen years ago   and grown
neglected   along the shores of the Danube
on the Danube in the Danube
-or breaking his legs behind runaway horses-
    with a Carnival quirk
    every Shrove Tuesday

                ×   ×   ×

      Of his riches
      a Patriarch
      erected a synagogue
    -   -for the people
His son
looked upon Lea
- -   of the people
      she sat in Synagogue
      -her hair   long as the Talmud
      -her tamarind eyes-   -
and disinherited
begat this Exodus   -

Imperial Austria taught the child
the German   secret patriotism
the Magyar tongue   the father
stuffed him with biblical Hebrew and the
seeds of science   exhorting him
    to vindicate
    his forefather's ambitions
The child
flowered precociously   fever
smote the father
       the widowed mother
took to her bosom   a spouse

of her own sphere
and hired
Exodus in apprenticeship
to such   as garrulously inarticulate
ignore   the cosmic cultures

Sinister foster-parents
who lashed the boy
to that paralysis of
the spiritual apparatus
common to
the poor
The arid gravid
intellect   of jewish ancestors
     the senile juvenile
     calculating prodigies of Jehovah
     -Crushed by the Occident ox
     they scraped
     the gold gold golden
     muck from off its hoofs-

moves Exodus   to emmigrate
     coveting the alien
     asylum   of voluntary military
     service   paradise   of the pound-stirling
     where the domestic Jew   in lieu
     of knouts   is lashed with tongues

×   ×   ×

     The cannibal God
shutters his lids of night   on the day's gluttony
the partially   devoured humanity
warms its unblessed beds   with bare prostrations
An insect   from an herb
errs on the   man-mountain
imparts   it's infinitesimal tactile stimulus
to the epiderm   to the spirit
of Exodus
stirring   the anaesthetised load
of racial instinct frustrated
impulse   infantile impacts with unreason
     on his unconscious

Blinking his eyes· · ·
at sunrise   Exodus
lumbar-aching   sleep logged   turns his ear
to the grit earth   and hears
the boom of cardiac cataracts
     thumping the turf
with his young pulse

He is undone!   How should he know
he has a heart   The Danube
gives no instruction in anatomy·
the primary
throb of the animate
a beating mystery
pounds on his ignorance
in seeming
death dealing·

(continued)

MINA LOY
(*The Little Review,* Spring 1923)

The black cat loops
     designs
across the rug
       up
     draped chinese curtains,
knocking the parokeets cage,
     ignoring bird fright,
However
     she could not compete
     with the Siamese kitten
whose
     crazy
       taut-electric
         antics
     were agile
       with
race-contemplated contortions
that apes and kings conspired
     in some dim

evolutionary

and perhaps fabulous

past

to cause.

Draftsman of lines

that fade while drawn

she disdained her public:

2 ladies · 1 Man ·

a bemused white dog

and a cathedral tower

glowering

through the open window.

ROBERT MCALMON

(*The Little Review*, Autumn–Winter 1924–1925)

THE DIAL

III

Buffalo Bill's
defunct
      who used to
      ride a watersmooth-silver
                stallion
and break onetwothreefourfive pigeonsjustlikethat
                        Jesus
he was a handsome man
               and what i want to know is
how do you like your blueeyed boy
Mister Death

E. E. CUMMINGS
(The Dial, 1920)

Dorothy

I
HER EYES

Her eyes hold black whips—
   dart of a whip
   lashing, nay, flicking,
   nay, merely caressing
   the hide of a heart—
and a broncho tears through canyons—
   walls reverberating,
   sluggish streams
   shaken to rapids and torrents,
   storm destroying
   silence and solitude!
Her eyes throw black lariats—
   one for his head,
   one for his heels—

and the beast lies vanquished—
    walls still,
    streams still,
    except for a tarn,
    or is it a pool
    or is it a whirlpool
    twitching with memory?

II
HER HAIR

Her hair
is a tent
    held down by two pegs—
    ears, very likely—
where two gypsies—
    lips, dull folk call them—
read your soul away:
one promising something,
the other one stealing it.
    If the pegs would let go—
    why is it they're hidden?—
and the tent
    blow away—drop away—
like a wig—or a nest—
    maybe
you'd escape
paying coin
to gypsies—
    maybe—

III
HER HANDS

Blue veins
    of morning glories—
blue veins
    of clouds—
blue veins
    bring deep-toned silence
    after a storm.
White horns
    of morning glories—

white flutes
   of clouds—
sextettes hold silence fast,
   cup it for aye.
Could I
   blow morning glories—
could I
   lip clouds—
I'd sound the silence
   her hands bring to me.
Had I
   the yester sun—
had I
   the morrow's—
brush them like cymbals,
   I'd then sound the noise.

IV

HER BODY

Her body gleams
like an altar candle—
white in the dark—
and modulates
to voluptuous bronze—
bronze of a sea—
under the flame.

ALFRED KREYMBORG
(*The Dial*, 1920)

II

O sweet spontaneous
earth how often have
the
doting

     fingers of
prurient philosophies pinched
and
poked

thee
has the naughty thumb
of science prodded
thy

    beauty   how
often have religions taken
thee upon their scraggy
knees squeezing and

buffeting thee that thou mightest conceive
gods
    but
true

to the incomparable
couch of death thy
rhythmic
lover

    thou answerest

them only with

        spring

E. E. CUMMINGS
(The Dial, 1920)

THE MEASURE

New England Verses

I
THE WHOLE WORLD INCLUDING THE SPEAKER

Why nag at the ideas of Hercules, Don Don?
Widen your sense. All things in the sun are sun.

II
THE WHOLE WORLD EXCLUDING THE SPEAKER

I found between moon-rising and moon-setting
The world was round. But not from my begetting.

III
SOUPE AUX PERLES

Health-o, when cheese and guava peels bewitch
The vile antithesis of poor and rich.

IV
SOUPE SANS PERLES

I crossed in '38 in the *Western Head*.
It depends which way you crossed, the tea-belle said.

V
BOSTON WITH A NOTE-BOOK

Lean encyclopaedists, inscribe an Iliad.
There's a Weltanschauung of the penny pad.

VI
BOSTON WITHOUT A NOTE-BOOK

Let us erect in the Basin a lofty fountain.
Suckled on ponds, the spirit craves a watery mountain.

VII
ARTIST IN TROPIC

Of Phoebus Apothecaire the first beatitude:
Blessed who is his nation's multitude.

VIII
ARTIST IN ARTIC

And of Phoebus the Tailor the second saying goes:
Blessed whose beard is cloak against the snows.

IX
STATUE AGAINST A CLEAR SKY

Ashen man on ashen cliff above the salt halloo,
O, ashen admiral of the hale, hard blue . . .

X
STATUE AGAINST A CLOUDY SKY

Scaffolds and derricks rise from the reeds to the clouds,
Meditating the will of men in formless crowds.

XI
LAND OF LOCUST

Patron and patriarch of couplets, walk
In fragrant leaves heat-heavy yet nimble in talk.

XII
LAND OF PINE AND MARBLE

Civilization must be destroyed. The hairy saints
Of the North have earned this crumb by their complaints.

XII
THE MALE NUDE

Dark cynic, strip and bathe and bask at will.
Without cap or strap, you are the cynic still.

XIV
THE FEMALE NUDE

Ballatta dozed in the cool on a straw divan
At home, a bit like the slenderest courtesan.

XV
SCÈNE FLÉTRIE

The purple dress in autumn and the belfry breath
Hinted autumnal farewells of academic death.

XVI
SCÈNE FLEURIE

A perfect fruit in perfect atmosphere.
Nature as Pinakothek. Whistle Chanicleer.

WALLACE STEVENS
(*The Measure*, April 1923)

Notes for an Epilogue

(*In a Restaurant*)
EVERYTHING is static, still
as in an antique miracle.

Air is held aloof—
taut in the vise
of an etheric woof.

People gnaw securely,
like mice,
or scurry
about in a terrific hurry.

Only the glare of
Silence glistens
everywhere and

Love is a cuckoo bird
dead in a Swiss clock:

                        (tick)

            (tack)
                    (tick)
        (tock).

WYNDHAM LEWIS
(*The Measure*, July 1925)

BROOM

If You Had Three Husbands

PRESENT HOMES

There then.

Present ten.

Mother and sister apples, no not apples, they can't be apples, everything can't be apples, sounds can't be apples. Do be quiet and refrain from acceptances.

It was a great disappointment to me.

I can see that here is a balcony. There never was a sea or land, there never was a harbor or a snow storm, there never was excitement. Some said she couldn't love. I don't believe that anybody said that. I don't mean that anybody said that. We were all present. We could be devoted. It does make a different thing. And hair, hair should not be deceiving. Cause tears. Why tears, why not abscesses.

I will never mention an ugly skirt.

It pleased me to say that I was pretty.

Oh we are so pleased.

I don't say this at all.

Consequences are not frightful.

Pleasure in a home.

After lunch, why after lunch, no birds are eaten. Of course carving is special.

I don't say that for candor.

Please be prepared to stay.

I don't care for wishes.

This is not a success.

By this stream.

Streaming out.

I am relieved from draught. This is not the way to spell water.

I cannot believe in much.

I have courage.

Endurance.

And restraint.

After that.

For the end.

This is the title of a conclusion which was not anticipated.

When I was last there I smiled behind the car. What car showed it.
By that time.
Believe her out.
Out where.
By that.
Buy that.
She pleased me for. . .   Eye saw:
Do it.

For that over that.

We passed away. By that time servants were memorable. They came to praise.
Please do not.
A blemish.
They have spans.
I cannot consider that the right word.
By the sime we are selfish, by that time we are selfish.
By that time we are selfish.
It is a wonderful sight,
It is a wonderful sight to see.
Days.
What are days.
They have hams.
Delicate
Delicate hams.
Pounds.
Pounds where.
Pounds of.
Where.
Not butter dogs.
I establish souls.
Any spelling will do.
If you look at it.
That way.
I am going on.
In again.
I am going on again in in them.

93

What I feel.
What I do feel.
They said mirrors.
Undoubtedly they have that phrase.
I can see a hat.
I remember very well knowing largely.
Any shade, by that I do mean iron glass. Iron glass is so torn, By what. By the glare. Be that beside. Size shall be sensible. That size shall be sensible.

Fixing.

Fixing enough.
Fixing up.
By fixing down, that is softness, by fixing down there.

Their end.

Politeness.
Not by linen.
I don't wish to be recalled.
One, day, I do not wish to use the word, one day they asked to buy that.
I don't mean anything by threads. It was wholly unnecessary to do so. It was done and then a gun. By that stand. Wishes.
I do not see what I have to do with that.
Any one can help weeping.
By wise.
I am so indifferent.
Not a bite.
Call me handsome.
It was a nice fate.
Any one could see.
Any one could see.
Any one could see.
Buy that etching.
Do be black.
I do not mean to say etching. Why should I be very sensitive. Why should I matter. Why need I be seen. Why not have politeness.
Why not have politeness.
In my hair.
I don't think it sounds at all like that.

Their end.

To end.

To be for that end.

I don't see what difference it makes.

It does matter.

Why have they pots.

Ornaments.

And china.

It isn't at all.

I have made every mistake.

Powder it.

Not put into boxes.

Not put into boxes.

Powder it.

I know that well.

She mentioned it as she was sleeping.

She liked bought cake best. No she didn't for that purpose.

I have utter confusion.

No two can be alike.

They are and they are not stubborn.

Please me.

I was mistaken.

Any way.

By that.

Do not refuse to be wild.

Do not refuse to be all.

We have decided not to withstand it.

We would rather not have the home.

This is not to teach lessons of exchange endurance and re-semblance and by that time it was turned.

Shout.

By.

Out.

I am going to continue humming.

This does not mean express wishes.

I am not so fanciful. I am beside that calculated to believe in whole pages. Oh do not annoy me.

Days.

I don't like to be fitted. She didn't say that.

If it hadn't been as natural as all the rest you would have been as

silly as all the rest.
 It's not at all when it is right.
 I wish for a cake
 She said she did.
 She said she didn't.

                    Gloom.

 There was no gloom.
 Every room.
 There was no room.
 There was no room.

 Buy that chance.
 She didn't leave me any money.
 Head.
 Ahead.
 I don't want to be visible or invisible.
 I don't want a dog named Dick.
 It has nothing to do with it.
 I am obliged to end.
 Intend.
 My uncle will.

GERTRUDE STEIN
(*Broom*, June 1922)

Sunset

stinging
gold swarms
upon the spires
silver

   chants the litanies the
great bells are ringing with rose
the lewd fat bells
                and a tall
wind
is dragging
the sea

with

dream

-s

E. E. CUMMINGS
(*Broom*, July 1922)

Three Portraits

I. PIANIST

ta
ppin
g
toe

hip
popot
amus Back

gen
teel·ly
lugu·
bri ous

          eyes
LOOPTHELOOP

as

fathandsbangrag

II. CARITAS

the skinny voice

of the leatherfaced
woman with the crimson
nose and coquettishly·
cocked bonnet

having ceased   the

captain
announces that as three
dimes and seven nickels and ten
pennies have been deposited upon

the drum there is need

of just twenty five cents
dear friends
to make it an even
dollar   whereupon

the Divine Average who was

attracted by the inspired
sister's howling moves
off
will anyone tell him why he should

blow two bits for the coming of Christ Jesus

?
??
???
!

nix, kid

III. ARTHUR WILSON

as usual i did not find him in cafes, the more dissolute atmosphere
of a street superimposing a numbing imperfectness upon such peri-
grinations as twilight spontaneously by inevitable tiredness of flang-
ing shop-girls impersonally affords furnished a soft first clue to
his innumerable whereabouts   violet logic of annihilation demon-
strating from woolworthian pinnacle a capable millenium of faces
meshing with my curiously instant appreciation exposed his hiber-
native contours,
aimable immensity impeccably extending the courtesy of five o'clock
became the omen of his prescience   it was spring by the way in
the soiled canary-cage of largest existence.

(when he would extemporise the innovation of muscularity upon the
most crimson assistance of my comforter a click of deciding glory
inflicted to the negative silence that primeval exposure whose elec-
tric solidity remembers some accurately profuse scratchings in a
recently discovered cave,   the carouse of geometrical putrescence
whereto my invariably commendable room had been forever subject
his Earliest word wheeled out on the sunny dump of oblivion)

a tiny dust finely arising at the integration of my soul i coughed

, naturally.

E. E. CUMMINGS
(*Broom*, July 1922)

Discourse in a Cantina at Havana

I.

Canaries in the morning, orchestras
In the afternoon, balloons at night.   That is
A difference, at least, from nightingales,
Jehovah and the great sea-worm.   The air
Is not so elemental nor the earth
So near.
         But the sustenance of the wilderness
Does not sustain us in the metropoles.

II.

Life is an old casino in a park.
The bills of the swans are flat upon the ground:
A most desolate wind has chilled Rouge-Fatima
And a grand decadence settles down like cold.

III.

The swans. . . . Before the bills of the swans fell flat
Upon the ground, and before the chronicle
Of affected homage foxed so many books,
They warded the blank waters of the lakes
And island canopies which were entailed
To that casino.   Long before the rain
Swept through its boarded windows and the leaves
Filled its encrusted fountains, they arrayed
The twilights of the mythy goober khan.
The centuries of excellence to be
Rose out of promise and became the sooth
Of trombones floating in the trees.

                   The toil
Of thought evolved a peace eccentric to
The eye and tinkling to the ear.   Gruff drums

99

Could beat, yet not alarm the populace.
The indolent progressions of the swans
Made earth come right; a peanut parody
For peanut people.

                 And serener myth
Conceiving from its perfect plenitude,
Lusty as June, more fruitful than the weeks
Of ripest summer, always lingering
To touch again the hottest bloom, to strike
Once more the longest resonance, to cap
The clearest woman with apt weed, to mount
The thickest man on thickest stallion-back,
This urgent, competent, serener myth
Passed like a circus.
                Politic man ordained
Imagination as the fateful sin.

Grandmother and her basketful of pears
Must be the crux for our compendia.
That's world enough, and more, if one includes
Her daughters to the peached and ivory wench
For whom the towers are built.   The burgher's breast,
And not a delicate ether star-impaled,
Must be the place for prodigy, unless
Prodigious things are tricks.   The world is not
The bauble of the sleepless nor a word
That should import a universal pith
To Cuba. Jot these milky matters down.
They nourish Jupiters.   Their casual pap
Will drop like sweetness in the empty nights
When too great rhapsody is left annulled
And liquorish prayer provokes new sweats: so, so:
Life is an old casino in a wood.

IV.

Is the function of the poet here mere sound,
Subtler than the ornatest prophecy,
To stuff the ear?   It causes him to make
His infinite repetitions and alloys
Of pick of ebon, pick of halcyon.

It weights him with nice logic for the prim.
As part of nature he is part of us.
His rarities are ours: may they be fit
And reconcile us to our selves in those
True reconcilings, dark, pacific words,
And the adroiter harmonies of their fall.
Close the cantina.   Hood the chandelier.
The moonlight is not yellow but a white
That silences the ever-faithful town.
How pale and how possessed a night it is,
How full of exhalations of the sea. . . .
All this is older that its oldest hymn,
Has no more meaning than tomorrow's bread.
But let the poet on his balcony
Speak and the sleepers in their sleep shall move,
Waken, and watch the moonlight on their floors.

This may be benediction, sepulcher,
And epitaph.   It may, however, be
An incantation that the moon defines
By mere example opulently clear.
And the old casino likewise may define
An infinite incantation of our selves
In the grand decadence of the perished swans.

WALLACE STEVENS
(*Broom,* Nov. 1923)

Four Poems

I.

when the spent day begins to frail
(whose grave already three or two
young stars with spades of silver dig)

by beauty i declare to you

if what i am at one o'clock
to little lips (which have not sinned
in whose displeasure lives a kiss)
kneeling, your frequent mercy begs,

sharply believe me, wholly, well
— did (wisely suddenly into
a dangerous womb of cringing air)
the largest hour push deep his din

of wallowing male (shock beyond shock
blurted)   strokes,   vibrant   with   the   purr
of echo pouring in a mesh
of following tone: did this and this

spire strike midnight (and did occur
bell beyond fiercely spurting bell
a jetted music splashing fresh
upon silence)— i without fail

entered became and was these twin
imminent lisping bags of flesh;
became eyes moist lithe shuddering big,
the luminous laughter, and the legs

whereas, at twenty minutes to
one, i am this blueeyed Finn
emerging from a lovehouse who
buttons his coat against the wind

II.

my smallheaded pearshaped

lady in gluey twilight
moving, suddenly

is three animals. The
minute waist continually

with an African gesture

utters a frivolous intense half of
Girl which (like some

floating snake upon itself always and
slowly which upward certainly is pouring) emits
a pose
            :to twitter wickedly

whereas the big and firm legs moving solemnly
like careful and furious and beautiful elephants

102

(mingled in whispering thickly smooth thighs
thinkingly)
remind me of Woman and

how between
her hips India is

III.

now that fierce few
flowers (stealthily)
in the alive west
begin

requiescat this six
feet of Breton big good
body,   which terminated
in fists hair wood

erect cursing hatless who
(bent by wind) slammed hard—
over the tiller; clattered
forward skidding in outrageous
sabots
          language trickling
pried his black
mouth with fat jibing
lips,

once upon a
(that is
over: and the sea heaving
indolent colourless forgets) time

Requiescat.
carry
carefully the blessed large silent him
into nibbling final worms

IV.

the wind is a Lady with
bright slender eyes (who

moves) at sunset
and who—touches—the

hills without any reason

(i have spoken with this
indubitable and green person "Are
You the wind?" "Yes" "why do you touch flowers
as if they were unalive, as

if They were ideas?" "because, sir
things which in my mind blossom will
stumble beneath a clumsiest disguise, appear
capable of fragility and indecision

— do not suppose these
without any reason and otherwise
roses and mountains
different from the i am who wanders

imminently across the renewed world"
to me said the) wind being A lady in a green
dress, who; touches: the fields
(at sunset)

E. E. CUMMINGS
(*Broom,* Nov. 1923)

Four Poems

1

The new cathedral overlooking the park
looked down from its tower
with great eyes today and saw
by the decorative lake a group of people
staring curiously at the corpse
of a suicide — Peaceful dead young man
the money they have put into the stones
has been spent to teach men of
life's austerity.   You died
and teach us the same lesson.
You seem a cathedral, celebrant of
the naked spring that shivers for me
among the long black trees

2

The stars, that are small lights,
are my nightly companions, my friends
now that I know them foreign.
The security I feel in them
cannot be broken.   Separate, inscrutable
uninterfering, like nothing
in my life — I walk with their sparkle
relieved and comforted or when
the moon moves slowly up among them
with flat shine then the night
has a novel light in it — curved
curiously in a thin halfcircle

3

By the road to the contagious hospital
under the surge of the blue
mottled clouds driving from the
northwest — a cold wind.   Beyond the
waste of broad muddy fields
brown with dried weeds, standing and fallen

patches of standing water
the scattering of tall trees

all along the road the reddish
purplish, forked, upstanding, twiggy
stuff of bushes and small trees
with brown leaves under them
leafless vines —

lifeless in appearance, sluggish
dazed Spring approaches —

They enter the new world naked
cold — uncertain of all
save that they enter — all about them
the cold, familiar wind —

Now the grass, tomorrow
the curl of wildcarrot leaf

One by one objects are defined—
It quickens: clarity, outline of leaf

But now the stark dignity of
entrance—Still, the profound change
has overtaken them—rooted they
grip down and begin to awaken

4

How has the way been found ?
Among wires
running through smoke
walking through and over
oily, stained waters—?
On the highest airs

WILLIAM CARLOS WILLIAMS
(*Broom*, Nov. 1923)

SECESSION

Day Coach

I

Tickets PLEASE
said the conductor, and Benjamin settled back
into his seat, and by this action wrapped
solitude about him like a cloak.

Strangers brushed past him
down the aisle, soiling only
the fringes of his mantel;
his eyes had turned
to watch the hills that so proceeded like awkward
vast dancers across his eyes;
to watch the moving
mist of his breath as it crept along the pane.

II

He says to himself
    — it is the placing
of the foot upon the step deposited by the porter;
      it is the leisurely
procession with baggage up a red plush aisle:
out of such gestures there grows
      the act of travel.

Johnstown, Pittsburgh: these cities
escape the grasp of the hand
these cities are pimpled on hills;
Manhattan is corseted briefly about with waters.
You climb into a train, give a tip, open a paper, light a
          cigar, and the landscape
jerks unevenly past.

Your knees straighten
automatically at Pittsburgh; a porter

takes the luggage, saying rapidly
   — this way to a taxi, Boss,
   this way to a taxi,
and the hills and fields of Pennsylvania quiver
behind you vaguely, the landscape of a dream.

III

As the other train passed he looked through the
plate glass of the dining car — the other — and saw
a fork suspended in the air and before it had finished
its journey he was peering into a smoking car with a
silver haze and four men playing cards over a suitcase
clamped to their knees. A world, a veritable world, as
seen beneath the microscope. A world in an envelope
sealed with the red tail light that proceeded gravely
past him up the track. A world sealed out of his world
and living for thirty-five seconds of his life.

IV

The lights of the train proceed
transversely across the water;
across the water strides
the shadow of the engineer;
the square barred windows move across the water
as if they marked a prison that exists
never between four walls, but only moves
continually across a world of waters.

V

His head drooped lower gradually; he dreamed
of the locomotive that boldly had deserted
the comfortable assurance of steel rails;
it turned and leaped
like a beast hunted along the wooded slope
BMMMP
     over logs, over stones and among
the trees that leaned away from it as it passed,
and all the time the engineer bending out of his cab
          and saying
     — The four fourteen will be on time at Youngsville
     the four fourteen will be on time WON'T it, Bill.

And the trees, reassured, lean back to their posts again.

VI

Time is marked not by hours but by cities; we are
one station before Altoona, one station beyond Altoona;
CRESSON: change cars for Luckett, Munster and all
points on the line that runs tortuously back into a
boyhood, with the burden of a day dropping like ripe
fruit at every revolution of the driving wheel, with a
year lost between each of the rickety stations: Beulah
Road, Ebensburg, Nant-y-glo; gather your luggage and
move it towards the door. BIG BEND.

VII

O voyagers, with you
I have moved like a firefly over the waters;
with you I was spit
like a cherry seed from the puckered lips of the tunnel.
Come: let us join our hands,
dance
  ring around the rosy, farmer in the dell
around this clucking locomotive. Come!
And out of the red cabooses huddled in the yards,
out of the engine cabs and roundhouses
will stream out silently to meet us
these others.
   Come!

VIII

Out of the group at the station, no form detached itself
to meet him; the circle of their backs
was a wall against him. He waited
until the checkerboard lights of the train had shown
phantasmally along the shale of the cut and vanished.
He buttoned his coat and stumbled into the darkness,
the darkness proceeded along with him until
he picked it up and wrapped it about his shoulders,
bending his shoulders under the weight of the darkness,
he stumbled away with his burden of bushes and hills.

MALCOLM COWLEY
(*Secession,* Spring 1922)

109

Poem

Meanwhile I observed him from a gable

to run along the street violently for they were thir-
teen and shout like maybe a siren I must tell Mr Bruce
I must tell Mr Robert Bruce I must tell Mr Robert Bruce
by five o'clock for they were thirteen at table

thus shouting as the clocks tolled five one clock ap-
ing another and he solely human amid the geometry of
houses wailed Too late too late for Babylon is falling

falling in flat brick walls folding against the street
like painted sets which after the orchestral triumph
of the fourth act come sprawling

I have watched crumbs of brick descend like fragments
of untidy

manna on the tablecloth at which the butler entered
with basketfired japan in an earthenware pot concealed
by a cosy and fishcakes blossoming around it by which
token also I knew that it was Friday alas was Friday

MALCOLM COWLEY
(*Secession*, Aug. 1922)

The Hothouse Plant

(Dedicated to Charles Demuth)

Pink confused with white
flowers and flowers reversed
take and spill the shaded flame
darting it back
into the lamp's horn

petal's aslant darkened with mauve

red where in whorls
petal lays its glow upon petal
round flamegreen throats

petals radiant with transpiercing light

contending
          above
the leaves
reaching up their modest green
from the pot's rim

and there, wholly dark, the pot
gay with rough moss.

WILLIAM CARLOS WILLIAMS
(*Secession*, Jan. 1923)

IV.

this evangelist
buttons with his big gollywog voice
then kingdomofheaven up behind and crazily
skating thither and hither in filthy sawdust
chucks and rolls
against the tent his thick joggling fists

he is persuasive

the editor cigarstinking hobgoblin swims
upward in his swivelchair one fist dangling scandal while
five other fingers snitch
rapidly through mist a defunct king as

linotypes gobblehobble

our lightheavy twic twoc ingly attacks
landing a onetwo
which doubles up suddenly his bunged hinging
victim against the
giving roper amid
screams of deeply bulging thousands

i too omit one kelly

in response to howjedooze the candidates new silk
lid bounds gently from his baldness
a smile masturbates softly in the vacant
lot of his physiognomy

his scientifically pressed trousers ejaculate spats

a strikingly succulent getup

but
we knew a muffhunter and he said to us Kid.
daze nutn like it.

E. E. CUMMINGS
(*Secession,* July 1923)

3 THE "PREDOMINANT FORCE"
of the Late 1920s to Early 1930s

Most art historians mark the end of cubism around 1925. Thus, Edward F. Fry:

> Cubism developed with extraordinary rapidity between the years 1907 and 1914. From 1914 until about 1925 there were a great many artists painting in a cubist mode, but this later phase produced relatively few stylistic innovations that had not already been anticipated to some extent during the pre-war years. By the mid-1920s, a crisis emerged in cubism as in European art generally, bringing to an end a period of almost twenty years during which cubism had been the predominant force behind an entire artistic generation.[1]

Although this summary may accurately reflect the history of visual cubism, in the verbal medium at least, cubism was alive and well long after 1925. *Absalom, Absalom!,* for example, which may accurately be described as the "supreme" American cubist novel, was not published until 1936. Many of Pound's *Cantos* were yet to be written, as were William Carlos Williams' *Paterson* (which was written successively from 1946 to 1958), George Oppen's *Discrete Series* (first published in 1932), and Louis Zukofsky's *"A"* (which itself spans fifty years of composition).[2] In short, cubism as a "predominant force" in the verbal arts was beginning its third and perhaps most important stage during the latter 1920s, one which was to reach its zenith just as the great economic crisis of the early 1930s crippled American and western European culture. For our present purposes, the most significant extensions of a cubist poetics are to be seen in the founding of such new journals as *Blues* and *Pagany* in America, and to a lesser degree *The Exile* and *transition* in Italy and France respectively. The latter two journals, both of which published a number of American poets, reveal again both the international and political dynamics of this verbal "revolution."[3]

113

Ezra Pound's *The Exile* (founded in 1927) was, like several of the other journals discussed so far, relatively short-lived. Pound's earlier association with *Blast,* as well as with imagism, vorticism, and futurism, make him an especially difficult figure to categorize (a fact which is, itself, amenable to the spirit of cubist multiplicity). Nonetheless, as Marjorie Perloff has argued, from as early as the publication of his "'memoir'" of Henri Gaudier-Brzeska in 1916, Pound's mode of composition tended toward the "'documentary' collages" which Perloff relates equally to futurism and cubism.[4] And Pound appears to have particularly promoted such compositions, both by himself and by others, in his expatriate journal of the late 1920s.

This is not to say that *The Exile* should be regarded as a strictly cubist (in particular, "synthetic cubist") journal, in the way that at least one critic regards Paul Reverdy's *Nord-Sud.*[5] Pound printed some of W. B. Yeats' poetry in this journal, including "Sailing To Byzantium" and "Blood and the Moon" (No. 3, Spring 1928). The opening issue prints Hemingway's "NEOTHOMIST POEM" as well: "The Lord is my shepherd, I shall not/ want him for long,"[6] and the second number includes Stella Breen's prose narrative, "My Five Husbands" (which may be regarded as a modern analogue to "The Wife of Bath's Tale").

Nevertheless, Pound's own poetry and that of Louis Zukofsky and William Carlos Williams—all American poets, whether expatriated or not—most clearly manifest the new poetic possibilities being realized in cubist poetry or, at the very least, poetry influenced and motivated by the cubist aesthetic revolution. The third issue, for example, includes "Part of Canto XXIII," which bears the amusing subscript: "The opening of this canto is too obscure to be printed apart from the main context of the poem." As with Eliot's *The Waste Land,* the verbal equivalent of collage is employed, in which objects or fragments of "materials drawn from disparate contexts" are juxtaposed—with the effect that "individual appearance and signification" are invariably altered.[7] The irony of the subscript further complicates the issue by presenting the absence of a larger context against which this fragment may be juxtaposed.

Even more remarkable is Zukofsky's "Poem Beginning 'The'," also included in the third number of this journal. (In fact, with the publication of this poem, Zukofsky begins to emerge as one of the single most important poets in this poetic climate—though literary critics have yet to afford him the canonized status given to Williams or Pound.) As with Pound's canto, the mode of composition is the collage, with the added complication that Zukofsky begins to explore the nebulous boundary

between poetic and musical composition—as he will do even more bril-
liantly in *"A"* (a synthetic cubist poem that evolves into musical scores).
Thus, the poem is divided into "movements," begins with the reference to
"olde bokes" and "good feith," yet appeals to the contemporary literary
climate, including most obviously Eliot's *The Waste Land* (and other works,
such as James Joyce's *Ulysses*, as well). The first movement, for example,
refers to the "Residue of Oedipus-faced wrecks,/ Creating out of the dead"
and the "waste land" with "wrathless skeletons . . . new planted." The
fourth movement somewhat humorously reinterprets Eliot's sterile land as
the "backseats which/ Are no man's land!"

In addition to this seminal poem, the fourth issue of *The Exile*
(Autumn 1928) includes Williams' "The Descent of Winter," which ex-
plores in an extended fashion the equally nebulous boundaries between
journal entries, narrative prose, and poetry. The poetic "entry" of 10/22, in
particular, is quite reminiscent of the analytic cubist strategies he had
used earlier in "The Red Wheelbarrow" but gains in sophistication by its
placement in an essentially synthetic cubist work. As Williams writes, self-
consciously, in the entry dated 10/23, "I will make a big, serious portrait of
my time."

The fourth issue of *The Exile* also includes Robert McAlmon's
"Gertrude Stein," an essay which testifies to the continued importance of
this writer, even if it is not entirely complimentary. It is included here, for
McAlmon (presumably intentionally) imitates in alternating passages the
kind of writing for which Stieglitz had praised her nearly two decades
before. The fourth issue of *The Exile* also includes Zukofsky's "Mr. Cum-
mings and the Delectable Mountains," an essay which contains a descrip-
tion of Cummings' artistic purpose that well describes most of the writers
discussed so far: "His intention is not to be serious, but to be very serious
and to get away with it" (*The Exile*, 4 [August 1928], 76–77).

Short-lived as it was, this journal thus made an important contribu-
tion to American cubist poetry, most specifically encouraging that facet
of cubist poetry that would later be realized in the "synthetic" works of the
complete *Cantos*, *"A"*, and *Paterson*.

*****

Of equal interest is *transition*, also begun in Europe in 1927. Among
the many well-known writers and artists to appear in the journal are
Williams, Man Ray, Juan Gris, Joyce, Stein, Picasso, Reverdy, Max Ernst,
and Picabia. And while other avant-garde movements inform this journal,

once again cubism remains a critical force both in the verbal and visual media. In addition to the works reprinted here, for example, the first issue reproduced Juan Gris' "Dish of Pears," which suggests the way in which synthetic cubism would modulate into abstraction.[8] As Henry Sayre has already pointed out, it is almost certain that this particular painting—as well as others by Gris—influenced Williams during this period; and it may also have been the provocation for Wallace Stevens' subsequent "Study of Two Pears," which concludes, "The shadows of the pears/ Are blobs on the green cloth./ The pears are not seen/ As the observer wills."[9]

The second number of *transition* (1927) includes Sidney Hunt's "white limp droop UP" and "design V," both of which explore (with great wit) the possibility of visually oriented poetry, suggesting again one direction that the attempt to create in words the effect achieved on canvas would take. Furthermore, Hunt's poem seems to combine the different strategies of Williams and Cummings into an eloquent evocation of absent color on the black-and-white canvas of the printed page, achieving thereby a tour de force of the translation of the visual medium to the verbal, back to the visual again. In so doing, the ambiguous status of the poem as an independent object or as a representational object becomes increasingly revealed to be essentially self-contradictory, with something of the same effect as Braque's 1912 "Hommage à J. S. Bach" (in which the word "Bach" and fragments of musical instruments evoke a musical quality simultaneously dismissed by the self-consciously flattened space of the canvas).

In the ninth number, Yvor Winters (who would abandon his interest in such verse around 1937)[10] experiments with "white space" and unusual line breaks, albeit somewhat conservatively, while Williams' "Winter" explores at the thematic level the equal importance of background and foreground (a strategy ultimately derived from Cézanne but quite characteristic of cubist paintings). Zukofsky's "Cocktails," which appears in a 1929 issue of this journal, shows in this instance a particularly deep affinity to Williams, rather than to Pound—a fact which may not be so surprising given that over several decades Zukofsky frequently edited Williams' verse—and suggests something of the mood created in Georgia O'Keefe's (non-cubist) city paintings produced during this period—in particular, "The Radiator Building-New York" (1927) in which Stieglitz' name is lit in red. In addition, the phrase "signs of/ 'ads'"—when, of course, "ads" *are* signs—compounds the problematic issue of referentiality in a way that is reminiscent of synthetic cubist paintings (especially when, as in Braque's "Woman with a Guitar" [1913] or Picasso's "Violin" [1914], painted words almost perversely refer to other signifying words, as in the daily newspaper).

116

Though not included here, it is important to note Eliot Paul's essay, "The Work of Pablo Picasso," which surveys the entire range and development of his oeuvre. Paul diminishes (incorrectly, I think) the artistic revolution figured by cubism, remarking that the "problem of space and the inter-relations of its divisions" troubled Giotto as well, before concluding that

> for a time, Picasso was carried away by his own discoveries but he soon decided that mere complication of detail was as bad for Cubism as it was for illustrative drawing. From that time on, he has striven for simplicity until in 1927 . . . his austerity is almost equal to that of Euclid.
>
> *transition* 13 (1928), 139–41

Of all the issues of this journal, the entire issue of June 1929, entitled "The Revolution of the Word," stands as its most remarkable achievement. This issue includes prose and poetry from writers of a wide array of nationalities and, more important, incorporates both verbal texts *and* paintings as instances of this new "word" — including some of Picasso's cubist works, such as his "Harlequin" series. From the United States, we find Gertrude Stein and Joseph Stella ("Brooklyn Bridge, 'Text and Painting'"). And although basically divided by country or continent, the one division entitled "Combat" reminds us of the continued impact of the Great War on the aesthetic "revolution" of this period. Taken in its entirety, this issue indicates the growing sophistication and diversity achieved during this period by writers and painters particularly concerned with the interrelation of visual and verbal texts. (The Contents page, which must serve as a marker for the whole issue, is reprinted in the Appendix.) The importance of this issue to American writers is suggested by the fact that in 1936 James Laughlin would dedicate his anthology, *New Directions in Prose and Poetry* to "THE EDITORS, THE CONTRIBUTORS, & THE READERS of *transition* who have begun successfully THE REVOLUTION OF THE WORD."[11]

Another important issue of *transition* (March 1932), which bears the title "The Vertical Age," begins with a section on "Anamyths, Psychographs and Other Prose-Texts," to be followed by "Metanthropological Crisis: a manifesto," "Poetry Is Vertical," "The Manic Personality," and "Homage to Joyce," before concluding with "Laboratory of the Word." The range of concerns suggested by this issue accurately reflects the range of aesthetic possibilities open to artists at the time. In particular, the final section includes Marius Lyle's remarkable "Scheme for Physical Improvement of Writers' Medium" (see Appendix), which succinctly summarizes the typographical effects and possibilities of the most analytical aspects of cubist literature. Self-consciously directed at a writers' "revolt" and "revolution," this work seems to me seminal not only in describing but also in illustrating a number of the strategies used by several of the poets discussed so far. The acute attention to the visual texture of language, in both this issue and the earlier "Revolution of the Word," reinforced the aesthetic that would support such subsequent works as Kurt Schwitters' "abloesung" (1933) or Barzun's remarkable "Fragment de l'universel poème" (1938).

*****

The energy fueling poetic creativity—and especially the energy fueling continued poetic experiments in a cubist fashion—suggested by *The Exile* and *transition* can be found in the late twenties with equal force in America in the poetry published in *Blues* and *Pagany* and, to a lesser degree, in other contemporaneous journals such as *Hound & Horn*. The mutual exchange between these journals may already have been suggested by the appearance of Williams and Zukofsky in *The Exile*—just as American writers had published in *Broom* several years before. In addition, as already mentioned, Williams and Winters appeared in *transition*. Louis Zukofsky appears in the February 1929 issues of both *transition* and *Blues* (number 15 and number 1, respectively), so that it may not be surprising that *Blues* should advertise *transition* on its inside cover.

Of the American journals begun in the late 1920s, however, *Hound & Horn* (founded in the same year as *transition* by Lincoln Kirstein, Allen Tate, and Yvor Winters) remains the most conservative. In fact, just as *Poetry* and *The Little Review* eventually became polarized for political/ aesthetic reasons, *Hound & Horn* became opposed to *This Quarter,* another small magazine published in Italy during this time, which dedicated its first number to Ezra Pound. Yet despite its relative conservatism, *Hound & Horn* is important for registering how widespread cubist poetry was at this time. S. Foster Damon's appropriately entitled "The Great Experiment" (1929) stands as the most remarkable poem to appear in this journal. Given the self-consciousness about poetic experimentation that we have witnessed in the poems discussed so far, this one proves particularly so, for it exhibits in miniature many of the developments we have been tracing over the preceding two decades. The poem begins, in fact, in a perfectly traditional way with rhymed couplets. Rapidly, however, it explores the possibilities of the prose poem before evolving into visual poetry. Given the force of cubism in the aesthetic experiments of this period, it is probably with great humor that Damon writes, "Meanwhile he posed his *cones and cubes . . .*" (emphasis added).

Williams' "Rain" appears in *Hound & Horn* the following year. While not as experimental as Damon's poem, "Rain" engages in an unusual verbal play with grammatical perspective in which one word may end a sentence while, simultaneously, beginning the next one, as the following example shows:

> The trees
> are become
> beasts fresh risen
> from
>   the sea—
> water
>
> trickles
> from the crevices of
> their hides—
>
> *Hound & Horn* 3, 1 (1929), 79

As a strategy, such verbal manipulation seems, once again, a specific counterpart to the manipulation of forms in cubist paintings, in particular the "interpenetration" achieved visually when one shape appears simultaneously to be different facets of multiple larger figures (most obviously in the work of Juan Gris during this period, but also as early as his 1913 "The Guitar").

This journal also prints A. Hyatt Mayor's essay "Picasso's Method" (mentioned above), which compares Picasso's pre-war cubist phase to the post-war mood. Mayor further compares Picasso's art to Pound's poetry and to Stravinsky's music, explicitly aligning all three artists and implicitly aligning the three media: "Picasso is by no means the only Proteus among modern artists. One thinks at once of Ezra Pound and Stravinsky" (*Hound & Horn* 3, 2 [Jan–March, 1930], 181). The next issue of *Hound & Horn,* in fact, prints three of Pound's *Cantos* (numbers XXVIII–XXX). Finally, the continued impact of cubism can be seen in Williams' 1932 "In the 'Sconset Bus," which repeats strategically the kind of simple play with visual perspective witnessed earlier in "The Red Wheelbarrow."

*****

The most important and successful American journals for publishing cubist poetry during this period, however, are *Blues*, founded in 1929 by Charles Henri Ford (with Williams as contributing editor), and *Pagany,* founded the following year by Richard Johns. As we might assume from the fact that Johns borrowed the title from Williams (specifically, Williams' 1928 *A Voyage to Pagany*),[12] these two journals are more than first cousins in their aesthetic concerns — they are virtually twins. Here we see the combined efforts of Zukofsky, Kenneth Rexroth, Pauline Leader, Parker Tyler, Henri Ford, Norman MacLeod, and others, all of whom were publishing in both journals and all of whom seemed committed to the prospect that, as for Gertrude Stein, "words and paint were equally material waiting to be formed."[13]

While the relatively large sampling here from each journal offers its own form of explication, it is worth noting that Williams essentially wrote the "manifestoes" for both magazines, in the form of "For a New Magazine" (*Blues* 1, 2 [March 1929]) and in the combined pieces, "Manifesto" and "The Work of Gertrude Stein," the latter of which was originally drafted as "Manifesto: in the form of a criticism of the works of Gertrude Stein," (*Pagany* 1, 1 [Jan.–March, 1930], 1, 41–46). Of these, the manifesto for *Blues* appears the more radical and political:

> Blues is a good name for it, all the extant magazines in America being thoroughly, totally, completely dead as far as anything new in literature among us is concerned. Anything that fractures the stereotyped is definitely taboo, now as always. In the common mind America is just recovering from the post-war hysteria of a few of the more bizarre writers of that unsettled time, returning to the normal paths of good literary practice. . . . But the young writers today must not be allowed to lose what those of 1914 and thereabouts won — even to be held as weakly as it is — with difficulty.

In contrast, the essay on Stein published in *Pagany* emphasizes far more the autonomous status of art that must not, Williams argues, seek to be "science, philosophy, history, the humanities, or anything else *it has been made to carry in the past*" (italics mine). Taken together, the manifestoes suggest that Williams' sense of the modern poetic revolution was its rejection of institutional connotations and its self-liberation as a medium (precisely the revolution achieved by cubist painters in the visual arts). No wonder, then, his reverence for Stein (who was utterly dismissed by Eliot, who was in turn denigrated by Williams) and his encouragement of such poets as Louis Zukofsky and George Oppen.

At least initially, *Blues* attempted to align itself with musical blues (rather than, for example, with Stravinsky), thus suggesting a conjunction between cubist poetry and blues that could be fruitfully explored. Nevertheless, only the first few issues of *Blues* seem to contain a significant number of poems specifically designed to evoke the sounds of blues in music, as well as the black dialect most frequently associated with that musical genre.[14] For instance, in the first issue Herman Spector published "A Wohmmn," part of which is cited below:

> i wann, i wann a wohmmn
> whose touch hrts.
> — — — — — — — —
> no haddit befaw
> i wann a wite wide wohmmn,
> promising maww.
>
> *Blues* 1, 1 (February 1929), 13

Possibly as a response to Williams' reinterpretation of the meaning of "Blues" (noted in "For a New Magazine" above), most of the subsequent contributors to *Blues* were preoccupied with the visual aspects of their verbal media. Later, the advertisement for *Blues* in *Pagany* would appropriately read:

> HANDS off B
> L
> U E S
> unless you can see print, hear sounds, and read words.
>
> (inside back cover, *Pagany* 2, 2 [Spring 1931])

Of the poems included here from *Blues,* Charles Henri Ford's "Group" is of particular interest for continuing the exploration of the possibilities of the prose poem. His later "Are Poems," published in the eighth number (1930), show a deep affinity with Walter Arensberg's "Ing" and "Arithmetical Progression of the Verb 'To Be.'" Parker Tyler's "Sonnet"—which is excellent in its own terms—shows the specific influence of E. E. Cummings. More important, perhaps, is its anticipation of Williams' "variable foot," a fact that is especially choice, given Williams' continued "inveighing against the sonnet" for not admitting "of the slightest structural change in its composition."[15]

In "Poem," published in the third issue (1929), Kenneth Rexroth, a cubist poet who also, as noted above, called Williams one as well,[16] says specifically,

> Come to color.
> *Between the edge of cube and cube* twilight thickens day deserts
> the eastward windows the cypress groves that grow along the
> westward sea. (italics mine)

In another poem published in the June 1929 issue of *Blues,* Rexroth calls attention to one obvious, essentially visual or typographical aspect of cubist poetry when his concern with color changes to the desire to "break backs of letters" (untitled, *Blues* 1, 5 [June 1929], 120).

The sixth issue of *Blues*, published in 1929, continues what had become a virtual tradition in these journals by billing itself as the "Expatriate" number, a fact that Williams perhaps ironically encouraged shortly before by asserting (largely in derision of Eliot) that "Poetry, like many another thing, causes men to leave life behind and go wherever the chase leads" ("A Note on the Art of Poetry," *Blues* 1, 4 [May 1929], 77). Not surprisingly, perhaps, Gertrude Stein appears in the expatriate number, with "George Hugnet," a short prose poem that deliberately conflates the relation a person achieves in society with a person's (or, more accurately, a writer's) relationship to either traditional or nontraditional grammar. In the same issue, Walter Lowenfels' "Antipodes," which is subtitled "from Finale of Seem," appears to be a specific response to Stevens' "The Emperor of Ice-Cream." Not only does the subtitle repeat, in a collage-like fashion, a phrase that appeared in Stevens' 1922 poem, but the opening section plays with "Sugar! Oh Cream!" while announcing that "Nothing rolls like a ball./ When the nogar man comes—." (Stevens' poem had called for the "roller of big cigars" to "whip/ In kitchen cups concupiscent curds" [*The Dial* 73, 1 (1922)].) Of the other poems from this issue included in this volume, Laurence Vail's "Meek Madness in Capri or Suicide for Effect" proves particularly interesting for exhibiting several different cubist strategies, including the effective use of white space typical of many cubist poems, as well as the grammatical manipulation of the verbal medium typical of Stein. In addition, the place in which this "madness" occurs is located specifically in "cautious cubes of room."

Although the number of cubist poems that appeared in this journal discourages individual explication of each poem (indeed, the relatively large number of poems reprinted here is still only a fraction of the cubist verse published in *Blues*), of particular merit is Williams' "The Attic Which Is Desire," a poem that not only borders upon concrete poetry, but that also addresses the verbal challenge of Zukofsky's "Cocktails" with its own "signs of/ 'ads'" (published in *transition* the preceding year). In addition, Williams' "The Moon—" (which "ride[s] upon the page/ by virtue of/ the law of sentences) dismantles a naive sense of pure representation by foregrounding both the text, and the medium with which the text is created, in much the same way that cubist paintings consistently violate normal expectations of representation in the visual medium.

In a somewhat similar fashion, Zukofsky's "Tibor Serly" calls attention to various media in its opening lines, while precluding any of them from representing with accuracy:

Red varnish
Warm flitch

Of cello,
They play

Scroll before
Them —

Blues 1, 9 (1930), 42

In fact, Zukofsky was a frequent contributor to *Blues*, though in a very different form than that which he presented to *The Exile*. The facet of Zukofsky's work most characteristic of his contributions to *Blues* might accurately be called his analytic cubist phase, promoted perhaps by his continued contact with Williams. As Neil Baldwin has pointed out, Zukofsky had an enormous impact on Williams' work, including specifically "The Descent of Winter" and "The Work of Gertrude Stein," even arranging the actual poems in some of Williams' books. The influence was mutual, however, so it is particularly revealing that Baldwin notes Williams' "deep confusion when confronted by examples of Zukofsky's poetry, from "Poem Beginning 'The'" through the various versions of 'A'."[17] Though not mentioned by Baldwin (and in spite of the fact that Williams could produce his own highly complex, synthetic works), the kind of poetry Zukofsky published in *Blues* (and in *Pagany* as well) was probably far more intelligible to Williams than were his longer, synthetic works.

I should also note that, while not of immediate concern to this chapter (though of relevance to the next), the Fall, 1930, issue of *Blues* prints, in translation, a long debate between Gottfried Benn and Johannes R. Becher called "Can the Poet Change the World?" Not surprisingly, they mention both Nietzsche and Marx in the course of trying to determine the poet's response to a "'new literary age'" prompted by "Soviet ideology." As Eugene Jolas notes in his introduction, the debate "synthesizes one of the important problems facing the poet today" (*Blues* 9 [1930], 5). Oversimplifying somewhat, Becher takes issue with Benn's assertion that the poet be allowed

> the liberty to shut himself off from contemporaries who consist partly of disinherited small stock owners and querulous utilitarians, and partly of Hertha-and-Poseidon-swimmers: he wants to go his own way.
>
> *Blues* 9 (1930), 8

An attitude immediately derided by Becher as "estheticism" and defended by Benn as "No, moral." Given the topic of the debate, which variously concerns Williams, Pound, Stanley Burnshaw, and even Wallace Stevens during this period, and given the actual socio-political developments of this time, the specific conjunction here of aesthetic/political concerns testifies again to the deeply political nature of this aesthetic development and anticipates the great controversies surrounding it that would finally erupt only a few years later.

Thus, while nearly as short-lived as *Soil* or *291,* and while relatively unknown (or at least not mentioned) by most critics, *Blues* is one of the most important journals for encouraging what we have been describing as a "cubist aesthetic" in American poetry. Within this context, Williams' concluding essay, "Caviar and Bread Again: A Warning to the New Writer," proves both poignant and intensely ironic:

> Experiment we must have, but it seems to me that a number of the younger writers has forgotten that writing doesn't mean just inventing new ways to say "So's your Old Man." I swear I myself can't make out for the life of me what many of them are talking about, and I have a will to understand them that they will not find in many another.
>
> If you like Gertrude Stein, study her for her substance; she has it, no matter what the idle may say. The same for Ezra Pound, for James Joyce. It is substance that makes their work important. Technique is part of it. . . .
>
> *Blues* 9 (1930), 47

This warning, perhaps ironically (but certainly problematically) published in the same year Williams praised Stein precisely for her revolutionary escape from the philosophical or humanitarian import long associated with poetry ("The Work of Gertrude Stein," *Pagany* 1, 1 [1930], 41–46), points to that more conservative side of Williams that is often ignored when considering his political side, or misrepresented when attending his "native" or "American" side. In addition, though he would clearly choose different authors, the statement above sounds very much like Stevens when he dismisses the poetry that is "modern in respect to form" in favor of that which is "modern in respect to what it says."[18] That Stevens would at least partially deride Williams some fifteen years later for being more "interested in the way of saying things than in what he has to say"[19] makes the irony here all the more acute and points to a critical area in which the best of our modern American poets began increasingly to misunderstand each other's poetics and purpose. Not only is it a misunderstanding that would permanently divide poets who had previously been part of the same climate and would surface radically in the disputes over "aesthetic autonomy" in the Bollingen prizes, it would also significantly contribute to many critical and theoretical disputes of our own day. It is, furthermore, a misunderstanding that for good or ill has given us a highly select and, I would argue, distorted "canon" of the poetic force and of the force of poetics in the first half of this century.

*****

Closely related to *Blues* in spirit and in contributors, the first issue of *Pagany: A Native Quarterly* (which appeared in the spring of 1930) includes Robert McAlmon, Kenneth Rexroth, Parker Tyler, Norman MacLeod, Charles Henri Ford, Louis Zukofsky, Gertrude Stein, Gorham Munson, and Yvor Winters (among others), as well as the essay by Williams, "The Work of Gertrude Stein," mentioned above. The most striking difference between the two journals is that whereas *Blues* published almost exclusively poetry, *Pagany* was far more likely to include prose as well, including the prose of various poets published in *Blues*. In this way alone, the two journals are powerful complements to each other, offering a fairly representative sampling of the concerns and writing of the times.

Of all its issues, however, the first one is most successfully what I would call "cubist" in nature (even though some subsequent issues include a few superior cubist poems). For example, Stein's "Five Words in a Line" (reprinted here) is followed by Williams' essay on her work, which is in turn followed by a poem (shading into a prose poem) by Rexroth that is dedicated to Williams. Henri Ford's "Three Poems," particularly "This Kind of Death," explore the possibilities of typography and punctuation in a manner akin to that of Cummings. Yvor Winters contributed three poems to this issue, "Wild Sunflower," "Idaho," and "To the Painter Polelonema," all of which are included here. All three appear, superficially, reminiscent of Williams and, in the case of "Wild Sunflower," of Williams' flower poems. Thematically, however, his attention to the "wormseething loam," the "hairy" thing "unfinished at the edges" anticipates Theodore Roethke, especially *The Lost Son.*

Sidney Hunt and Edouard Roditi, in subsequent issues of the first volume, again explore the typographical possibilities of cubist verse, in particular the possibilities of white space. Of all the works published in the first volume of *Pagany*, Parker Tyler's poem "Dream of the Erotic" — with the subtitle, *"An Essay in Articulate Typography"* (italics mine) — is the most important, combining, as it does, strategies of Mina Loy, Cummings, Williams, and Winters.

In the subsequent volumes, the influence of cubism in the verbal medium remains quite strong (even if less consistent), as evidenced in

several remarkable poems. I should call special attention to the sophisti-
cated verbal manipulation in which Stein engaged by following Georges
Hugnet's "Enfances" (with the possibility of a homophonic on "N-fances")
with "Poem Pritten on Pfances of Georges Hugnet." And though not
included here, it is important to note that *Pagany* printed Pound's Cantos
XXX–XXXIII in the summer of 1931. Yet of all the poems to appear in this
journal, Zukofsky's "'A': First Movement, 'Come Ye Daughters'" is the
most important to this study, prefiguring his seminal epic-length *"A"*,
finally completed almost fifty years later. The specific lines in which he
plays with

> Feet off ground:
> As beyond effort, playing —
> Music leaving no traces.
> Nor any conscious effort,
> Nor boiling to put pen to paper

collapses the concerns about revolutionizing metrical feet, poetic stanzas,
musical scansion, and (implicitly) the tradition of any perspective
(whether visual, verbal, or musical) that is ultimately derived from "linear"
concerns. We are reminded of the way in which Picasso collapses the same
artistic traditions in his 1913 "Violon au Café" or that Braque did in such
paintings as the 1913 "Woman with a Guitar"; both of these works fracture
not only traditional perspective, but at least implicitly musical and verbal
structures as well with their fragments of musical instruments and printed
words.

*****

While largely unknown, *Pagany*, together with *Blues*, signifies the
degree to which the cubist aesthetic had fully integrated American poet-
ics by the beginning of the third decade of this century. In the particular
case of Zukofsky, who is so prominent in both of these American journals,
Blues and *Pagany* provide something of a testing ground for the continued
work of one of the major poets of this century. But more important, they
demonstrate the sustained attempt of some of our most conscientious
writers to create in revolutionary language nothing short of social revolu-
tion. As James Laughlin would say only a few years later in his anthology
of *New Directions,*

> I believe then, that experimental writing has a real social value, apart from
> any other. . . . For however my contributors may see themselves I see them

as agents of social reform as well as artists. Their propaganda is implicit in their style and in probably every case (originally, at least) unconscious.[20]

Whether the political stance of these writers was ever unconscious is, to my mind, quite debatable. Laughlin is nonetheless correct in his analysis that the change in language could or should instigate a change in social structures. As feminist theorists (most especially those from France) have recently been demonstrating, language is inextricably bound within social conventions that it either perpetuates or subverts. The possibility, however, that no meaningful language *can* escape traditional systems is a possibility that would lead another great cubist poet, George Oppen, to enter a period of poetic silence as political protest. Oppen's gesture thus ironically anticipates one facet of the next phase of American cubist poetry, a phase in which the force of cubism in American verse declines quite dramatically.

THE EXILE

Poem Beginning "The"

Because I have had occasion to remember, quote, paraphrase, I dedicate this poem to Anyone and Anything I have unjustifiably forgotten. Also to J. S. Bach (309), Bede's *Ecclesiastical History* (248, 291), Max Beerbohm (245), Beethoven's *Ninth Symphony* (310–312), Broadway (134), Geoffrey Chaucer (1st Movement, Title), College Cheer (45), E. E. Cummings' *Is Five* (38), Dante (66), Norman Douglas' *South Wind* (14), Elijah, the Prophet (24), T. S. Eliot's *The Waste Land* and *The Sacred Wood* (25–27), John Erskine (184, 185), Heinrich Heine (266, 267, 269, 316), Robert Herrick (187, 188), Horace (141), Horses (224–237), Aldous Huxley's *Those Barren Leaves* (12, 18), Henry James (2nd Movement, Title), Jewish Folk Song (191, 270–286), James Joyce (13, 20, 28, 29), D. H. Lawrence (8, 19, 133), Christopher Marlowe's *Edward II* (46, 47), Modern Advertising (163), George Moore (24), Marianne Moore (22), Mussolini (74, 75), Myself (130, 142, 167, 309), Obvious (Where the Reference Is Obvious), Walter Pater's *Renaissance* (165), Peer Gynt (281–285), Poe's *Helen* (168–182), Popular Non-Sacred Song (4, 5, 36, 37, 288, 289), Ezra Pound (15, 18), Power of the Past, Present and Future (Where the reference is to the word Sun), E. A. Robinson's *Children of the Night* (132), Sophocles (6), Oswald Spengler (132), Max Stirner (199–202), Symbol of our Relatively Most Permanent Self, Origin and Destiny (Wherever the reference is to the word Mother), The Bible (1–3, 9, 313, 314), The Bolsheviki (203, 323), The French Language (31, 33, 51, 292), The King's English (166), *The Merchant of Venice* (250–265), The Yellow Menace (241–242), University Extension (70), Villon (21), Franz Werfel (68), Virginia Woolf's *Mrs Dalloway* (52), Yehoash (110–129, 205–223, 318–330).

Figures and References in Parenthesis are to line in *Poem Beginning "The."*

Poem Beginning "The"

First Movement: "And out of olde bokes, in good feith"

1   The

2   Voice of Jesus I. Rush singing

3   in the wilderness

4   A boy's best friend is his mother,

5   It's your mother all the time.

6   Residue of Oedipus-faced wrecks

7   Creating out of the dead,—

8   From the candle flames of the souls of dead mothers

9   Vide the legend of thin Christ sending her out of the temple,—

10   Books from the stony heart, flames rapping the stone,

11   Residue of self-exiled men

12   By the Tyrrhenian.

13   Paris.

14   But everywhere only the South Wind, the sirocco, the broken
      Earth-face.

15   The broken Earth-face, the age demands an image of its life and
      contacts,

16   Lord, lord, not that we pray, are sure of the question,

17   But why are our finest always dead?

18   And why, Lord, this time, is it Mauberley's Luini in porcelain, why
      is it Chelifer,

19   Why is it Lovat who killed Kangaroo,

20   Why Stephen Daedalus with the cane of ash,

21   But why les neiges?

22   And why, if all of Mary's Observations have been made

23   Have not the lambs become more sapient drinking of the Spring;

24   Kerith is long dry, and the ravens that brought the prophet bread

25   Are dust in the waste-land of a raven-winged evening.

26   And why if the waste land has been explored, travelled over,
      circumscribed,

27   Are there only wrathless skeletons exhumed new planted in its
      sacred wood,

28   Why—heir, long dead,—Odysseus, wandering of ten years

29   Out-journeyed only by our Stephen, bibbing of a day,

30   Oh why is that to Hecuba as Hecuba to he!

31   You are cra-a-zee on the subjects of babies, says she,

32   That is because somehow our authors have been given a woman's
      intuition.

33   Il y a un peu trop de femme in this South Wind.

34   And on the cobblestones, bang, bang, bang, myself like the
      wheels—

129

35 The tram passes singing
36 O do you take this life as your lawful wife,
37   I do!
38 O the Time is 5
39   I do!
40 O the Time is 5
41   I do!
42 O do you take these friends as your loves to wive,
43 O the time is 5
44   I do!

45 For it's the hoo-doos, the somethin' voo-doos
46 And not King's onelie, but the wisest men
47 Graue Socrates, what says Marlowe?
48 For it was myself seemed held
49 Beating — beating —
50 Body trembling as over an hors d'oeuvres —
51
52 And the dream ending — Dalloway! Dalloway —
53 The blind portals opening, and I awoke!

54 Let me be
55 Not by art have we lived,
56 Not by graven images forbidden to us
57 Not by letters I fancy.
58 Do we dare say
59 With Spinoza grinding lenses, Rabbaisi,
60 After living on Cathedral Parkway?

    Second Movement: International Episode
61 . This is the aftermath
62 When Peter Out and I discuss the theatre.
63 Evenings, our constitutional.
64 We both strike matches, both in unison,
65   to light one pipe, my own.
66 'Tis, 'tis love, that makes the world go round and love is what I
        dream.
67 Peter is polite and I to me am almost as polite as Peter.
68 Somehow, in Germany, the Jew goat-song is unconvincing —
69   How the brain forms its visions thinking incessantly of the
        things,

130

70 Not the old Greeks anymore,—
71 the things themselves a shadow world scarce shifting the
   incessant thought—
72 Time, time the goat were an offering,
73 Eh, what show do we see to-night, Peter?
74 "Il Duce: I feel God deeply."
75 Black shirts—black shirts—some power is so funereal.

76 Lion-heart, frate mio, and so on in two languages
77 the thing itself a shadow world.
78 Goldenrod
79 Of which he is a part,
80 Sod
81 He hurried over
82 Underfoot,
83 Make now
84 His testament of sun and sky
85 With clod
86 To root what shoot
87 It sends to run the sun,
88 The sun-sky blood.

89 My loves there is his mystery beyond your loves.
90 Uncanny are the stars,
91 His slimness was as evasive
92 And his grimness was not yours.

93 Do you walk slowly the halls of the heavens,
94 Or saying that you do, lion-hearted not ours,
95 Hours, days months, past from us and gone,
96 Lion-heart not looked upon, walk with the stars.
97 Or have these like old men acknowledged
98 No kin but that grips of death,
99 Of being dying only to live on with them,
100 Entirely theirs,
101 And so quickly grown old that we on earth like stems raised
   dark
102 Feel only the lull, heave, phospher change, death, the
103 One follow, the other, the end?

104 Our candles have been buried beneath these waters,
105 Their lights are his,

106   Ship-houses on the waters he might have lived near.
107   Steady the red light and it makes no noise whatever.
108   Damn it! they have made capital of his flesh and bone.
109   What, in revenge, can dead flesh and bone make capital?
110   And his heart is dry
111   Like the teeth of a dead camel
112   But his eyes no longer blink
113   Not even as a blind dog's.

114   With the blue night shadows on the sand
115   May his kingdom return to him,
116   The Bedouin leap again on his *asilah*,
117   The expanse of heaven hang upon his shoulder
118   As an embroidered texture,
119   Behind him on his saddle sit the night
120   Sing into his ear:

121   Swifter than a tiger to his prey,
122   Lighter than the storm wind, dust or spray,
123   The Bedouin bears the Desert-Night,
124   Big his heart and young with life,
125   Younger yet his gay, wild wife
126   The Desert-Night.

127   Some new trappings for his steed,
128   All the stars in dowry his meed
129   From the Desert-Night.

130   I've changed my mind, Zukofsky,
131   How about some other show—
132   "The Queen of Roumania," "Tilbury," "The West-Decline,"
133   "Hall's Mills," "The Happy Quetzalcoatl"
134   "Near Ibsen," "Dancing with H. R. H.," "Polly Wants a New Fur
           Coat,"
135   "The Post Office"—
136   Speaking of the post office, the following will handicap you
               for the position,
137   my dear Peter,
138   Your weight less than one hundred twenty-five pounds,
139   One half of a disabled veteran, and probably
140   the whole of an unknown soldier,
141   That's indomitaeque morti for you.

142   Is it true what you say, Zukofsky,
143   Sorry to say, My Peter Out.

144   "Tear the Codpiece Off, A Musical Comedy,"
145   Likewise, "Panting for Pants,"
146   "The Dream That Knows No Waking."

Third Movement: In Cat Minor
147   Hard, hard the cat-world.
148   On the stream Vicissitude
149   Our milk flows lewd.

150   We'll cry, we'll cry,
151   We'll cry the more
152   And wet the floor,
153   Megrow, megrow,
154   Around around,
155   The only sound

156   The prowl, our prowl,
157   Of gentlemen cats
158   With paws like spats

159   Who weep the nights
160   Till the nights are gone—
161   —And r·r·run—the Sun!

Fourth Movement: More "Renaissance"
162   Is it the sun you're looking for,
163   Drop in at Askforaclassic, Inc.,
164   Get yourself another century,
165   A little frost before sundown,
166   It's the times don'chewknow,
167   And if you're a Jewish boy, then be your Plato's Philo.

168   Engprof, thy lectures were to me
169   Like those roast flitches of red boar
170   That, smelling, one is like to see
171   Through windows where the steam's galore
172   Like our own "Cellar Door".

173   On weary bott'm long wont to sit,
174   Thy graying hair, thy beaming eyes,

175 Thy heavy jowl would make me fit
176   For the Pater that was Greece,
177   The siesta that was Rome.

178 Lo! from my present — say not — itch
179   How statue-like I see thee stand
180 Phi Beta Key within thy hand!
181   Professor — from the backseats which
182 Are no man's land!

183 Poe,
184 Gentlemen, don'chewknow,
185 But never wrote an epic.

Fifth Movement: Autobiography

186 Speaking about epics, mother,
187 How long ago is it since you gathered mushrooms,
188 Gathered mushrooms while you mayed.
189 It is your mate, my father, boating.
190 A stove burns like a full moon in a desert night.
191 Und in hoyze iz Kalt. You think of a new grave.
192 In the fields, flowers.
193 Night on the bladed grass, bayonets dewed.
194 It is your mate, my father, boating.
195 Speaking about epics, mother, —
196 Down here among the gastanks, ruts, cemetery-tenements —
197 It is your Russia that is free.
198 And I here, can I say only —
199   "So then an egoist can never embrace a party
200   Or take up with a party?
201   Oh, yes, only he cannot let himself
202   Be embraced and taken up by the party."
203 It is your Russia that is free, mother.
204 Tell me, mother.

205 Winged wild geese, where lies the passage,
206 In far away lands lies the passage.
207 Winged wild geese, who knows the pathway?
208 Of the winds, asking, we shall say:
209 Wind of the South and wind of the North
210 Where has your sun gone forth?
211 Naked, twisted, scraggly branches,

212 And dark, gray patches through the branches,
213 Ducks with puffed-up, fluttering feathers
214 On a cobalt stream.
215 And faded grass that's slowly swaying.
216 A barefoot shepherd boy
217 Striding in the mire;
218 Swishing indifferently a peeled branch
219 On jaded sheep.
220 An old horse strewn with yellow leaves
221 By the edge of the meadow
222 Draws weakly with humid nostrils
223 The moisture of the clouds.
224 Horses that pass through inappreciable woodland,
225 Leaves in their manes tangled, mist, autumn green,
226 Lord, why not give these bright brutes—your good land—
227 Turf for their feet always, years for their mien.
228 See how each peer lifts his head, others follow,
229 Mate paired with mate, flanks coming full they crowd,
230 Reared in your sun, Lord, escaping each hollow
231 Where life-struck we stand, utter their praise aloud.
232 Very much Chance, Lord, as when you first made us,
233 You might forget them, Lord, preferring what
234 Being less lovely where sadly we fuss?
235 Weed out these horses as tho' they were not?
236 Never alive in brute delicate trembling
237 Song to your sun, against autumn assembling.

238 If horses could but sing Bach, mother,—
239 Remember how I wished it once—
240 Now I kiss you who could never sing Bach, never read
        Shakespeare.
241 In Manhattan here the Chinamen are yellow in the face, mother,
242 Up and down, up and down our streets they go yellow in the face,
243 And why is it the representatives of your, my, race are always
        hankering for food, mother?
244 We, on the other hand, eat so little.
245 Dawn't you think Trawtsky rawrthaw a darrling,
246 I ask our immigrant cousin querulously.
247 Naw! I think hay is awlmawst a Tchekoff.
248 But she has more color in her cheeks than the Angles—Angels—
        mother,—

249 They have enough, though. We should get some more color,
     mother.
250 If I am like them in the rest, I should resemble them in that,
     mother,
251 Assimilation is not hard,
252 And once the Faith's askew
253 I might as well look Shagetz just as much as Jew.
254 I'll read their Donne as mine,
255 And leopard in their spots
256 I'll do what says their Coleridge,
257 Twist red hot pokers into knots.
258 The villainy they teach me I will execute
259 And it shall go hard with them,
260 For I'll better the instruction,
261 Having learned, so to speak, in their colleges.
262   It is engendered in the eyes
263   With gazing fed, and fancy dies
264   In the cradle where it lies
265   In the cradle where it lies
266 I, Senora, am the Son of the Respected Rabbi,
267 Israel of Saragossa,
268 Not that the Rabbis give a damn,
269 Keine Kadish wird man sagen.

Half-Dozenth Movement: Finale, and After

270 Under the cradle the white goat stands, mother,
271 What will the goat be saddled with, mother?
272   Almonds, raisins.
273 What will my heart be bartering, mother,
274   Wisdom, learning.
275 Lullaby, lullaby, lullaby, lullaby.
276 These are the words of the prophet, mother,
277 Likely to save me from Tophet, mother—
278 What will my heart be burning to, mother,
279   Wisdom, learning.
280 By the cat and the well, I swear, my Shulamite!
281 In my faith, in my hope, and in my love.
282 I will cradle thee, I will watch thee,
283 Sleep and dream thou, dear my boy!
284   (Presses his cheek against her mouth.)

285 I must try to fare forth from here.
286 I do not forget you,
287 I am just gone out for to-night,
288 The Royal Stag is abroad,
289 I am gone out hunting,
290 The leaves have lit by the moon.
291 Even in their dirt, the Angles like Angels are fair,
292 Brooks Nash, for instance, faisant un petit bruit, mais tres net,
293 Saying, He who is afraid to do that should be denied the
          privilege,
294 And where the automobile roads with the gasoline shine,
295 Appropriately the katydid—
296 Ka-ty did. . . . Ka-ty didn't. . . .

297 Helen Gentile,
298 And did one want me; no.
299 But wanted me to take one? yes.
300 And should I have kissed one? no.
301 That is, embraced one first
302 And holding closely one, then kissed one? yes.
303 Angry against things, iron I ring
304 Recalcitrant prod and kick.
305 Oh, Baedekera Schonberg, you here
306   dreaming of the relentlessness of motion
307 As usual,
308 One or two dead in the process what does it matter.

309 Our God immortal such Life as is our God,
310 Bei dein Zauber, by thy magic I embrace thee,
311 Open Sesame, Ali Baba, I, thy firefly, little errant star, call here,
312 By thy magic I embrace thee.

313 O my son Sun, my son, my son Sun! would God
314 I had died for thee, O Sun, my son, my son!

315 I have not forgotten you, mother,—
316 It is a lie—Aus meinen grossen leiden mach ich die kleinen
          lieder,
317 Rather they are joy, against nothingness joy—
318 By the wrack we shall sing our Sun-song
319 Under our feet will crawl
320 The shadows of dead worlds,

321   We shall open our arms wide,
322   Call out of pure might—
323   Sun, you great Sun, our Comrade,
324   From eternity to eternity we remain true to you,
325   A myriad years we have been,
326   Myriad upon myriad shall be.

327   How wide our arms are,
328   How strong,
329   A myriad years we have been,
330   Myriad upon myriad shall be.

LOUIS ZUKOFSKY
(*The Exile*, Spring 1928)

Part of Canto XXIII

(*The opening of this canto is too obscure to be printed apart from the main context of the poem*)

Precisely, the selv' oscura,
And in the morning, in the Phrygian head-sack,
Barefooted, dumping sand from their boat,
'Yperionides!
     And the rose grown while I slept,
And the strings shaken with music,
Capriped, the loose twigs underfoot;
We here on the hill, with the olives
Where a man might carry his oar up,
And the boat there in the inlet;
As we had lain there in the autumn
Under the arras, or wall painted below like arras
And, above, with a garden of rose-trees,
And thrum of sound from the cross-street;
As we had stood there,
Watching road from the window,
Fa Han and I at the window,
And her head bound with gold-cords,
Cloud over mountain; hill-gap in mist, like a sea-coast.

Leaf over leaf, dawn-branch in the sky
And the sea dark, under wind,

The boat's sails hung loose at the mooring,
   Cloud like a sail inverted,
And the men dumping sand by the sea-wall
And the olives there on the hill
   Where a man might carry his oar up.

And my brother De Maensac
Bet with me for the castle,
And we put it on the toss of a coin,
And I, Austors, won the coin toss and kept it,
And he went out to Tierci, a jongleur
And on the road for his living,
And twice he went down to Tierci,
And took off the girl there that was just married to Bernart.
And went to Auvergne, to the Dauphin,
And Tierci came with a posse to Auvergnat,
And went back for an army,
And came to Auvergne with the army
But never got Pierre nor the woman.
And he went down past Chaise Dieu,
And went, after it all, to Mont Ségur,
   after the end of all things,
And they hadn't left even the stair,
And Simone was dead by that time,
And they called us the Manicheans
Wotever the hellsarse that is.

And that was when Troy was down, all right,
   superbo Ilion. . . .
And they were sailing along
Sitting in the stern-sheets
Under the lee of an island
And the wind drifting off from the island.
"Tet, tet. . . .
   what is it?" said Anchises.
"Tethnéké," said the helmsman, "I think they
Are howling because Adonis died virgin."
"Huh! tet. . . ." said Anchises,
   "well, they've made a bloody mess of that city."

"King Otreus, of Phrygia
"That king is my father."

and saw then, as of waves taking form,
As the sea, hard, a glitter of crystal,
And the waves rising, but formed, holding their form;
No light reaching through them.

Explicit Canto xxiii
Adolphe 1920: "uno degli sforzi piu insigni e spasimosi di questi ultimi tempi
per imprigionare nella renitente materia dell' arte il mistero della vita."

Corriere della Sera
24 June, 1927

EZRA POUND
(*The Exile*, Spring 1928)

Excerpt from **The Descent of Winter**

9/27

"What are these elations I have
at my own underwear?

I touch it and it is strange
upon a strange thigh."

*   *   *

9/29

My bed is narrow
in a small room
at sea

The numbers are on
the wall
Arabic 1

Berth No. 2
was empty above me
the steward

took it apart
and removed
it

only the number
remains
. 2 .

140

on an oval disc
of celluloid
tacked

to the whiteenameled
woodwork
with

two bright nails
like stars
beside

the moon

9/30

There are no perfect waves—
Your writings are a sea
full of misspellings and
faulty sentences.   Level.   Troubled.
A center distant from the land
touched by the wings of nearly
silent birds that never seem
to rest, yet it bears me
seriously—to land, but without
you.

This is the sadness of the sea—
waves like words all broken—
a sameness of lifting and falling mood.

I lean watching the detail
Of brittle crest, the delicate
imperfect foam, the yellow weed
one piece like another—

There is no hope, or maybe
a coral island slowly
slowly forming and waiting
for birds to drop the seeds
will make it habitable

10/9

  and there's a little blackboy
  in a doorway

141

scratching his wrists

The cap on his head
is red and blue
with a broad peak to it

and his mouth
is open, his tongue
between his teeth —

10/10

   Monday
        the canna flaunts
   its crimson head

   crimson lying folded
   crisply down upon

        the invisible

   darkly crimson heart
   of this poor yard

   the grass is long

        October tenth

1927

10/13   a beard . . . not of stone but particular
hairs purpleblack . . . lies upon his stale breast

10/21

   In the dead weeds a rubbish heap
   in flames: the orange flames
   stream horizontal, windblown
   they parallel the ground
   waving up and down
   the flamepoints alternating
   the body streaked with loops
   and purple stains while
   the pale smoke, above,
   steadily continues eastward —

   What chance have the old?
   There are no duties for them

no places where they may sit
their knowledge is laughed at
they cannot see, they cannot hear.
A small bundle on the shoulders
weighs them down
one hand is put back under it
to hold it steady.
Their feet hurt, they are weak
they should not have to suffer
as younger people must and do
there should be a truce for them

10/22

that brilliant field
of rainwet orange
blanketed

by the red grass
and oilgreen bayberry
the last yarrow
on the gutter
white by the sandy
rainwater

and a white birch
with yellow leaves
and few
and loosely hung

and a young dog
jumped out
of the old barrel

10/23

I will make a big, serious portrait of my time. The brown and
creamwhite block of Mexican onyx has a poorly executed replica of
the Aztec calendar on one of its dicefacets the central circle being a
broadnosed face with projected hanging tongue the sun perhaps
though why the tongue is out I do not know unless to taste or gasp in
the heat, its own heat, to say it's hot and is the sun. Puebla, Mexico,
Calendario Azteca, four words are roughly engraved in the four
corners where the circle leaves spaces on the square diceface this is
America some years after the original, the art of writing is to do

work so excellent that by its excellence it repels all idiots but idiots are like leaves and excellence of any sort is a tree when the leaves fall the tree is naked and the wind thrashes it till it howls it cannot get a book published it can only get poems into certain magazines that are suppressed because because waving waving waving waving waving waving tic tack tic tock tadick there is not excellence without the vibrant rhythm of a poem and poems are small and tied and gasping they eat gasoline, they all ate gasoline and died, they died of—there is a hole in the wood and all I say brings to mind the rock shingles of Cherbourg, on the new houses they have put cheap tile which overlaps but the old roofs had flat stone sides steep but of stones fitted together and that is love there is no portrait without that has not turned to prose love is my hero who does not live, a man, but speaks of it every day

1. continued (the great law)

What is he saying? That love was never made for man and woman to crack between them and so he loves and loves his sons and loves as he pleases. But there is a great law over him which—is as it is. The wind blowing, the mud spots on the polished surface, the face reflected in the glass which as you advance the features disappear leaving only the hat and as you draw back the features return, the tip of the nose, the projection over the eyebrows, the cheek bones and the bulge of the lips the chin last.

2

I remember, she said, we had little silver plaques with a chain on it to hang over the necks of the bottles, whisky, brandy or whatever it was. And a box of some kind of wood, not for the kitchen but a pretty box. Inside it was lined with something like yes, pewter, all inside and there was a cover of metal too with a little knob on it, all inside the wooden box. You would open the outer cover and inside was the lid. When you would take that off you would see the tea with a silver spoon for taking it out. But now, here are the roses—three opening. Out of love. For she loves them and so they are there. They are not a picture. Holbein never saw pink thorns in such a light. Nor did Masaccio. The petals are delicate. it is a question if they will open at all and not drop, loosing at one edge and falling tomorrow all in a heap. All around the roses there is today, machinery leaning upon the stem, an aeroplane is upon one leaf where a worm lies curled. Soppy it seems and enormous, it seems to hold up the sky for it has no size at all. We eat beside it — beside the three roses that she loves. And an oak tree grows out of my shoulders. Its roots are my arms and my legs. The air is a field. Yellow and red grass are writing their signature everywhere.

10/27

And Coolidge said let there be imitation brass filigree fire fenders behind insured plateglass windows and yellow pine booths with the molasses-candygrain in the wood instead of the oldtime cake-like whitepine boards always cut thick their faces! the white porcelain trough is no doubt made of some certain blanched clay baked and glazed but how they do it, how they shape it soft and have it hold its shape for the oven I don't know nor how the cloth is woven, the grey and the black with the orange and green strips wound together diagonally across the grain artificial pneumothorax their faces! the stripe of shadow along the pavement edge, the brownstone steeple low among the office buildings dark windows with a white wooden cross upon them, lights like fuchsias, lights like bleeding hearts lights like columbines, cherry red danger and applegreen safety. Any hat in this window $2.00 barred windows, wavy opaque glass, a block of brownstone at the edge of the sidewalk crudely stippled on top for a footstep to a carriage lights with sharp bright spikes, stick out round them their faces! Stop in black letters surrounded by a red glow, letters with each bulb a seed in the shaft of the L of the A lights on the river streaking the restless water lights upon pools of rainwater by the roadside a great pool of light full of overhanging sparks into whose lower edge a house looms its center marked by one yellow windowbright their faces!

10/28

born, September 15, 1927, 2nd child, wt. 6 lbs. 2 ozs. The hero is Dolores Marie Pischak, the place Fairfield, in my own state, my own county, its largest city, my own time. This is her portrait: O future worlds, this is her portrait — order be God damned. Fairfield is the place where the October marigolds go over into the empty lot with dead grass like Polish children's hair and the nauseous, the stupifying monotony of decency is dead, unkindled even by art or anything — dead: by God because Fairfield is alive, coming strong. Oh blessed love you are here in this golden air, this honey and dew sunshine, ambering the houses to jewels. Order — is dead. Here a goose flaps his wings by a fence, a white goose, women talk from

145

second story windows to a neighbor on the ground, the tops of the straggling backyard poplars have been left with a tail of twigs and on the bare trunk a pulley with a line in it is tied. A cop whizzes by on his sidecar cycle, the bank to the river is cinders where dry leaves drift. The cinders are eating forward over the green grass below, closer and closer to the river bank, children are in the gutters violently at play over a dam of mud, old women with seamed faces lean on the crooked front gates. Where is Pischak's place? I don't know. I tink it's up there at the corner. What you want? —

Here one drinks good beer. Don't tell my husband. I stopped there yesterday, really good. I was practically alone, yes.

Some streets paved, some dirt down the center. A Jew has a clothing store and looks at you wondering what he can sell. And you feel he has these people sized up. A nasty feeling. Unattached. When he gets his he'll burn it up and clear out in a day. And they do not suspect how nicely he has measured them. They need stuff. He sells it. Who's that guy I wonder. Never seen him around here before. Looks like a doctor.

That's the feeling of Fairfield. An old farm house in long tangled trees, leaning over it. A dell with a pretty stream in it below the little garden and fifty feet beyond, the board fence of the Ajax Aniline Dye Works with red and purple refuse dribbling out ragged and oily under the lower fence boards. No house is like another. Small, wooden, a garden at the back, all ruined by the year. Man leaning smoking from a window. And the dirt, dry dust. No grass, or grass in patches, hedged with sticks and a line of cord or wire or grass, a jewel, a garden embanked, all in a twenty foot square, crowded with incident, a small terrace of begonias, a sanded path, pinks, roses in a dozen rococco beds.

Knock and walk in: The bar. Not a soul. In the back room the kitchen. Immaculate, the enameled table featured. The mother nursing her from a nearly empty breast. She lies and sucks. Black hair, pencilled down the top flat and silky smooth, the palmsized face asleep, the mother at a point of vantage where under an inside window raised two inches she can govern the street entrance.

Who's that?
A woman. Oh that old woman from next door.

146

The father, young, energetic, enormous. Unsmiling, big headed, a nervous twitch to his head and a momentary intense squint to his eyes. She watches the door. He is in shirt sleeves. Restless, goes in and out. Talks fast, manages the old woman begging help for a bruised hand. A man who might be a general or president of a corporation, or president of the states. Runs a bootleg saloon. Great!

This is the world. Here one breathes and the dignity of man holds on. "Here I shall live. Why not now? Why do I wait?"

Katharin, 9, sheepish, shy — adoring in response to gentleness so that her eyes almost weep for sentimental gratitude, has jaundice, leans on his knee. Follows him with her eyes. Her hair is straight and blond.

On the main river road, a grey board fence over which a grove of trees stick up. Oaks, maples, poplars and old fruit trees. Belmont Park, Maggyar Home. For rent for picnics. Peace is here — rest, assurance, life hangs on.

Oh, blessed love, among insults, brawls, yelling, kicks, brutality — here the old dignity of life holds on — defying the law, defying monotony.

She lies in her mother's arms and sucks. The dream passes over her, dirt streets, a white goose flapping its wings and passes. Boys, wrestling, kicking a half inflated football. A grey motheaten squirrel pauses at a picket fence where tomato vines, almost spent, hang on stakes.

Oh, blessed love — the dream engulfs her. She opens her eyes on the trouble bosom of the mother who is nursing the babe and watching the door. And watching the eye of the man. Talking English, a stream of Maggyar, Polish what? to the tall man coming and going.

Oh, blessed love where are you there, pleasure driven out, order triumphant, one house like another, grass cut to pay lovelessly. Bored we turn to cars to take us to "the country" to "nature" to breathe her good air. Jesus Christ. To nature. It's about time, for most of us. She is holding the baby. Her eye under the window, watching. Her hair is bobbed halfshort. It stands straight down about her ears. You, you sit and have it waved and ordered. Fine. I'm glad of it. And nothing to do but play cards and whisper. Jesus Christ. Whisper of the high school girl that had a baby and how smart her mama was to pretend in a flash of genius that it was hers. Jesus Christ. Or let us take a run up to the White Mountains or Lake Mohonk. Not Bethlehem (New Hampshire) any more, the Jews have ruined that like lice all over the lawns. Horrible to see. The dirty things. Eating everywhere. Parasites.

And so order, seclusion, the good of it all.

But in Fairfield men are peaceful and do as they please — and learn the necessity and the profit of order — and Dolores Marie Pischak was born.

10/28

On hot days
the sewing machine
        whirling

    in the next room
    in the kitchen

and men at the bar
    talking of the strike
    and cash

10/28

a flash of juncos in the field of grey locust saplings with a white sun powdery upon them and a large rusty can wedged in the crotch of one of them, for the winter, human fruit, and on the polished straws of the dead grass a scroll of crimson paper — not yet rained on

10/28

in this strong light
the leafless beechtree
shines like a cloud

it seems to glow
of itself
with a soft stript light
of love
over the brittle

grass

148

But there are
on second look
a few yellow leaves
still shaking

far apart
just one here one there
trembling vividly

10/29

The justice of poverty
    its shame its dirt
are one with the meanness
    of love

its organ in a tarpaulin
    the green birds
the fat sleepy horse
    the old men

the grinder sourfaced
    hat over eyes
the beggar smiling all open
    the lantern out

and the popular tunes—
    sold to the least bidder
for a nickel
    two cents or

nothing at all or even
    against the desire
forced on us

10/30

To freight cars in the air

all the slow
    clank, clank
    clank, clank
moving above the treetops

the
    wha,   wha

THE "PREDOMINANT FORCE"

of the hoarse whistle

    pah,   pah,   pah
    pah, pah, pah, pah, pah

    piece and piece
    piece and piece
moving still trippingly
through the morningmist

long after the engine
has fought by
             and disappeared

in silence
        to the left

[continued]

WILLIAM CARLOS WILLIAMS
(*The Exile*, Autumn 1928)

TRANSITION

white limp droop UP
    h
      r
        o
          u
            g
              h
        p *i* *n*   *k*
        t
         o
        R
      R E   Drooping
      E D
        D   droopink
          kto ww

          white

S<small>IDNEY</small> H<small>UNT</small>
(*transition*, May 1927)

Bison

O eye of grief
O fire of hairy
earth

        gunpowder
of the beating
rock!

      You
clove the silence
stared into the sun
O bed of burning
horns

      O swarming
blood that stored black
honey in your flesh

151

THE "PREDOMINANT FORCE"

thighed with the storm!

YVOR WINTERS
(*transition*, Dec. 1927)

Cocktails
and signs of
"ads"

flashing,
light's waterfalls,

Bacchae
among electric lights

will swarm the crowds
streamers of the lighted

skyscrapers

nor tripping
over underbrush

but upon pavement

and not with thyrsus
shall they prick

the body of their loves
but waist to waist

laugh out in gyre —
announced then upon stairs,

not upon hills,
will be their flight

when passed turnstiles,
having dropped

coins
they've sprinted up

where on the air (elevated)
waves flash — and out —

leap
signaling — lights below

LOUIS ZUKOFSKY
(*transition*, Feb. 1929)

HOUND & HORN

The Great Experiment

WHOEVER heard of a laboratory
in a skyscraper's top story!
Was it genius or merely queer
to seek exalted atmosphere?
Perhaps he found significance
in seeing citizens as ants;
perhaps he merely preferred to soar
above jerky traffic roar;
perhaps there was something in the air
he found up there.
But nobody bothers about ascent
as long as a man pays his rent.

Meanwhile he poised his cones and cubes
'Twixt huge mirrors and sweating tubes,
And at night a million candle-power
Flashed purple and green like an air-mail tower.
No one asked why, for no one cared,
Though sons of Belial sometimes stared
At a sky-scraper top that blinked and glared.

Night-long a brain surveyed the Deep
And puzzled out problems, even in sleep,
Mingling chemical speculations
With geometrical equations
And psychical anatomy
Such as no ancient could foresee.

. . . .

Division of soul and body
Is sacrifice to Nobodaddy
Who scuttles the ship effectively
That should explore the Central Sea.

But to empty the skull as one empties a chalice
And wander through the body as through a palace

Ancient, decayed with neglect, yet still splendid;
To ascend stairs that no man for ages has ascended. . . .

Van Helmont, in his *Oriatrike*,
Records (see "A Mad Idea") that his psyche
For two hours was loosed from its normal nexus
And functioned quite well through his solar plexus.
"Mad"? — a clear case of sense-transference;
But he'd missed the point of that little occurrence.
He stumbled indeed on his consciousness' floor,
His toe in the lock of the secret trap-door.
The wolfsbane was clearly but complemental,
And drugs are both violent and accidental.

Involved with this was the whole problem of astronomy, gravitation-geometry being the first key, if we ignore the assumptions of Einstein on an interlocking of ideas for which words furnish no formula as yet. Abstractions applied to profoundest personality, a reversal, a wriggling through, backward as it were, or inward (but here the words deceive, in spite of themselves).

Then again, the practical dangers; for palaces inhabited only in one small room for centuries inevitably sink apart here and there: a wall crumbles, exposing sheer brick to moonlight; staircases fall away in darkness; fissures open in the marble floorings, especially when intricately tessellated; centuries of rain-drip corrode and groove; essential locks rust together into flimsy skeletons. But worst of all, the danger is best expressed by saying that fumbling or haste alike may tie a knot which straining will only tighten, where nice technique should tie no knot at all, and a strong pull brings the string straight again.

Now all was ready; he would be
Columbus of Infinity.
— Red square of sunlight on the wall,
Circular sun red in the west —
He sat himself twixt square and ball
And closed his eyes as though to rest;
Reached with his right hand for the switch;
Found it, and quickly snapped it on;
Heard the machinery start with a twitch,
And opened his eyes to — a swift green moon?

Before him cube and fire-ball sped
Roaring prismatic from green to red
Faster and faster—the world was whirling—
Or was he himself in his chair twirling—?
From right to left, flashing, roaring
Faster and faster—his chair was soaring;
The skyscraper spun like a slender spindle;
He felt his whole body swell, yet dwindle. . . .

Quicker—
      quicker—
           flicker—
                  quicker—
Flicker quicker flickerflicker
Flickerflurr—rr—blurr—rr—

Rroar—rr—rroo— rroooooooooooooooooooooooooooooo
rr   oo
rr   *The stars, in their slow posturings*   oo
rr   *Below the horizon of the brain,*   oo
rr   *Are bright foam circling on deep springs*   oo
rr   *That pulse and pause and pulse again.*   oo
rr   oo
rr   *Their vast geometries of force*   oo
rr   *—Cat's cradle of infinities—*   oo
rr   *Pour upward from the single source*   oo
rr   *Into enormous vortices.*   oo
rr   oo
rr   *Plunge in! and let yourself be sucked*   oo
rr   *Beneath the glowing foam, between*   oo
rr   *The moving currents, through the duct*   oo
rr   *That leads into the last serene.*   oo
rr   oo
rroar—rr—rreee—rr— rroooooooooooooooooooooooooooooo
rr   oo
rr   *We gods, in our vast posturings,*   oo
rr   *Complete the dance predestinate;*   oo
rr   *No anguished prayers, no magic rings,*   oo
rr   *Can cause one step to hesitate.*   oo
rr   oo
rr   *The fiercest feat of outer air*   oo
rr   *Dashes as vain against our glory*   oo

rr   *As thunder-breakers blare and flare*   oo
rr   *Against a granite promontory.*   oo
rr   oo
rr   *The silver fountains of our force*   oo
rr   *Outcircle from our happiness;*   oo
rr   *We see, but care not for their course*   oo
rr   *Through planes and cycles numberless.*   oo
rr   oo
rr   *The pure act soaks into the marsh*   oo
rr   *Lying about our marriage-feasts,*   oo
rr   *Diffused and quaking from the harsh*   oo
rr   *Gales roaring and tumbling like huge beasts.*   oo
rr   oo
rr   *Here rot the knotted living forms*   oo
rr   *Bound breast to back, each other's prey:*   oo
rr   *Husband and consort linked like worms,*   oo
rr   *Sucking the sick life-blood away.*   oo
rr   oo
rr   *The pure act filters up through mud,*   oo
rr   *Through clutching roots and clotted slime,*   oo
rr   *Past beings ravenous on salt blood*   oo
rr   *Sucked leech-like in the night of time.*   oo
rr   oo
rr   *Compressed into one monstrous shape*   oo
rr   *They merge and slowly brutify;*   oo
rr   *Mother with child, and man with ape,*   oo
rr   *The live with dead, the truth with lie.*   oo
rr   oo
rr   oo
rr   oo
rr   *Here sit enthroned the skeletons*   oo
rr   *Who with their pointing fingers freeze*   oo
rr   *The tortures and oblivions*   oo
rr   *That crowd the marsh about their knees.*   oo
rr   oo
rr   *Yet through the stinking marsh still bubble*   oo
rr   *The silver fountains of our force,*   oo
rr   *And rising over stump and stubble*   oo
rr   *Into the third world take their course.*   oo
rr   oo
rroar — rr — rreee — rr —— rroooooooooooooooooooooooooo

rr .... oo
rr ..... *Dispersed, yet unpolluted still,* ..... oo
rr ..... *They rise as mist, and then attain* ..... oo
rr ..... *Another form, when they distill* ..... oo
rr ..... *Into the firm curves of a brain.* ..... oo
rr .... oo
rr ..... *Then warm the brain, till it release* ..... oo
rr ..... *The perfume of the primal skies,* ..... oo
rr ..... *That ultimately shall unfreeze* ..... oo
rr ..... *Our happiness as battle-cries.* ..... oo
rr .... oo
rr ..... *Fight not the living, for their shapes* ..... oo
rr ..... *Dissolve to other shapes instead:* ..... oo
rr ..... *Always the inmost soul escapes.* ..... oo
rr ..... *So aim your dagger at the dead.* ..... oo
rr .... oo
rroar — rr — rreee — rr —— rrooooooooooooooooooooooooooo
rr .... oo
rr ..... *Meanwhile we dance, and dancing watch* ..... oo
rr ..... *The shadows of our pageantry* ..... oo
rr .... oo
rr ..... *That leap and mingle, splotch and blotch,* ..... oo
rr ..... *To farcical catastrophe.* ..... oo
rr .... oo
rr ..... *Meanwhile we feast, and deeply quaff;* ..... oo
rr ..... *Seeing their wants, their clumsy guile,* ..... oo
rr ..... *We roar with laughter — we can laugh* ..... oo
rr ..... *For it is hollow all the while.* ..... oo
rr .... oo
rroar — rr — rreee — rr —— rrooooooooooooooooooooooooooo
rr .... oo
rr ..... (Sitting somewhere, he managed to twitch ..... oo
rr ..... Off, with his left hand, the switch.) ..... oo
rr .... oo
rrooooooo — rr — oooo — rr — rr —— mmmmmmmmmmmmmm
rr .... mm
rr ..... *The veil conceals a mask: the mask* ..... mm
rr ..... *Conceals a face; the face conceals* ..... mm
rr ..... *A word; the word . . .* ..... mm
rr .... mm
rr .... mm

rr He opened his eyes; the room was twirling mm
rr As water in a cup keeps swirling. mm
He staggered to the window. In the east mm
A green sun glared, and sank, and ceased. mm
He stumbled. Everything was wrong. mm
A cool breeze blew the words of a song mm
Out of his brain. He stumbled—cursed: mm
Somehow the whole room was reversed. mm
He walked like a clumsy child just learning mm
Because he felt the vast world turning, mm
mm
mm

Tilting upward away from the sun mm
And backward, to black oblivion. mm
The corridor ran the other way, mm
As though it were seeking yesterday. mm
Bells?—no, the clash of the elevator door; mm
Then it rose with the strength of an eagle-of-war; mm
And soared fifty stories—to the ground-floor! mm
mm

The street was murmurous as a wood in June. mm
In the west was rising a purplish moon. mm
All the masks lifted, when he went by, mm
And the music they released filled the whole sky. mm
mm

Then silently beside him there appeared mm
A woman's figure, anciently endeared mm
And since forgotten; but now freshened, clearer, mm
As a familiar statue in a mirror mm
Leaps with its primitive vitality. mm
Her voice surged with the rhythms of the sea. mm
mm

mmmmmmmmmmmmmmmmmmmmmmmmmmm
m
What m Weather!—Weather!—The whole
lovely m universe speaks always and of nothing
weather m but weather. It utters its sunrises
this m and rainbows and bursts of stars in
evening! m an everlasting discourse of incredible
m beauty. Weather is the speech of the
m universe; emotions are the weather of

	m	the soul. Oh, glorious that it should be so!
	m	
	m	
Are you	m	But Space is endless—how can I find
walking	m	her there? Time also is endless—
my way?	m	she slips between the seconds.
	m	
How well	m	Calm-eyed, the eternal Aphrodite re-
you are	m	joicing goes to her immortal love, that
looking!	m	never now shall be snared in any
	m	golden net, even for the divine laughter.
	m	
What	m	High above the dimensions, we Gods
are	m	stand upon our pedestals, never guessing
you	m	the wars sculptured upon the panels below.
saying?	m	On earth we sank in sodden tragedy;
	m	while above, we celebrated our marriage-
	m	feast, amused at the drama enacted for
	m	our pleasure.
	m	
Ha!	m	Recall Dr. Fludd on the Lute of the
ha!	m	Universe; then remember that the micro-
ha!	m	cosm contains macrocosm *in essentiis.*
	m	Wherefore believe me, believe me, that
	m	here is the slender instrument of love,
	m	as yet untuned, unplayed. Linger a
What	m	little, tightening the knobs precisely;
is the	m	then, when the chords echo from the hollow
matter?	m	body, sweep the strings with the white
	m	plectrum, meanwhile fingering the

melody. . . .

m m m m m m
m
mmmmmmmmmmmmmmmmmmmmmmmmmmmmmmmmmm
m
mmmmmmmmmmmmmmm
m
m
m
mmm

. . . .

159

—just a temporary aberration
due to the accumulation
of nervous impulse in the brain.
Perfectly sane! Perfectly sane!
But cases are known (this point is the worst)
of people curiously reversed;
to you, his brother, I may confide
his heart is on his right side.
Oh, harmless—nothing in the blood;
a rest in the country will do him good.
Keep him from work a month and more.
—Perfectly harmless—Mind the door!—

S. FOSTER DAMON
(*Hound & Horn,* July–Sept., 1929)

Rain

As the rain falls
so does
your love

bathe every
open
object of the world—

In houses
the priceless dry
rooms
of illicit love
where we live
hear the wash of the
rain—

There
paintings
and fine
metalware
woven stuffs—
all the whorishness
of our

    delight

sees
from its window
the spring wash
of your love
        the falling
rain—

The trees
are become
beasts fresh risen
from
    the sea —
water

trickles
from the crevices of
their hides—

So my life is spent
      to keep out love
with which
she rains upon

    the world

of spring

    drips

so spreads

    the words

THE "PREDOMINANT FORCE"

far apart to let in

      her love —

And running in between
the drops

      the rain

is a kind physician

      the rain
of her thoughts over
the ocean
        every

where

    walking with
invisible swift feet
over

    the helpless
        waves —

Unworldly love
that has no hope
    of the world

    and that
cannot change the world
to its delight —

The rain
falls upon the earth
and grass and flowers
come
      perfectly

into form from its
         liquid

clearness

      But love is
unworldly

      and nothing
comes of it but love

following

and falling endlessly
from
      her thoughts

WILLIAM CARLOS WILLIAMS
(*Hound & Horn*, Oct.–Dec., 1929)

In the 'Sconset Bus

UPON the fallen
cheek

a gauzy down —
And on

the nape
— indecently

a mat
of yellow hair

163

THE "PREDOMINANT FORCE"

stuck with
celluloid

pins
not quite

matching it
— that's

two shades
darker

at the roots —
Hanging

from the ears
the hooks

piercing the
flesh —

gold and semi-
precious

stones —
And in her

lap the dog
(Youth)

resting
his head on

the ample
shoulder his

bright
mouth agape

pants restlessly
backward

WILLIAM CARLOS WILLIAMS
(*Hound & Horn,* July–Sept., 1932)

BLUES

Group

OPTIONAL

foreword

persimmons are on the trees on the quaggy ground too but do
not eat one that isn't soft for it will pucker your mouth but
anyway you are beautiful whether your mouth is puckered or
not

poem

o maleness o lovers or animals kisses oh bitter (as orangepeel)
and seekers of forests of brass and footprints

i run with slow steps and am aroused from a narcosis of squalor

my hands are warmed on icy foreheads and my thighs made cold
with consecrate lusts
ochrefaced men move into a numbness
why am i hostile to the keepers of gardens and the keepers of
cities
an existence is nullified in the omega of a cracked hickorynut

let only a tree be your lover
take only sand for a marriagebed
use sun for raiment and rain for a sacrament
rain rages on the riversurface
rain pursues a vagrancy and is an impetus for death by drowning

ELEGY

when the layers of smoke have faded into a staleness brick walls
are maudlin and four o'clock is once more in travail
a car overturns with a scream of brakes and a scream of fear and i
catch my breath which is sour with bootleg
o cankerous complexity of a city morning and four a m
men pull into a coldness and sparrows like dead leaves are
agitated by a sullen wind
clothes stuffed with flesh and blood begin to move along the

165

sidewalks
whistles at six a m sob a threnody for broken bones

To Be Pickled In Alcohol

I

if brains pickled in alcohol prove anything don't say sweetly *it may*
be hurtn you but it's killin me
words said sweetly said even nicely are not an antitoxin

here is a tic for your nose and cheek and a paperhat to be gay
with
o fingers and the twitching of a head
you will know the glued standing and see many locomotives rush
to a destruction

II

i rumble on the narrow streets and find an expiation for this
chaos
he said *it's red like that all over looking* and i choked a cigarette butt
looking in my glass i am sure that i resemble a traffic squall or a
sudden snow
a promise has been too insistent and i mold stickily bread into a
hanging
if a watch ticks shatter your unrest against abnormality

who has said a gray day now is a penitent

i hold tightly to an ivy wreath and a shudder
with torn nails i build grandly the last madhouse for a burned
dream

CHARLES HENRI FORD
(*Blues*, March 1929)

Sonnet

I smell an oriental luxury
from him
     his suit is brown
                I smell an or-
iental lux
     I love his nose
          ury

from him
      's slender hook
                  I smell an or-
ien
      and he is strong as rope
                  tal lux-
ury from
      excellently built
                him
                   I
I dream of
      smell an oriental lux-
ur
      him at night that
                y from him
                  he
                   I
makes love to me yes
                smell an orien-
ta luxury from
      strenuous love
                him
sweet marvelous
                I smell an orien-
tal
      he's in busi
                luxury from him
ness
    I
      a Jew and O his sex ap
                smell
an
   peal
      rien
         him
            from
              ury
                lux
                 smell

PARKER TYLER
(*Blues*, March 1929)

167

Poem

Across the morning I spear the articulate flight of a bird and make of it the design of my private disguise against the uncertain morning.

(Once, the earth hanging half-way like an imaginary shadow remarked the palpitations of your white heart, bird; you carried your flight ever nearer to the sun-vortex; that was your reply.)

Forget the trembling bird   remember only the triumphant solution of the sweep, Earth—but O do not unravel it!   seeking the dusty count of one more 'clarity'   You can find merely an endless swirl of gauze contriving somehow wantonly within the relativity of space to be singularly free.

PAULINE LEADER
(*Blues*, May 1929)

Frustrations: Four from Tension

why ears

why should you lie dead
at ten o'clock then carelessly
talk and rise into a gold awakening

then (tell me) why
should you as fondling
a sprig of heliotrope
draw in the scent through
two
chiseled
nostrils

why are you never specific

the morning is definite the wind is
you
are a ghost on horseback
or the image of a hotness caught in ice
you are the loophole in a hangrope
and i forever harmonious
discords sagging about your head and ears

n.b.

there the over
ripe fruits
bursting in the garden sending
putridbukes to the finelypowdered
o
there is a nuditydecay

observe the syphlipocks and vari
ously is it is
it necessary

note) then) the gaudy taxis
losing in the very brightness
hardly butterflies neg
lect the details

thirsts not slaked
with can-da-dry-and
corn but
wishes laughably are o

slough the bition of an applebiting
here is the focus of a withholdgiving
darling
jangle in a seeth of straw
ber
ries
and love the last of sickles on a hair

denudation of tributes

this
is the orchid
resisting the tracing
oh
                              this
spiderweb spanning your
thumb and the forefinger
looking as a mole's course
rankles in the buttercup
false as
spangles or the rainbow's
sickening in a paleness

laxly on the object
haunting and the filling as a pipeorgan's
notes say
incentive in the snowdrift
speeding for the hummingbird
reasoned on exposure
judas dangling from the loverope
pressing to a pullmancar
jostled by the mob at
(1)   christ's death
(2)   wilde's judgment
(3)   valentino's funeral and the burning of the
      sherrynetherland tower
                    lastly
lovers in exodus
stompsway to the *so long blues*
drugged by electrons
shivering in the subway
gods three now
ejected for a toolonghungering

poem

i stood in
great drafts and
felt the cries of centuries blow
by me touching my forehead i
averted my face from a sadness threatening
to slit my abdomen with a very
thin knife i stood
listening to the
dark lips
forcing flame and hunger from a saxophone
i knew
feelessly
the liquid bodies of frustrations
i knew them filling
throat and nostrils i recalled
her saying drowning
is should be

a
love
ly
death

CHARLES HENRI FORD
(*Blues*, May 1929)

George Hugnet

George and Genevieve Geronimo with or with whether they thought they were with whether. They thought that they with whether.

Without their finding it out. Without. Their finding it out. With whether.

George whether they were about. With their finding their whether it finding it out whether with their finding about it out.

George with their finding it with out.

George whether their with their it whether.

Redoubt out with about.

Without out whether it their whether with out doubt.

Azure can with our about.

It is welcome welcome thing.

George in are ring.

Lain away awake.

George in our ring.

George Genevieve Geronimo straightened it out without their finding it out.

Grammar makes George in our ring which Grammar makes George in our ring.

Grammar is as disappointed not is as Grammar is as disappointed.

Grammar is not as Grammar is as disappointed.

George is in our ring. Grammar is not is disappointed. In are ring.

George Genevieve in are ring.

GERTRUDE STEIN
(*Blues*, July 1929)

Antipodes

(from Finale of Seem)

Nothing rolls like a ball.
When the nogar man comes—
blowing by the flow of grace—
speaking of silver linings, lash
    lovelisness, duodraulic lovejoy—
you light the tiny gas flame.
Hot piano! Through the remarkable
    princible of two air space
knowledge is power rolled out.
Beneath its almost magical double action
a dash,
with hardly a tremor
a new beat.
Oh Sugar! Oh Cream! Oh Muffets!

        Spring was her discontent.
        She tired of her face
        and at the Galeries Lafayette
        cut short the glory of the universe.

To a ribbon of fine spun wheaten threads
thin light alloy
goes on in an endless cycle
like a perpetual cocktail.

        She bobbed her hair in April.
        One relates
            people walking
        with rows of standing taxis
        and confines
            poetry
        to pavements.
        Then where, O spring, will you park?

Do your andirons belittle or enlarge
    upon the beauty of your mantle?
Lola Casnati, skin analyst,
stalking the streptococcus hemolyticus,
    crisply simple, as rhythmic,

whereof she speaks an announcement:
are the goal — a goal?

> *Still,*
> *something of her stalwart tresses*
> *stalks the bleak imagined pavement*
> *of April in my mind.*
> *I shall see her in the mornings —*

For knowing man
the unique flat-backed
scientifically measured for water-absorption
how much of beauty?
Boxing. And then, as if inspiration had been
    wheeled
and the gaily coloured handles
a beautiful non-rusting steel
a scarlet ash crackle with laughter
and yet the sweetest songs are silent still.

> *O weep with me for Neaera's hair,*
> *sunk never to rise again*
>   *to mix*
> *its fresh infrequent fragrance*
> *with the morning rolls*
>   *making*
> *every cup of coffee*
> *the beginning of a week end.*

Speedy beads, make the most of sunlight.
Youth   Youth   Youth
You must wash your face, too.

> *Gone are the tangles of Neaera's hair.*
> *I am left too desolate*
> *with half my empire*
>   *on a barber's floor.*

This is lysol time
The stars are bound for Barcelona.

> *A taxi! A taxi!*
> *To Nineveh! — Rome!*
> *No two people walk alike.*

*I shall
search the antipodes
to find
Spring where Helen lies
constantly out of season.*

There was a time when a bath was just a bath.
Now it is much more.
Dust your bath on. . .

If only powder were magic;
If you could use it to achieve
JUST BEAUTY, to have again
the undimned velvet,
to have the mirror on the wall
say: Sal Hepatica, powdery beauty,
the fairest of them all. . .

Cosmetics can never hide the truth.
Her hair is dry; her hair is oily;
He has dandruff; O America!
Nothing rolls like hair-free limbs
spiked to wampas baby stars.
. . . *Zip!*
Step on it, Mother.

WALTER LOWENFELS
(*Blues*, July 1929)

Meek Madness in Capri or Suicide for Effect

SCENERY

That   he-wind howled   the sea
scooped hollow on one   side
mounted t'other

waters
surmounting waters surmounting
waters surmounting waters
surmounting waters surmounting
waters surmounting waters
surmounting   wa. . . . .

174

Vesuvio : Woe

lava will smell of rubber
crater boil over

the wet wrath shifted
tilted   sudden I spy
the bottoms of the fairy isle
monstrous maroon
fouling a fresh sahara   baby pink
a' shiver with shy shrimps
frenziedly drying
                    dying

yon winds   .   .   .   the lowly olives
bow   metal leaf squeaking
lean   a livid agony
the good roots float
smug muds in feline waters
oiled but rude to boat
and tidy swimming lady
Santa Lucia swoons   in white hermetic
rooms   gorge barber tenors
crude eggs
        pale tapes
                gay garlics
eyes   bonny ebon stars
glazed with the ache of money

up stairs of warped mush wood
sews sour mother   puny
mosaics of rag   she sews
and owes   money for minestrone

up to his hips in storm
that most distinguished beggar
drips
        dissolves
a rag in elemental slop
he is   a sop
in raging soup

THE "PREDOMINANT FORCE"

he melts and
         melts
what shall I do soft saint   with my lone sou
boots are my only musics

the wind goes black   the erring
girls   gargle with tidal oceans
their bosoms   bladders
hold love above the seas
crooning for cuddlers

the bloated brothels float
creamed skins and pink electrics
the bay churns rats
now the pitch cracks
it cr-crr . . .

cr-crr-cracks   a slippery half moon slides
continually crosswise   then

falls &

     .
     .
     .
     .
     .
     .
     .

     falls

bobs up
     pops
into my cautious cubes of room
it burns blue cold
cauterizes   my eye ball
whites the coal
and now it is threading the key hole

s
  l
    a
      n
       t
      s

        skids
      skids

cloud has no whim   no skill
to halt that fall   so
easy-greasy-easy

RUSE

hard and twice   lest it flutter   I shall tie my heart
bore a hole sly in the middle of the wind
dig me a quiet hot spot
sit there
and chuckle
and later   smiling
I shall slide into the embassy like a knife
or shall it be a brothel
a chic church
and rip the passports
stopping the slits with birdies

the girls
their pink and mauve kimonas flapping like dogs' ears
shall make their faces naked
their gums obscene
while fronting those shops of bosom
delicatessen thighs
the virgin yankee bishops
will sweat aside
most stiffly
grease spots of vice
while the suburban secretaries
and my wife . . . . .

THE "PREDOMINANT FORCE"

but I am a knife in the mannish wind
I'll slip beneath their skirts
gartered about their hearts
for safety   gimlet those spinster
bladders   leaking pale   water colour
drop by drop
                          those
kind kind   souls

the wind he-she   .   .   .   dearies
my knives are butter

old right arm   cardboard
drowsy and numb with thumbs
drowsy and numb with thumbs
my sex a drooping lily

the luke hearth lulls
subtle variants of comas
death   lending to   jerky life
customs of silence   stillness
a mild and monstrous stupour
in head   a noble null
a stone to lay in bed
by wife   instead of   sex mechanics

still there are   humdrum funs
plump matrimonial puns   vague aches
said to have root far back
far down   in mystic mines
purses and easy journeys
in swift plush chairs   a heap of
Firm Flush Fact   for

the wife has a fortune in iodine
she loses a handkerchief
                          and   lo
                          her hearth doth stop
she had five laundresses last month
the angel

that bitchwind .   .   .   we mouthing
worthwhile semitic computations
bitterly adding   triumphantly subtracting
full busy   the dear thin dame

the sane soup gongs
quick   do it   do it
mister poet
one madness
if cheap   bright-oh

DEED

yon catty breeze   .   .   .   pillowed
against thy seldom curious bosom
tiny
but taut with numbers
like a fat cautious bank
lay I my own vague head
good oppenheim
Madonna of the Sums

galling the gallop of thy diminishing division
a vexing unit while thou lassoest zeros
I'll peel me quick
naked but unexciting   miseree
tiptoe a something high
a roof   a lash   a head note
and now
to death   mayhap
amusement

leap I   leap I

I'll say I'm imperial eagle
germany   tamany
I'll say I'm a sparrow
paper arrow
day after tomorrow

when the wife comes down to count the wash
she'll slip in a familiar squash

THE "PREDOMINANT FORCE"

she will send many wires

| to my mother | to my sister |
| to her mother | to her sister |

she will write many letters

| to her mother | to her sister |
| to my mother | to my sister |

she will make it up with the baby's nurse
she will worry

sister   why worry   oh why worry sister
the end in the end is the end of ends
thy young man was a mess

> a mess
> a mess
> a mess
> a mess
> a mess

the she-wind blubbered   babe Phoebus pissed
a fin de siécle albumen   the 'elp
melo-snivel-dramatic
whined the plates   quaint dust
broomed from beneath the matrimonial bed
unwarlike   cobwebbed the worried wife
frenziedly signing checks
cocktailing funeral mourners

the fairy breeze   .   .   .   nay tickle not
my horizontal bone   you naughty
away   I am most dead
hence not without grandeur
of sorts   it is not meet to scratch
beyond extremis   dead? very.
the final journey should have an air
begad   my coffin is no taxi

Laurence Vail
(*Blues*, July 1929)

Cessableinack

one i(me)? or tiberius
walk down-optional asphalt walk
lounge here
                                                        &
                                                                     there lounge
walk asphalt walk
                                             lounge there
                                  &
here lounge
walk asphalt optional-up walk
lenagaynst bulging bank
fulla
            hard
                        cold
                                    gold
lenagaynst taylashop
                                fulla
                    pants
       &
vests
nleenon kaphaydors
i(me)? or tiberius
two deyall
                glideslide
                                b form e
azi lounge & lounge
endeyre allyn accessable
azi c demdeyre

CESSABLEINACK CESSABLEINACK
CESSABLEINACK CESSABLEINACK

rings imyears
ittrings ittrings ittrings

hell wenwill its top

GOD dammittal lattimmad DOG

three i(me)? or tiberius
wrayped every l(l × l = l) uvdem
n i wrayped demmon

lawns non beds
in shacks
                    &

                    palaces in
budday worrayped in myd dreams
had visions huvem sleeping
wimmee imi bed
n inner morning
                    phweet

                         phweet
       day wergone
buddayre allyn accessable
endee damned word (le verbe)
rings n rings n
       RINGS N RINGS
CHRIST INNER MOUNTAINS
wonchews top
       de word (le verbe)
                    ringingimyears
                         i(me)?

AUGUSTUS TIBERIUS
(*Blues*, Fall 1929)

Poem to F. M.

I

to dream a part a part to dream
                                   is
to awake wake wishing for the whole
a dream a whole a waking mystery
of sleep's dream an intangible . . .

                                   yet
as the arc of waking sleep shows
dawn traduced
                    the dream intrudes
its images and colors dream intrudes
its images and colors on the yearning mind
that stretched and moaned
all night

now
        on the clear lines
of the dawn sees fade the dream's
apotheosis fade
the dream's unclear apotheosis
in the waking and the noise
                :the arcs
toward shoes and socks
and further still the washbowl gaunt
and hard and morbid
          toward
these which from dream's arcs slide
inevitably

II

to the new sun to
the new sun will
be shown the stanch skin of
the movement which at
one o'clock
        at two o'clock
will justify a name
          a business
an organism
         neither glad nor sorry — but
for dream's sake
when the washbowl left (the
cloth spread out) there is
a noticeable tread toward the
improbable in stone a noticeable
tread more noticeable
          waking
dream to salve the footsteps grown
more violent than heartbeats
beating of the stone
        at
three o'clock at four

III

and o
the stone immortal

183

                          the
immortal stone: the fibre not:
the form
           is ready to pour
into any dream reality but not
this dream
for not this form of
the immortal stone flows through
these streets now too familiar
for anything but this
                          one
                                    dream
one dream that never
comes back with its easy
feet

                    IV

that stone should dictate
these bright sure irrelevancies
to which sky is an accomplice and
I add: the myriad
of waters and the meadows
is the weight to shut my eyelids
to accept dream's substitute
for anything the last
hour left me with:
                          o
only this has
              surely has
                          could
only this direct my dreamsnared feet
toward quavering apprehension of
the stone the day
has left me with
is all a
         all a
like a cir-
cle
    and the stone which flesh is can
evade the washbowl and the after stroll

V

is all to slip beneath
the coverlet
to act much as a
dream would act
                    and acting
not betray the dream the dream
hung surely on the lashes' lash
inviolable as a stone: hung
where no window in the morning
looks upon a finished building
and the welcome feet to frustrate sun:
                                        no
as though in that other land
there were
no rising or no joy
at all but what the dream sees
faintly faintly
                in the morning eyes
as just before

PARKER TYLER
(*Blues*, Spring 1930)

Two Poems

THE ATTIC WHICH IS DESIRE
the unused tent
of

bare beams
beyond which

directly wait
the night

and day—
where storms

sobbing and
whispering

confess—
Here from the
street by
***
  S
*   *
  O
*   *
  D
*   *
  A
*   *

ringed with
running lights

the darkened
pane

exactly
down the center
is
transfixed

   THE MOON—
diving
through bedrooms
makes the car
ride upon the page
by virtue of
the law of sentences
Bulleting
through roofs
behind reedy trees
it is the night
waking to
smells of lechery

WILLIAM CARLOS WILLIAMS
(*Blues*, Spring 1930)

Are Poems

JUNCTURE

Things have to do with each other, nothing inviolable
caught between the flexuous mind, the impermanent heart
but has a closeness with dry mirth, not not but painlessly.

Much should be foresworn; forgiven even sooner than committed;
(oh the blood might be lost like water sliding from a roof—
and the back of the victim drooping settle into an argent
  stillness).

This is the day when color will be drawn from faces;
hours changeable, uncaught will move evenly toward nightfall.
Let us then measure the dimensions of a cry: clear, solid and
  unalterable.

ARE POEM

esp. if red
can set rocking anyway
on a thumbjoint anybody's head:

though,

one taking in and out a big breath postponing sickness,
some nerves in whenever unlight makes sunlight
shall be not very strung:

morning (with night
early on the side of it)
and sleep, being what a small death, are.

CHARLES HENRI FORD
(*Blues*, Spring 1930)

Tibor Serly

(from *Two Dedications*)
Red varnish
Warm flitch

Of cello,
They play

Scroll before
Them — Sound

Breaks the
Sunset! — Kiss

With wide
Eyes — With

Their music
The (no?)

Pit, weather
Of tears

Which plagues
Us — Bodies

Of waves
Whose crests

Spear air,
Here rolls

The sea —
Go chase

It — a
Salt pact

Ranged over
Bars — white

Ribs pervade
In constant

Measures the
Rounds — Its

Wet frosting,
A kiss

Opens nothing.
Bend head

No! lips
Not this

An assumed
Poise among

Crowds! Blue—
Withdraws sunset—

Tones sound—
Pluck—dissonant—

Stops sing
The welter.

LOUIS ZUKOFSKY
(*Blues*, Fall 1930)

PAGANY

Poem

falling off a fence MARYANN
maryann color of old honey
falling off maryANN
or being seduced under lilacs (maryann)
mating with lilacs:
MARYANN mother of twin black children

falling off no more fences
falling no more

remembering slimly: maryANN color of dead honey,
lilacs, Lilacs, LIlacs, LILAcs, LILACs, till she die.

> the ripe sweet scent of lilacs where they had tricked her,
> had taken the la de do brilliancy of running on fences,
> MARYANN tricked by beauty, dying slowly of beauty,
>   maryann,
> color of black honey, dreaming no more.

KATHLEEN TANKERSLEY YOUNG
(*Pagany*, Jan.–Mar., 1930)

Five Words in a Line

> Five words in a line.
> Bay and pay make a lake.
> Have to be held with what.
> They have to be held with what they have to be held.
> Dependent of dependent of why.
> With a little cry.
> Make of awake.
> Five words in a line.
> Four words in a line.
> They make it with it being please to have withheld

with with it.

Four words in one line.
If to pay by postage.
At all to delay to pay by postage.
If he is he then he will follow me but will he. With them.
With will he.
Really. Five words in a line.
There is every way to-day to say in with a whitened
end with it.
Pardon there with ours.
It is very little that will. That in that in that will.
Four words in one line.
Have withhold. Have withheld.
Six words in one line.
They were alike. With them. They went with wish. If they had
the possibility of annoyance.
Six words in one line.
They are as well as alike.
Three were by theirs allied.
If they were true to usual. A refusal. Made carriage with
a weeding.
Without varied vary roses.
But with them.
Withhold.

They look at him and they know what he thinks.
Now they could when they look at him.

When they were married by him this made away.

Barred to be barred.

Why little a long a lain made with a piled with adapt.

Very benevolently she left for him.

If she could with and did dazzle.

Why were they changing two in yet or all day.

It is very happily that it is with added that it is as it is a gold
or is told.

Commence again that we like waving.

Once every day once a day they make it do. By this time a

part of it is impressed favorably with keeping. If not by and with allowance. They mean that if they know.

What does it look like if it looks like it.

They came to the country and they asked them not to and they did a little at a time with whom with flourishes.

Jenny Solomon

Matter pan has acuteness in return she said with they did.

Only now nearly known names a press with them.

A Sofa

Married a presently for them and known. It might be larger.

It might not be as high as with them.
To come back.
If it looks like it.
Without it.
With it.
If it looks like it with it.
Four words in each line.
If it does it looks as it does it looks like it.
Does look like it.
It does look like it.
Five words in a line is right.
By never being suspicious and always being careful she has never been robbed.

GERTRUDE STEIN
(Pagany, Jan.–Mar., 1930)

For W. C. W.

Into the Shandy Westerness

a

Do you understand the managing?
Mornings like scissors.
Leaves of dying.
Let event particle e. Point track m-n.
Congruence. Yes? that's what you thought it would be?

A flag waves, a kite climbs. Clouds climb, advancing impalpable edges. The whole mottled sky turns slowly on its zenith, the same clouds go round and round the horizon.

As A is.

A triangular chessboard squared in two tones of grey. P to K3, Kn x B. It's very cold under the table. A cold window.

When he was little he used to go out to the barn and put his cheek against a cow and cry and cry. When he swam in the pasture creek the little fish tickled his legs.

Something is going to cut.

Something is going to break.

I don't see it I can't hear it but it's swinging.

One goes swiftly back. One goes forward. Two move to the left. A Voice. The steel column bores and bores into the ground. Presently the air is filled with ammonia fumes.

We will sing hymn number 366, "Art thou weary, art thou languid" 366, MY number, MY bleeding number. So I ups and tells 'em WHY I was weary WHY I was languid.

b

As B is.

Orange green yellow blue red violet.

Is there anybody there said the stranger. Is there any reason why after all these difficulties we should be subjected in this particularly humiliating manner?

Orange. Row after row of shining minute faces. Green. A slight lurch and the the floor begins to climb smoothly steadily up up everything clatters against the altar. The celebrant is embarrassed.

White disks fly from the cylindrical heads of the spectators and disappear out of the windows. Presently only their palpitating necks are left; hollow, dark purple inside.

It's pleasant to think of the cottages along the mountain side. The alfalfa ripening in the afternoon. The thin smoke of evening. The chill nights.

Assorted solutions, neat packages of peace were distributed by officious archangels. There was much unemployment, long breadlines everywhere in the dusty cities, quiet, no traffic, much patience. We came on, collecting visas, wasting our substance in bribes, asking, Who is king in this kingdom, who is your ruler, by what do you measure?

193

c

Whenever I think of England I see Wyndham Lewis
standing in a high freezing wind on the plain where Mordred
and Arthur fought, dressed only in his BVDs painfully extracting
thorns from his chapped buttocks. It grows dark rapidly.

When I think of France I see Marcel Duchamp on Michigan
boulevard in a raccoon coat and a number of young americans
praying before a roller-coaster from which middle aged
frenchmen strapped to bicycles leap into tubs of coca-cola.

Ta-tum-ta-tee* I love you
There'll ne'er be none above you
Even when you do
Fa down and go boom
BOOM boom BOOM boom   boom

d

Now the blue flowers return the gravel mornings.
Now the immaculate mistresses
And those we loved from afar.

It's yellow in the sunlight and blue around the corner and
it's all been so simple. The grey furry plants and the white hands.
The considerations, the ablatives. The conversation about death.
The lace parasol.

He was naturally very neat.

He was particular about his neckties and very proud of his
razors. They gleamed on maroon plush. His watch lost sixty
seconds every four weeks neither more nor less. He sat on the
screen porch smelling faintly of citronella and spoke slowly and
distinctly about love. Then he died. And she hadn't made up her
mind. So she walked under the lace parasol avoiding the decayed
catalpa blossoms that littered the sidewalk.

e

It grows dark. A shitepoke flies up from the canal. That's a
shitepoke he says to the boy. For supper hasenpfeffer. The rabbits
are getting at the tomato sets, bad. Tourists are camping down at
the wood lot at the corners. You can see their fire from the back
door. When they came for water Nero snapped at the man. Now
he looks over at their fire and barks every few minutes. On both

sides of the walk about every ten feet all the way to the gate
bushel baskets are turned upside down over the peonies. As it gets
darker they disappear.

KENNETH REXROTH

(*Pagany*, Jan.–Mar., 1930)

*The reader may substitute any four syllable word he chooses.

Three Poems

POEM

After the moon's
light went out
after the rained
on solemnly sand
frangible before the sun's
coming and
even before i asked it: what could have remained?

Suggestion of eyes
tightly blue-lidded: not lips
too twistedly still: oh after the sunrise
only hands unfeelingly
resting in their own apocalypse.

THESE TOO

for the steaming of the fruitful flesh . . .
for the tearing . . .
one had the whites vitric . . .
plunging from the scaffold in a flaccid streak . . .
another nestling in the cavern . . .
drew a newspaper closer . . .
oh the ringing into a tremor . . .
oh the ringing . . .
oh the tremor . . .
oh the . . .
ing . . .
oh . . .
r . . .

This Kind Of Death

is slowbleeding looking on your face slow
dying on your nakedness like this
(but gradually numbly)
electrolytical resolving
notangent
single focus and foci
oh darling let a touch be
like a broken jerk and broken neck by hanging like
hotlead without crying
out not a fang on entrails
not a slowebbing looking on your face and a
dying
like
thi
s
.

Charles Henri Ford
(*Pagany*, Jan.–Mar., 1930)

Three Poems

Wild Sunflower

Sunflower! gross of leaf and porous,
gummy, raw,
with unclean edges,

        fury
of the broken but unbeaten
earth, it leers
beside our door!

       Grip

hard to the dry
airy logs, scoured
clean with sun. Hold fast
to what you are in spite of
the wormseething loam,
the boiling land. And give
me love, slow love

that draws the turbid
loam up into sun!

> But
fiercely this thing
grows, is hairy, is
unfinished at the edges,
gulps the sun and earth, will
not be beaten
down nor turn away.

> IDAHO
Life sucks away
through jagged
cuts

> man clings
to shrinking rock
and shingle: twisting
crab strong as the waning
tide

> he concentrates
to this, holds on
with back and hoe bent

> > angry
root, clawed, smoked
and dying

the hills!
hairylidded eye.

> To The Painter Polelonema
You wring life
from the rock
from gold air
violent with odors
smoking wrath

you seize life
in the naked hand
crush, smelt it,
temper—
in a single grip

that lasts for years

it is
for this one lives

and drives a
brain into the rock
and bursts the veins
with love —

        of rock!

no sparrow
cracks these seeds

that no wind blows.

YVOR WINTERS
(*Pagany*, Jan.–Mar., 1930)

Is Pleasure

to look at
to see   the sl ow l owering of a
to hear the sl ow urge of   sea
to see
       the sl ow descend so even of
        a   stage   curtain   to
hear the surge of
            to feel the cool
flanks of
       to taste the to feel the cool
of him to taste feel the sea to see
to taste the wet kisses of to hear
to taste the wet kisses of her

sof sound an.d s ur ge   mo not on ous
of slow dr opp ing cur tain

to look at   wet
       cool slow wet   pools

SIDNEY HUNT
(*Pagany*, Apr.–June, 1930)

Snow-Ghost

Bleak air a fear
a dreaming monster turning
slowly that will
flake way

             in hollow gloam
age spiralling in Time

Draw back

the shining blind
the vibrant membrane
singing back a
dream

      come to me
where I stand O
where I sifting change

invisible save on the plane of light

I look both ways and wait

Behind the window, waterclear
volcanic trees of winter
against crumblng sky.

YVOR WINTERS
(*Pagany*, July–Sept., 1930)

Dream of the Erotic

    (*An Essay in Articulate Typography*)

whenever sky blues
are a forest interval and on
a plane of superrooted being:
                          lips
lie prostrate dazed and
                  dreaming
                      :flowers
grow magnificently gold with
ages on their pet-
als then

will
            breeze come

faintly
            as I prostrately : before : with
only quivering nostrils was
                              : : but mod-
erately mad with
                  scent
and over me will spread
a robe of scent for waking change
                                  to
num:ber petals in eye-dropping
                              still: :
                                        ness

till the tall trees
                    in
their grandeur : see : a : bird
                              go
flagging its great lust
                        toward
storied flowers (
                  drive its beak deep
                  in their sleeping
                  hearts,, till they must give
                                              the
                  plumage of their hon-
                  ey one
                        :great yel: :
                        low
                              flower
                  drop-
                  ping dead
)
where rest and rest are
coupled in a sane
disorder of the mind
                    O
it were vain to
                think

the mist is taken from the
                              evening
flower for the sun to drink
                      up
                        at
the dawn : : what change : is this
                              for
flowers re-
        do-
             lently
                  kept
                      in
silence unfulfilled by : :
breaking, though
it were vain too to seek
the flo-
        wer
unclosed when silence with
                        a
hammer strikes the sun
                  and
jungles quiv-
          er
              back
to immemorial : : : sleep
O now:
        these lips
              are know-
ing not the oth-
          er scent
                :except as
brother to the
             air and: all: the sky
of suns and moons as I
             am thinking
                  hark-
ening not but to the
             timeless breeze : : :
                    these

THE "PREDOMINANT FORCE"

fall

    :

      :

      ing,,, ah

            these fall

               :

                 ing,,,, lips

                      give

succor to the

         flower

            rinsed

               in ennui

and : : : :

they fall toward

      PURPLE

          ennuied

              jung·

                 les

                    as

the sun

      falls

        in: the sky with

             flash: and

din of moment and : : yet not

          a

          sun

that winks its day to·

         ward darkness or

furrow of the

      moon

        : : : is

any scarlet streak like

         this!

to : drink : thee : in : a : breath (—

          O

SUN-TORMENTED FLOWER

)

PARKER TYLER
(*Pagany*, Oct.–Dec., 1930)

Enfances

1

Enfances aux cent coins de ma mémoire
si ma mémoire est l'oeuvre de la passion,
enfances décimées par les nuits
si les nuits ne sont qu'une maladie du sommeil,
je vous poursuis avant de dormir, sans hâte.
Sans hâte, mais plié sous des tâches ingrates,
tête nue et transpirant de fièvre,
je vous mesure au trajet de la vie
et vos insoumissions, enfances, sont muettes,
enfances si l'enfance est ce silence
où gravement déjà s'installe la mort
et si ma main n'a pas retrouvé sa solitude,
et c'est avouer que je vous laisse libres
hors de mon destin que d'autres voulurent court,
à vos robes d'indienne, à vos plaisirs sanguins.

2

Enfance dans la laine
en dépit des semaines,
enfance dans la rue
sans adieu et sans mal
et jouant avec le hasard,
au rire des cotonniers
comparez vos corps nus,
enfance dans la cour
avec des oiseaux comme des chiens
annonçant les voleurs sans talent,
j'ai vécu cette enfance
et tant d'autres encore,
ayant du sang mêlé de nord
et de midi, ici et là,
où je naquis et où je voyageai
et tous les noms sont là
au courant de l'invisible
et de ce que l'amour n'a pas brouillé.

3

J'ai parlé de tant d'années
que la mémoire a ornées
de ce qu'inventèrent leurs complices.
Mes souliers n'étaient point usés
d'une course au soleil
dans les places où seules
les ombres des arbres prouvaient des arbres
qui ne cachaient pas du soleil.
Alors on criait et la main alors
réfléchissait et se sentait cruelle.
Je joue, je suis fort,
ma faim me donne raison.
L'amour déjà et ses dons
naissaient avec le sang.
J'ai battu mes pensées et les bois:
partout les filles trouvaient des prétextes
à ne rien passer sous silence,
des prétextes à lever leur jupe pour apprendre
et leur rire étaite donné au mauvais élève,
gagné par lui au temps du premier tabac.
Restait à prouver l'irrémédiable:
le visage masqué par l'inconnu, sans peur,
des heures elles restaient à genoux
devant les garçons déculottés
et les chiens ne s'en allaient pas.
Mon sexe se souvient ici
de ses premiers soupirs.

Rien à cacher,
je le dis à tous:
mon sexe a respiré
entre leurs mains moites.

4

Je suis dans mon droit,
on m'a trahi si fidèlement.
J'ai payé le prix des mots
et ce n'est pas un amusement.
Un oiseau, m'a-t-on dit,
a passé entre le ciel et moi.

On ne m'a pas parlé de toi,
j'ai cessé d'écouter, j'ai feint
de découvrir un incendie
dans la substance de ton oeil.
Les animaux sont beaux
parce qu'ils sont nus.
A l'intérieur aussi.

5

Tout ce que j'ai tu,
le partage de la conscience,
tout ce qui s'est dérobé,
le perpétuel et le visible,
et quelque adieu nocturne,
notre premier dialogue,
la croissance des graines,
tun n'avais rien d'autre au front
que le sable de la mémoire
au fil de l'eau où j'ai lavé
ma pensée et ainsi de suite,
à tes pieds l'histoire de la terre
et quelque chose de très rare
que je ne connaissais pas,
enfance prédite par la magnésie.

6

Dénombrée l'éxigence,
dénommée la fallace,
les grands se sont trompés
en fondant une famille.

L'enfance est née de l'enfance
dans l'indifférence surmontée
et longuement vécue
sortira sa parole.

Quelque erreur insolite.

7

Ai-je longtemps rapproché
de mon appétit

ces empereurs qui cachent
leur tendresse peinte?

Recouvert de mon sang
ces livres d'enfants fouettées?
Et tout ce plaisir avec feu
puis bien plus vite

avec une écolière sans devoir
ou les copiant sur l'ennui,
noire des taches de l'écriture
et blanche de percale,

à cause de l'amour
qu'on joue sous les tables,
tapis jusqu'au sol,
par les après-midi sans mère.

8

Tu doutais de toi à compter les jours
qui te séparaient d'un ennui habitable
et tu te criais avant de courir:
j'ai ma tête et j'ai ma voie.
Il ne faut pas répondre à l'enfance.
Enfance, il y avait des mots et des présences
que tu n'osais pas t'avouer
et l'ombre t'accablait de ses malédictions.
Le soleil t'avait donné cette ombre
cette ombre pour aimer et pour te conquérir.
Tu chantes pour oublier cette conquête,
ton départ et celui des clartés nomades.
Mais alors, tu te couchais des semaines
en feignant d'être malade
et si l'on criait comme aux révolutions
tu étais sûre de ta fièvre puerpérale:
le doute s'installait en toi magnifiquement
avec l'amour.

9

Me voici lourd de circonstances,
profond dans mes appétits
et mon intelligence est animale.
J'avais compris d'une façon ou d'une autre

qu'on pût rester des heures devant l'amour.
Les promenades devant le dernier train
n'empêchaient pas d'aimer et davantage.
L'enfance et l'enfance de la poitrine,
les belettes en parlent entre elles.
Je n e capitule pas devant vos avantages,
j'appelle et ma voix va droit,
où tu m'entends, m'entends-tu?
J'ai quitté ma chemise ancienne
et nu devant mon âge je sais,
je sais que tu m'entends
comme tu dois m'entendre, avec joie,
parce que je parle de ma solitude
et de ma solitude à la tienne
et qu'entre l'une et l'autre de ces cités infaillibles
il y a une houle qui va et qui vient,
tout ce que le parole désenchante.
Devant témoin je parlerai de cela
et de ceci qui me tient au mouillage
malgré le vent, les courants et la marée.
Mon tangon est ta pensée,
ta pensée una manie étrangère à la séduction.
J'ouvre de mes audaces brûlées
la pulpe du silence, cent fois par nuit,
je contourne l'édifice de notre dédain
et j'entre par la porte de l'accident.

10

Enfance apprise dans les livres d'aventures,
enfance en but au miracle des mécaniques,
enfance sans lecture des mauvais livres,
enfance sans rêve et préférant la vie
où tu mettais ta lumière d'anarchie,
enfance montée dans l'amour des batailles
et dans la haine des règles et des soldats,
enfance silencieuse dont la rebellion
si blanche s'augmentait de blancs calculs,
enfance qui complotais un théâtre
où jouait le peine de mort son rôle
de gestes graves appris par la révolte,

enfance qui contenais la beauté des déserteurs,
enfance que dire de plus de ton enfance,
sous le front des inductions, ferme,
je te vis en moi et n'ai point changé
et je puis médire de mon angoisse,
maudire toutes les tares du désespoir.
Ma poitrine si blanche contre le cauchemar
et cette inégalité font que je puis vivre.

11

Voici que la maladie me donne une voix plus forte:
je suis malade, je suis grand: on m'a volé,
tout le monde est là et je suis en colère,
les splendeurs de la maladie battent contre mes côtes.
Mes bras ont bruni et l'enfance sent la viande.
Dans une ville lointaine ma tête solitaire,
par delà les murs ma voix qui frappe,
au-dessus de ma tête mon bras veineux,
mes amis furent jugés au tribunal de l'enfance.
L'indifférence des victimes pèse sur l'injustice
et celles qu'on n'éxécute pas nous méprisent.
Mais la maladie me rend invulnérable,
lâchement j'aurais pu rire ou me tuer moi-même.
J'ai appelé les noms, puis à bout de coeur
j'ai craché sur le reste ne valant pas ma violence,
sûr alors d'avoir de droit de parler et de vivre,
le droit d'être dans mon tort par plaisir,
comme la peste et la famine.

12

Ma faim est large, mon appétit démesuré.
Je peux parler longtemps sans médire
mais tout me blesse et je sais haïr.
Ce pays que je vois pour la première fois
à ma timidité confie les soins du voyage,
tout ce qu'une absence crée d'incertitude,
tout ce que la surprise a gagné sur l'amour,
et c'est si haut que je pense à mon orgueil
qu'aucun regret de mes humiliations subies pour toi
n'éxerce mon enfance à redouter la nuit,

la nuit et ces dons que tu m'as faits,
ces dons où se tatoua ton indifférence
sous la forme et le chant d'un regard particulier.
Enfance, je te nomme au centre du monde,
au centre de mon coeur tu te nommes toi-même,
tu te nommes la course à l'exemple de ma faim,
enfance homicide à l'exemple de ma faim.

13

L'imprudence a dérangé les simples,
déjoué les mesures de la honte.
L'enfance se décrit et se plait
dans les maisons de bois où dort le charbon,
derrière les palissades dont on fait les bateaux.
Du doigt elle invente l'équilibre du repos,
l'orgueil du regard avec de frais contrastes
et nourrit son plaisir du repos des marées,
quand la mémoire file au plus près du vent,
ce sont les souvenirs d'un voyage en projet.
Ailleurs s'en va l'enfance et la table vacante
de l'eau, du sel et du pain reste embarrassée
et des artichauts et du lard, du fromage et des abricots.
Elle bâtit sa maison sur l'heure de nos mots,
se prête au jeu des phrases où jeune l'oubli,
où tournent les prisonniers et les esclaves du hasard,
tandis que s'éxilent l'inconstance et la perfidie.

14

Que me disent amour et ses tourelles?
J'ai perdu la plus belle en ouvrant la main,
en changeant de pas j'ai trompé le silencieuse,
rira l'éternelle en tuant la plus belle,
la morte a su garder son domaine,
en refermant les bras j'ai tué l'éternelle,
l'enfance a renié, renié la souveraine
et c'est ainsi que vont les semaines.

15

De quelle couronne légère
fleurir l'adultère?

209

Jamais les jours, jamais les nuits
n'ont donné de preuves à la terre.
J'aurais résolu le problème,
en saurais-je plus de moi-même?
J'ai faim et soif à vie,
à vie purge ta peine,
en pure perte.

16

La louange a choisi parmi vos corps ensemble
la méthode qui rectifie vos brusques chagrins
et toutes celles, enfances, toutes celles qui sont mortes
portent un ruban clair et la manie de la danse.
L'onaniste se souviendra-t-il de cette fille en deuil
drapée d'un deuil si limpide et qui l'excitait tant
après les robes soulevées en visite, en secret
et qu'il vit pâlir devant une image obscène.
Chaque jour, elle pâlit davantage, chaque visite,
jusqu'à mourir à l'ombre sure le jeune homme nu.
Dormir où tu dors, Angélina, si Angélina
que le bain réveille au milieu de son parcours
ton collier de sommeil et l'infidèle pensée
d'où ta solitude descend vers nous de si loin,
comme tu dors, Patricia, dois-je le dire, Patricia,
dont l'obscurité recule à chaque outrage,
au mépris des rêves, c'est dormir avec soin
sur ton jeune amour solitaire et sans vêtement,
où d'autres ne verraient que de l'herbe.

17

Sans sortir de l'enfance tu as vingt-trois ans
et tu traverses une rivière sans penser à moi.
Si tu dormais en vérité, quitterais-tu si vite
cette tête et ce bras lancés contre ton mensonge?
Et me voici sur ta table au secret de mon malheur
parce que je ne puis croire, je ne puis croire à tes robes
et parce que je n'ai pas menti décidément
et que tu pars pour longtemps sur un fleuve qui s'éloigne.
Nous aurons ensemble croisé dans des mers réelles
et ton absence c'est l'alignement des feux verts.

210

J'ai fait semblant de dormir à voir ma tête,
mais chantait le chant que tu aimais chanter
et c'était bien ta tête qui dormait, d'un oeil,
sourde à tous les mots et c'étaient bien les mots
que chantaient ce chant, ta tête et ton sommeil.
Et me voici sorti de l'ombre, vêtu comme d'habitude,
vêtu couleur de légumes et j'aime ce chant
que je n'aurais pas dû connaitre dans ma tête
si ta tête était restée sur l'autre versant.

18

Quand je dors, c'est merveille:
le sommeil sort de mon angoisse,
ce que je hais le mieux en moi-même,
et l'amour et sa fatigue font dormir.

19

Si je parle de vous,
nus entre mes repas,
jeux des vêtements
ou villes que ne touchent
ni les éponges ni les cargos,
maisons détruites par la vie,
objets à portée du front,
crimes, cris des coqs au pôle,
nourritures trop faibles pour l'appétit,
c'est que vous êtes mes familiers
et les familiers de l'enfance,
enfance à la bouche laiteuse.
En un mot les mois s'éveillent
et la surface candie de l'averse.
La balle a franchi le bois
et blessé l'enfance à genoux.
Les chants éclatèrent contrairement
et mille mains rougirent
pour écrire au tumulte.
Après la pluie, unique sentinelle,
sans mot d'ordre le soleil
s'il brûla mon corps au fond,
fit de ma pensée une brûlure.

J'ignorais en passant mon temps
près de toi et de ton enfance, enfance,
les amers plaisirs du plaisir
et ton enfance, cette femme,
cette femme comme une femme
et pas plus et pas moins,
comme une femme et c'est tout
et c'est davantage qu'une fontaine,
plus que la mer, plus et plus,
alors j'ai pris de l'herbe et de l'herbe
sur mon dos et sur mon ventre
et partout sur tes traces:
l'heure brûlait au centre de l'heure,
l'éveil passait, dépassait
le bout de notre tête.

20

Ma maison de bois a perdu son profil
au profit du tien. Si j'en tenais rancune
au vent qui l'emmène, serais-tu celle
que nomment les mois au coeur des horoscopes?
Et je serais moins encore cet arbre dont ton repos
prit la fourche principale pour deux bras vivants
et cette tête bouclée sans avenir et sans pardon
pour mon imagination dant la fourche est la foudre,
parce que la masturbation m'habille de tes robes
et me pousse vers toi, vers toi et le travail.

21

Au hasard des édredons rouges
j'use mon corps et ma vie,
mon enfance absente à la canicule.

22

J'aime t'avoir comme une mauvaise habitude
quand nous sommes couchés dans ta chambre.

23

Où es-tu, si loin et si près,
que je vois avec peine

l'enfance et ses manies
et qu'un même rire
devient notre sillage
et qu'une même tristesse
nous dit de même
que l'eau s'éloigne de nos collines.
Et ton écriture s'éfface
sur ma poitrine lavée.
Le plaisir mourut en chemin
d'un climat à un autre
et son ombre ne bouge plus.
J'avais tout paré pour la vie
et mon appareillage, il est vrai,
fut loin de tous et sans ironie.

24

Enfance, qui t'endormais pour ne pas perdre ton temps,
je t'ai apprise au premier cinéma.
Je te tiens par la main et tu caches sous ta tête
cet éclat de mon diadème, ce que fut ma conscience,
mais ce n'est pas de cela qu'il s'agit ni d'oubli
ni de souvenirs, il s'agit de ce mot retrouvé,
de ce geste si futile qui font que les souvenirs
sont morts, morts et sans lendemain
et qui font que la vie vous tient par la main
et ne cache rien à ceux qu'elle oublie,
même à ceux qu'elle oublie.

25

J'ai incendié ma vie.
De ses forêts rougies
sortaient des animaux sauvages.
Ma confiance a puisé sa force
de bâtir, en vous, sources marines,
et celle de vivre avec mes ongles
cet amour si fragile né d'un fouet,
cette âme surprise par les drogues,
cette aventure où j'ai laissé
du sang pour créer ma vie.
Sur ton front sans humeur

213

tes faveurs ont écrit mon front
et ton visage s'est levé
sur un mur plus neuf
où mon sang a nommé tes avantages.
Ai-je gagné sur ton malheur
cet air de forêt qu'a ma chambre vide
et vide aussi de tes branches.
Quand le vent a soufflé
au vasistas ta distraction,
j'ai mesuré dans la nuit solide
la distance des ports,
au compas la distance,
au compas le trajet magnifique,
au compas mon domaine.
Quelque fois avançait ta main
hors de ta manche trouée
et tes doigts sans fatigue
roulaient les cordages, les cordages,
avec la volonté du navigateur.

26

Embarquons, partons aux Indes,
vanille, vanille,
toutes les nourritures se valent.
Gabrielle, trio de neige,
Eugénie, Yvonne, l'ordre
a changé son courant d'amour,
l'ordre des mots dans ta bouche,
enfance réveillée par mes désordres.
Sous la pluie sérieuse
quand tournait le vent,
quand remontait le vent
du phare au rocher de la Jument,
en cachant ta tête
tu premais ce vent
pour ma pensée et sans mal
tu tendais ton bras
vers la croisée où mon absence
a mis le silence au rang de la lumière,
ton absence dans ma solitude,
ce don que la lumière avait fait à ma mémoire.

214

27

J'ai vielli en une veille,
trois veilles et j'ai perdu,
j'ai perdu trois têtes,
trois têtes et je n'y reconnais
plus la mienne.
Je te retrouve, enfance,
je te tutoie, enfance,
mais parler de toi
c'est parler d'elle et de notre pacte
et je te mêle à nos plaisirs adultes
où jamais tu ne quittais nos épreuves.
Je rétablis ta présence sans mémoire
à l'aide de mes mains et devant ton absence.
L'odeur de l'amour est une odeur de jour,
de jour en jour une odeur d'herbe en plein jour,
le mouvement de ta tête sur mon ventre
aidait la naissance de la pensée,
l'extraordinaire mélange du feu et de l'eau
après l'immobile regard sous le front.
Ma pensée c'est une fontaine qui s'achève en fontaine.

28

Le chemin finit par un gros paysage
et ta jalousie sous un chapeau sans bord.
Et ma voix est une feuille
au fur et à mesure de ton avenir,
je dors en écrivant et grandi de ton ombre
parce que je n'ai pas demandé de preuves à ton amour,
je serre dans mes bras ton épithète.

29

J'ai mis un costume d'été
pour paraitre gai.
Et le roi s'était avancé
Pour dire sa pensée.
La reine prenait son bain
et ne disait rien.
L'enfance avait pris la reine
et lui disait sa peine.
Le roi sur la terrasse,

la reine dans le palais d'en face,
et personne ne savait
ce qui se passait,
mais le roi était en gris clair
et la reine pleurait
pour un crime de l'enfance.

30

Enfances aux quatre coins du monde,
dans cette ville où l'on me fit vivre,
parti avec une valise à ma taille, à la mer,
et ignorant le langage des enfants,
renaissez-vous au présent de ce coeur
qu'une chanson a mis à l'ouvrage.
Imaginez-vous les honneurs de la forêt
et cette longue promenade de la forêt
et ce rire blanc dans son infirmerie.
Vos manies ont distrait mes habitudes,
celles qui sont relevées à chaque quart de nuit,
du parcours de la vie et du paysage,
des soupçons de maladie que le jour dédaigne,
mais toi, mon enfance que je prénomme,
toi que je nomme ma salubrité,
à choisir tes préjugés tu devins femme
et si je fus ton préjugé san contrôle,
toutes les fleurs sont à mon nom
dans tes bras et autour des maisons.
La musique naquit de nos conventions,
un décor que l'enfance imposait à l'enfance,
un manque à notre goût pour le silence
et de mémoire je chante ta gymnastique.
Enfances, imaginez-vous les honneurs de la forêt
et ce vent palmé qui crée une apologie.

GEORGES HUGNET
(*Pagany*, Winter 1931)

Poem Pritten on Pfances of Georges Hugnet

1

In the one hundred small places of myself my youth,
And myself in if it is the use of passion,
In this in it and in the nights alone
If in the next to night which is indeed not well
I follow you without it having slept and went.
Without the pressure of a place with which to come unfolded
folds are a pressure and an abusive stain
A head if uncovered can be as hot, as heated,
to please to take a distance to make life,
and if resisting, little, they have no thought,
a little one which was a little which was as all as still,
Or with or without fear or with it all,
And if in feeling all it will be placed alone beside
and it is with with which and not beside not beside may,
Outside with much which is without with me, and not an
Indian shawl, which could it be but with my blood.

2

A little a little one all wooly or in wool
As if within or not in any week or as for weeks
A little one which makes a street no name
without it having come and went farewell
And not with laughing playing
Where they went they would or work
it is not that they look alike with which in up and down as
chickens without dogs,
Coming to have no liking for a thief which is not left to
have away,
To live like when
And very many things
Being with me with them
with which with me
whoever with and born
and went as well
Meant,
Five which are seen
And with it five more lent.

As much as not mixed up,
With love.

3

I often live with many months with years of which I think
and they as naturally think well of those
My littlest shoes which were not very much without that care
left there
where I would like the heat
and very nearly find that trees have many little places that
make shade.
which never went away when there was sun
In a way there were cries and it was felt to be the cruelest yet
I am very happy in my play
and I am very thirsty in hunger
Which is not what is always there with love
And after all when was I born.
I can touch wood and think
I can also see girls who were in finding
and they will laugh and say
and yes say so as yes as yes with woe
And now they with me think and love love that they told
with hide and even
It is as if all fields would grow what do they grow, tobacco
even so,
And they will not delight in having had,
Because after no fear and not afraid,
they have been having that they join as well,
And always it is pretty to see dogs.
It is no double to have more with when they met and in
began who can.
There is very little to hide,
When there is everything beside
And there is a well inside
In hands untied.

4

I follow as I can and this to do
With never vaguely that they went away
I have been left to bargain with myself
and I have come not to be pleased to see

They wish to watch the little bird
Who flew at which they look
They never mentioned me to it,
I stopped to listen well it is a pleasure to see a fire which
does not inspire them to see me
I wish to look at dogs
Because they will be having with they wish
To have it look alike as when it does

5

Everything is best of all for you which is for me.
I like a half of which it is as much
Which never in alone is more than most
Because I easily can be repaid in difficulty of the hurry left
Between now not at all and after which began
It could be morning which it was at night
And little things do feed a little more than all
What was it that was meant by things as said
There is a difference between yet and well
And very well and when there was as much which is as well
as more
And it is very likely made away again
Very nearly as much as not before
Which is as better than to have it now
Which it is taken to make my blood thin.

6

It is very likely counting it as well
Named not alas but they must lend it for
In welcome doubt which they need for deceit
They face a little more than most and made it.
They will be born in better than at least
with not at all relieved and left away a little said
Which is not with made not useless.
Unless is used with where like what.

7

A very long a little way
They have to have
In which array
They make it wring

Their tendering them this.
It is whatever originally read read can be two words smoke
can be all three
And very much there were.
It is larger than around to think them little amiably
What is it said to incline learnt and places it as place
as which were more than the two made it do.
Remember not a color.
Every little boy has his own desk.

8

Who leaves it to be left to like it less
which is to leave alone what they have left
They made it act as if to shout
Is when they make it come away and sit.
Nobody need say no nor yes.
They who had known or which was pressed as press
They might with thought come yet to think without
With which it is to like it with its shell,
A shell has hold of what is not withheld
It is just as well not to be well as well
Nevertheless
As when it is in short and long and pleasure
It is a little thing to ask to wait
It is in any kind of many chances
They like it best with all its under weight
And will they miss it when they meet its frame,
A frame is such that hours are made by sitting
Rest it in little pieces
They like it to be held to have and hold
Believe me it is not for pleasure that I do it.

9

Look at me now and here I am
And with it all it is not preparation,
They make it never breathless without breath
And sometimes in a little while they wait.
Without its leaving.
It is mine to sit and carefully to be thought thorough
Let it be said that it is said let me alone,
You alone have a way to think and swim,

Leave it as well
And noises have no other.
It is in their refrain that they sing me.
It just can happen so.

10

Did he hear it when it was as said
And did he sing it when he sang a song
And did he like it when it was not said
And did he make it when he went along
There is a little doubt without which meant
That he did go that he went that he was not sent,
Who could send whom
Which went which way where
It is alike that they say that this is so
In any little while more may be most
Most may be most and best may be most best
It is at once a very little while
That they eat more when many are more there
Like it alike
Every little while they twitch and snore
It is a hope of eating all alike
That makes them grow
And so say so.

11

Here once in a while she says he says
When it is well it is not more than ill
He says we say she says
When it is very well it is not more than still it is not more
than ill
And all he says it is and all and very well and very much that
was of very ill.
And anyway who was as strong as very strong with all and
come along,
It is a height which makes it best to come to be a matter
that they had
Alike in not no end of very well and in divide with better
than the most,
And very well who knows of very well and best and most
and not as well as ill.

It could be made as curly as they lie which when they think
with me
Who is with me that is not why they went to be just now.
Just now can be well said.
In imitation there is no more sign that if I had not been
without my filling it with absence made in choosing extra bright.
I do mind him, I do mind them I do mind her,
Which was the same as made it best for me for her for them.
Any leaf is more annoying than a tree when this you see see
me she said of me of three of two of me.
And then I went to think of me of which of one of two of
one of three of which of me I went to be away of three of two of
one of me.
Any pleasure leads to me and I lead them away away from
pleasure and from me.

12

I am very hungry when I drink,
I need to leave it when I have it held.
They will be white with which they know they see, that darker
makes it be a color white for me, white is not shown when I am dark
indeed with red despair who comes who has to care that they will let
me a little lie like now I like to lie I like to live I like to die I like to lie
and live and die and live and die and by and by I like to live and die
and by and by they need to sew, the difference is that sewing makes it
bleed and such with them in all the way of seed and seeding and
repine and they will which is mine and not all mine who can be
thought curious of this of all of that made it and come lead it and
done weigh it and mourn and sit upon it know it for ripeness
without deserting all of it of which without which it has not been
born. Oh no not to be thirsty with the thirst of hunger not alone to
know that they plainly and ate or wishes. Any little one will kill
himself for milk.

13

Known or not known to follow or not follow or not lead.
It is all oak when known as not a tree,
It is all best of all as well as always gone when always sent
In all a lent for all when grass is dried and grass can dry
when all have gone away and come back then to stay.

Who might it be that they can see that candied is a brush that bothers me.

Any way come any way go any way stay any way show any way show me.

They ask are peas in one beets in another one beans in another one,

They follow yes beets are in one peas are in one beans are in one.

They hear without a letter which they love, they love above they sit and when they sit they stare.

So when a little one has more and any one has more and who has more who has more when there can be heard enough and not enough of where.

Who has more where.

14

It could be seen very nicely
That doves have each a heart.
Each one is always seeing that they could not be apart,
A little lake makes fountains
And fountains have no flow,
And a dove has need of flying
And water can be low,
Let me go.
Any week is what they seek
When they have to halve a beak.
I like a painting on a wall of doves
And what do they do.
They have hearts
They are apart
Little doves are winsome
But not when they are little and left.

15

It is always just as well
That there is a better bell
Than that with which a half is a whole
Than that with which a south is a pole
Than that with which they went away to stay
Than that with which after any way,
Needed to be gay to-day.

16

Any little while is longer any little while is shorter any little while is better any little while for me when this you see then think of me.

It is very sad that it is very bad that badly and sadly and mourn and shorn and torn and thorn and best and most and at least and all and better than to call if you call you sleep and if you sleep you must and if you must you shall and if you shall when then when is it then that Angelina she can see it make it be that it is all that it can have it color color white white is for black what green which is a hope is for a yellow which can be very sweet and it is likely that a long tender not as much as most need names to make a cake or dance or loss or next or sweetening without sugar in a cell or most unlikely with it privately who makes it be called practice that they came. They come thank you they come. Any little grass is famous to be grass grass green and red blue and all out but you.

17

He is the exact age he tells you

He is not twenty-two, he is twenty-three and when this you see remember me.

And yet what is it that he can see.

He can see veritably three, all three which is to be certainly. And then.

He tells of oceans which are there and little lakes as well he sings it lightly with his voice and thinks he had to shout and not at all with oceans near and not at all at all, he thinks he is he will he does he knows he was he knows he was he will he has he is he does and now and when is it to be to settle without sillily to be without without with doubt let me. So he says. It is easy to put heads together really. Head to head it is easily done and easily said head to head in bed.

18

When I sleep I sleep and do not dream because it is as well that I am what I seem when I am in my bed and dream.

19

It was with him that he was little tall and old and just as young as when begun by seeming soldiers young and bold and with a little change in place who hopes that women are a race will they be thin will they like fat does milk does hope does age does that no one can think when all have thought that they will think but have not bought no without oceans who hears wheat do they like fish think well of meat it is without without a change that they like this they have it here it is with much that left by him he is within within within actually how many hear actually what age is here actually they are with hope actually they might be bespoke believe me it is not for pleasure that I do it. They often have too much rain as well as too much sun.

They will not be won.

One might be one.

Might one be one.

20

A little house is always held
By a little ball which is always held,
By a little hay which is always held
By a little house which is always held,
A house and a tree a little house and a large tree,
And a little house not for them and a large tree.
And after all fifteen are older than one two three.

It is useful that no one is barred from looking out of a house to see a tree even when there is a tree to see. She made it mentioned when she was not there and so was he.

21

He likes that felt is made of beaver and cotton made of trees and feathers made of birds and red as well. He likes it.

22

He likes to be with her so he says does he like to be with her so he says.

23

Every one which is why they will they will be will he will he be for her for her to come with him with when he went he went and came and any little name is shame as such tattoo. Any little ball is made a net and any little net is made for mine and any little mine that any have will always violate the hope of this which they wore as they lose. It is a welcome, nobody knows a circumstance is with whatever water wishes now. It is pleasant that without a hose no water is drawn. No water is drawn pleasantly without a hose. Doublet and hose not at all water and hose not at all any not at all. Not at all. Either not at all by not at all with me. When this you do not hear and do not see believe me.

24

They were easily left alone they were as easily left alone they were as easily left alone with them. Which makes mistakes mistakes which are mistakes who mistakes mistakes let them see the seal what is the difference between seal and school what is the difference between school and singing school and seeing school and leaving school and sitting in a school. They know the difference when they see the screen which is why leaves are dry when rain is thin and appetising which can be when they win. They win a little exercise in win. Win and win. Perhaps with happens to be thin. It is not easy to be led by them. Not easy to be led and led and led to no brim. In doubt not with them. Not in doubt not with them. Leave it to me to know three from three and they did leave it to him.

25

It is easy to mingle sails with steam oil with coal water with air, it is easy to mingle everywhere and to leave single everywhere water and air oil and coal butter and a share it is a share to ask them where and in a little they will have it there they like it there they had it to prepare and to be a comfort to them without care. It is a need to see without a glare of having it come in does it come in and where. They like a little dog to be afraid to have a nightingale be told a chicken is afraid and it is true he is she is and where whenever there is a hawk up in the air. Like that. It makes anybody think of sail-boats.

26

Little by little two go if two go three go if three go four go if four go they go. It is known as does he go he goes if they go they go and they know they know best and most of whether he will go. He is to go. They will not have vanilla and say so. To go Jenny go, Ivy go Gaby go any come and go is go and come and go and leave to go. Who has to hold it while they go who has to who has had it held and have them come to go. He went and came and had to go. No one has had to say he had to go come here to go go there to go go go to come to come to go to go and come and go.

27

In a little while they smile in a little while and one two three they smile they smile a while in a little while a little smile with which to smile a while and when they like to be as once in a while it is about the time with which in which to smile. He can smile and any smile is when to smile. It is to show that now that he can know and if to smile it is to smile and smile that he can know and any making it be ready there for them to see to change a smile to change a smile into a stare and very likely more than if they care he can care does and will and not to have to care and this is made with and without a need to carry horses horses without sails sails have an ocean sometimes just the land but to believe to have relief in them who can share horses sails and little less a very little less and they like them. It does it hope. They come they see they sew and always with it a hope is for more not more than yesterday but more to-day more to-day more to say more to-day. A little long and birds can drink with beaks and chickens do and horses drink and sails and even all.

28

A clock in the eye ticks in the eye a clock ticks in the eye.

A number with that and large as a hat which makes rims think quicker than I.

A clock in the eye ticks in the eye a clock ticks ticks in the eye.

29

I love my love with a v
Because it is like that
I love myself with a b
Because I am beside that
A king.
I love my love with an a
Because she is a queen
I love my love and a a is the best of them.
Think well and be a king,
Think more and think again
I love my love with a dress and a hat
I love my love and not with this or with that
I love my love with a y because she is my bride

I love her with a d because she is my love beside
Thank you for being there
Nobody has to care
Thank you be being here
Because you are not there.
And with and without me which is and without she she can
be late and then and how and all around we think and found that
it is time to cry she and I.

30

There are a few here now and the rest can follow a cow,
The rest can follow now there are a few here now.
They are all all here now the rest can follow a cow
And mushrooms on a hill and anything else until.
They can see and sink and swim with now and then a brim.
A brim to a hat
What is that,
Anyway in the house they say
Anyway any day
Anyway every day
Anyway outside as they may
Think and swim with hearing him,
Love and song not any song a song is always then too long
to just sit there and sing
Sing song is a song
When sing and sung
Is just the same as now among
Among them,
They are very well placed to be seated and sought
They are very well placed to be cheated and bought
And a bouquet makes a woods
A hat makes a man
And any little more is better than
The one.
And so a boat a goat and wood
And so a loaf which is not said to be just bread
Who can be made to think and die
And any one can come and cry and sing.
Which made butter look yellow
And a hope be relieved

228

By all of it in case
Of my name.
What is my name.
That is the game

GERTRUDE STEIN
(*Pagany*, Winter 1931)

"A"

FIRST MOVEMENT: "COME YE DAUGHTERS"

A
  Round of fiddles playing Bach —
    The double chorus.
       "Come, ye daughters, share my anguish —"
    Bare arms, black dresses
      "See Him! Whom? —"
    Bediamond the passion of our Lord,
      "See Him! How? —"
His legs, blue tendons bleeding,
Tinsel over his ribs
      "O Lamb of God most holy —"
Black, black full dress in the audience —
Dead century where is your motley,
Country people in Leipzig,
      Easter,
Matronly flounces,
        — starched, heaving,
Belly freighted — boom!
Cheeks of the patrons of Leipzig —
"Going to Church? where's the baby?"
"Ach, dort eilt sich der Kappellmeister —"
"Johann Sebastian! (twenty-two
      children!)."

      According to Matthew,
    Composed seventeen twenty-nine,
    Repeated here at Carnegie,
That was Thursday, 'twenty-eight, the fifth evening of April,
    April, and the autos honking outside, all those

that were parked there.
    (*"Hearts turned to thee"*)
   German lady
  Auch ich war in Arkadien geboren.
The lights dim, and the brain when the flesh dims.
Hats picked up from under seats.
Galleries darkening.
    "No suh!
Not past that exit, Zukofsky!"
"Agh, Satan! Agh — gh!"
Ecdysis: the serpent coming out,
     gradual molting,
Blood staining the floor as the foot stepped,
Bleeding chamfer for shoulder:
"Not past that exit, Zukofsky!"
"Devil! what! — ?"
"Blood of your desire to graft what you desire,
Consider the Angels who sang in the boys' choir
God's cherubs,
If seen near the ocean, stripped white skins, red coat of the
  sunburn, —
They have mothers."
"No, Satan, not heart that bled
Over boys' voices, nor blood
Flowing for lost sons, —
I have harbored perfection."
And as one who under the stars
Spits free across the sand dunes, and the winds
Blow thru him, and his spit seems to drown worlds,
I lit a cigarette, and passed free
Beyond the red light of the exit.

Asmodeus fading to "Camel" smoke,
Greasy, solicitous, eyes longing minutes after,
Smiling, a tramp's face,
Lips looking out of a beard
Hips looking out of ripped trousers
    and suddenly
Nothing.
But about me, the voices of those who had
    been at the concert,

Feet stopping everywhere in the streets,
Stopping of turned necks for chatter:
"Poor Thomas Hardy   he had to go so soon,
It was he who admired so our recessional
                     architecture,
What do you think of our new Sherry-Netherland!"
"Lovely soprano,
Is that her mother, lovely lines,
I admire her very much!"
And those who had perused the score at the concert,
The immature pants that filled chairs
Patrons of poetry, business temples erected to arts and letters,
                   The cornerstones of waste paper,
"Such lyric weather!" chirping
Quatrain on quatrain, empty and
The sonneteers when I consider again and over
                      again
             Limp wet blanket pentameters
Immured holluschickies, dead honor men
Persisting thru polysyllables,
Mongers in mystic accretions,
The stealers of "melange adultere de tout,"
The Americanizers of the Classics,
                   Tradition!
(To them word of great contours).
And raping women with horses.

And on one side street near an elevated,
Lamenting contemporaneousness,
Foreheads wrinkled with injunctions:
"The Pennsylvania miners again on   the lockout,
We must send relief to the wives and children —
What's your next editorial about, Carat?
We need propaganda, the thing's
                becoming a mass
                   movement."

And I.
Upon the feast of that Passover,
The blood's tide as the music's
A thousand fiddles as beyond effort

THE "PREDOMINANT FORCE"

Playing—playing
Into field and   forgetting to die,
The streets smoothed over as fields,
Not even   the friction of wheels,
Feet off   ground:
As beyond effort, playing—
Music leaving no traces
Not dying, yet leaving no traces.
Nor any conscious effort,
Nor boiling to put pen to paper.
Perhaps a few things to remember
(Three there stealing in   thru the music
As pioneers moccasined stealing in thru the music).

Atheling—"There are different techniques   ,
Men write to be read, or spoken,
Or declaimed, or rhapsodized,
And quite differently to be sung;"
Carlos—"I heard him agonizing,
I saw him *inside;*"
Estlang—"Everything which
We really are and never quite live."
Far into (about three) in the morning,
The trainmen the most wide awake
                    "Weary, broken bodies," calling
Station on station, under earth
A thousand fiddles as beyond—
                    "Cold stone above thy head—"
                    Trainmen chanting

And again:

                    "He came and found them—
                    Sleeping, indeed their eyes were
                                        full of sleep."

Good night . . .

So the next day the reverses,
As if the music were only a taunt,
As if it had not kept, flower-cell in flower, liveforever
                    before the eyes, perfecting,—
I thought that was finished, Zukofsky,
Existence not even subsistence,

Worm eating the bark of the street tree,
Smoke sooting skyscraper chimneys,
That which has been looking for substitutes, tired,
Ready to give up the ghost in a cellar.

Remembering what?
Love, in your lap, in a taxi, unwilling—
A country of state roads and automobiles,
But the greatest number idle, shiftless, disguised on streets,
The excuse of the experts
'Production exceeds demand so we curtail employment,'
And the Wobblies hollering reply,
Yeah! but why don't you give us more than a meal
                    to increase the consumption!
While the great Magnus, before his confreres in industry,
Swallow tail, eating a sandwich,
"Road map to the stomach," grinning,
To a chart pointing, and between bites.

Dogs cuddling to lamposts
Lonely—look—what—maybe broken forged iron—
"We ran 'em in chain gangs, down in the Argentine,
Executive's not the word, use *engineer,*
Single-handed, ran 'em like soldiers,
Seventy-four yesterday, and could run 'em today,
Been fishin' all Easter
Nuthn' like nature for hell-fire!"
                    "Ye lightnings, ye thunders
                    In clouds are ye vanished?
                    Open, O fierce flaming pit!"

                              LOUIS ZUKOFSKY
                              (*Pagany*, Summer 1932)

4 The WANING OF CUBISM
in the Late 1930s to Early 1940s

As the various works included above amply show, the development and subsequent spread of cubist poetics in America continued with great intensity throughout the 1920s well into the 1930s. In 1932, for example, William Carlos Williams founded the second of his journals named *Contact*, just as George Oppen was composing *Discrete Series*, a volume that extends and modifies the possibilities of cubist verse. In addition, many of Ezra Pound's *Cantos* remained to be written, as did many of the books of Louis Zukofsky's *"A"*. In 1937, Wallace Stevens would publish what I regard to be his supreme synthetic cubist poem, "The Man with the Blue Guitar," while Williams continued the poetic experimentations that would ultimately culminate in *Paterson*. In fact, the impact of verbal cubism appears to have been felt throughout American poetry by the beginning of the 1930s. For example, although H. D. was developing more specifically what we have now come to call "revisionist" poetry during this period, something of the cubist aesthetic seems to have influenced her work as well, as the following excerpt from her 1931 "Sigil"[1] suggests:

Sigil

January 21, 1931

IF YOU take the moon   in your hands
and turn it round
(heavy, slightly tarnished platter)
you're there;

if you pull dry seaweed   from the sand
and turn it round
and wonder at the under-side's bright amber,
your eyes

look out as they did here
(you don't remember)
when my soul turned round,

perceiving the other-side of everything,
mullein leaf, dogwood leaf, moth wing
and dandelion seeds under the ground.

It is also true, however, that something of the great energy and
originality which fueled the development of American cubist poetry
throughout the twenties began to wane between the first and last years of
the thirties—essentially between the onset of the Great Depression and
the advent of World War II. Many of the more successful journals dis-
cussed above chose to or were forced to dissolve during this period, while
others (repeating the pattern already traced in Europe) turned more
exclusively toward surrealism. At the same time, at least in America, a new
conservative trend arose among American poets, so that even though
Stevens would publish "The Man with the Blue Guitar" during this period,
it is clear that by the end of the decade, he and other poets such as Yvor
Winters had ceased to favor the kind of poetic experimentation so charac-
teristic of the teens and twenties. In this regard, it proves especially ironic
that, while Stevens could not have known the kind of personal chaos
which now appears to have been the destructive inspiration for such
famous works of Picasso as his "Weeping Woman" (1937) and even "Guer-
nica" (1937),[2] he explicitly questions the ultimate consequences of the
destructive potential of cubism in the fifteenth canto of "The Man with
the Blue Guitar":

Is this picture of Picasso's, this "hoard
Of destructions," a picture of ourselves,

Now, an image of our society?
Do I sit, deformed, a naked egg,

Catching at Good-bye, harvest moon,
Without seeing the harvest or the moon?

Things as they are have been destroyed.
Have I?

It is precisely the question of *deformity*, in all its senses, that encouraged
Stevens (as well as others) to abandon the avant-garde—especially as the
ring of "Rien! Rien!" began to sound more ominous and fanatical in some
of the surrealist works—and to turn instead more energetically to the
realm of ideas and formal control which would ultimately be realized in
such poems as "Notes toward a Supreme Fiction."

In addition, I would argue that the combined interests of poetics and politics which had animated the American poetic experimentation of the early part of this century appear to have diverged during this decade, though only superficially so. Thus while James Laughlin would argue in 1936 that he had abandoned his prior faith in the "economist" for the "poet — the word-worker — who must lead,"[3] several new journals that appear more committed to political action than to poetically inspired reform (such as *The Marxist, The New Historian, The New Viewpoint,* and *Revolt*) were begun during this period.

Still, it is far from accurate to claim that cubism in American verse disappeared entirely during this period. Though it was not seen, perhaps, as frequently in the small magazines, nor pursued with such energy among groups of sympathetic poets, from a certain perspective cubist poetry appears to have become so thoroughly disseminated during this period, and so successfully absorbed by certain individual poets, that it may have subsequently become almost unrecognizable by its sheer familiarity. For example, after the publication of Stevens' remarkable poem mentioned above, the *Cantos* (many of which were written during and after the Second World War) were concluded, the completed *Paterson* was finally published in its entirety in 1973, and the finished *"A"* did not appear until the 1970s. Only recently have we begun to recognize the common cubist aesthetic behind these great American works. But in doing so, we also find a formidable foundation — however ironically cubism may be called a foundation — and an equally formidable tradition which has been realized, variously, over the subsequent years in the verse of Theodore Roethke, Robert Duncan, Charles Olson, and more recently in the work of L = A = N = G = U = A = G = E poets such as Ron Silliman. The end of the "cubist moment" in American verse is thus ultimately nothing but a fiction, even if it is true that by the mid-1940s the poetic climate in America had changed in obvious and significant ways.

Most obviously, the kind of collaborative effort among American poets in creating this new American verse was largely diffused by the end of the 1930s, and certainly by the middle of World War II. And although the cubist aesthetic appears to have continued to affect deeply several poets' poets (if not academicians' poets), it never achieved in the most critical sense what Gerald Bruns describes metaphorically as cultural "binding":[4]

> From a phenomenological point of view, it is in the question of a how a text becomes binding upon a community that the subject of politics and interpretation begins to emerge with proper clarity and as a substantive issue. One needs to speak here of the conditions that enable a text to

become forceful and to hold a community in its power. This community does not need to be a community of readers or interpreters.

Though speaking specifically of legal texts, the question of the relationship achieved between community and "text" is, with only a minor adjustment, critical to the question of the relationship achieved between the larger American community and cubist "texts" — or the cubist aesthetic, in general. For despite the sustained attempt of many of our best poets in the first part of this century to critique (rather than merely reflect) certain pending developments in our culture, such critiques appear not to have proved "binding" at all. It may even be true that not only did the new poetics fail to achieve a significant integration with society during this period (an integration clearly disdained and avoided by some of the more radical, if not anarchist, poets), but subsequently no poetics, no poetry, perhaps no individual poet at all has regained the place in cultural consciousness that was deemed not only possible but even probable by Walt Whitman. It is thus not merely how and why a text becomes binding that needs further serious study, but how and why a text — or the principle controlling a specific group of texts — does *not* become binding that needs equal attention as well.

Although this subject ultimately extends far beyond the realm of the present study, it appears that the unexpected economic crisis of the early 1930s — a crisis that was critically different in relation to society from the kind of "social revolutions" that had been occurring worldwide for nearly two hundred years — left a radical, even scandalous rift in American consciousness that has not and — perhaps cannot — be healed. During the Great Depression the rift between actual survival and American conscience (rather than mere consciousness) — between the pressing need for the dollar and the empowering belief in social dreams which had consistently animated American history and culture — widened to a point where the possibility for the convergence of poetic inspiration (and poetic production) with the economic structure (without which, the former cannot survive) was almost systematically precluded. Such a rift has not narrowed, but rather has widened with the subsequent, alarming confluence of economic and military concerns through World War II, the Korean War, the Vietnam War, and undefined wars in Central America. It may be that it was only during the Vietnam War, when this very confluence was challenged by a significant portion of our society, that anything like socially significant *poetry* (not merely popular verse) was almost realized again. This fact suggests something of the necessary conditions for the possibility of future poetic success in this country.[5]

Whether or not poetry will ever regain its historically central place in human culture remains to be seen. What is most important about the fourth phase in American cubist verse, at least in terms of this study, is the various attempts to fan the "fiery" breath that had fueled this "vital page in literary history" before its occasionally contemptuous and often painful dismissal. As Katinka Loeser would note in a poem written during the middle of World War II (included below), poetry had become "false and unfit": it was now "the time of prose"—and, one might add, a "time" which would herald the future development of prose in the form of criticism itself and, almost concurrently, new developments in the visual medium which have recently come to dominate our culture in the form of "videos."

Of the various poets considered so far, it is finally William Carlos Williams who provides the most visible link between the early development of cubist verse on American "soil" and its continued support (though we should note that Louis Zukofsky, coming a generation after Williams, was equally important from the late 1920s through recent times). In addition to contributing to nearly every magazine mentioned in this work, and in addition to his intimate involvement with *Blues* and *Pagany*, in 1932 he founded the second *Contact* specifically to promote the "significance of all writing which is the writing itself" ("Comment," *Contact*, 1, 1 [February 1932], 7–9).

The aesthetic/political conflict, however—or at least the ambiguity about the nature and extent of the involvement of aesthetic with political concerns—which began to be more prevalent during the thirties can also be seen in the various statements Williams published in the second *Contact*. For instance, in the opening "Comment" just cited, he adds that

> The words themselves must stand and fall as men. A writer has no use for theories and propaganda, he has use for but one thing, the word that is possessing him at the moment. . . . *A magazine without opinions or criteria other than words . . . such a magazine would be timely to a period such as this*. It can never be a question of its being read by a million or by anybody, in fact. (italics mine)

Notably, this apologia for his "effrontery" in beginning yet another new magazine sounds very much like Alfred Stieglitz' 1912 defense of Gertrude Stein's writing (published in *Camera Work*)—which was also a remarkably ingenious, if subversive, defense of Picasso's new cubist paintings[6]—as if Williams wished to strip poetry from the political rhetoric that had come to accompany most literary "manifestoes" after the beginning of the Great War.

However, *this* critical change, so contrary to the earlier call for political and poetic "revolution," appears to have its locus not in the Great

War, but in the Great Depression. Williams in fact appeals to the eco-nomic crisis of the times in the same "Comment": "You might say: People are in distress the world over, writing will not relieve them. . . . Why not take the money there is for a magazine like this and give it away — as food — to the bums, for instance, living in packing cases over near the East River these winter nights?" Yet, with an interesting gesture for a man so often revered for social concerns, Williams distinguishes the "value" of words (specifically of "good writing") from monetary value with a state-ment which ironically anticipates the later Stevens: "What in the world good are we any of us anyhow — except hypothetically, a pure question of the imagination?"

Despite the implicit, if not explicit, elitism of his opening "Com-ment," in the third issue of *Contact* Williams published another "Com-ment" which refocuses and refines his faith in the power of words as a social concern:

> There is a heresy, regarding the general character of poetry, which has become widely prevalent today and may shortly become more so through academic fostering*: it is that poetry increases in virtue as it is removed from contact with a vulgar world.
>
> I cannot swallow the half-alive poetry which knows nothing of totality.
>
> It is one of the reasons to welcome communism. Never, may it be said, has there ever been great poetry that was not born out of a commu-nist intelligence. They have all been rebels, against nothing so much as the schism that would have the spirit a lop sided affair of high and low.
>
> *Contact* 1, 3 (1932)
> (Williams' asterisk in the text refers to the recent
> appointment of Eliot at Harvard.)

Thus, at least when it comes to a certain kind of aesthetics (typified here by Eliot), evaluations — "opinions and criteria" — not only appear justifi-able but are grounded specifically in political rationale. The extension which *Contact* might suggest is that it is finally impossible for any maga-zine to be an organ "without opinions or criteria other than words."

Whatever actual criteria Williams was using in accepting or solicit-ing work for his new journal, it is not surprising that in his first issue he included several of the writers who were already publishing together as a kind of group. Cummings' poems include the somewhat scatological "'let's start a magazine'" and his now well-known "r-p-o-p-h-e-s-s-a-g-r," as well as "mouse)Won" and "ondumonde.'" Zukofsky's poems are quite similar to those published in *Blues* — the second one, in fact, is devoted to "Empty Bed/ Blues" — while Parker Tyler's "Poem" (actually a prose poem) demonstrates the continued influence of Gertrude Stein. Yet it is with more than a little humor that Williams also included "Micky [sic] Mouse and American Art" in this issue, an essay in which Diego Rivera argues that in the future all revolutionary "pictures and statues and poetry and prose" which might survive "the general cleansing of the world" will be regarded with "passionate curiosity":

> And the esthetes of that day will find that MICKEY MOUSE was one of the genuine heroes of American Art in the first half of the 20th Century, in the calendar anterior to the world revolution.
>
> *Contact* 1, 1 (February 1932), 39

Despite a first issue that seemed to promise the furthering of cubist poetry, the second *Contact* finally published far more prose than poetry. With the notable exceptions of Williams' own "The Canada Lily" and "The Cod Head" and Zukofsky's "Song 9" (see p. 257), subsequent issues of this magazine did little to promote or develop cubist verse. In fact, in the third issue, Yvor Winters published "Sonnet to the Moon," which is largely regular in form (and in title), even if somewhat fashionably cynical, as in such lines as "The lucent, thin, and alcoholic flame/ Runs in the stubble with a nervous aim" (*Contact* 1, 3 [1932], 48). In general, *Contact* proves most notable for the lengthy bibliography of little magazines compiled by David Moss, and the sections of what would be Nathanael West's *Miss Lonelyhearts* rather than for its poetry, a fact which anticipates the relatively rapid diminishment of cubist verse over this decade.

*****

Something of the continued interest in cubism in America poetry can be found during this period in *Trend* (different from *The Trend* discussed in Chapter One), although without the self-consciousness and exclusivity that mark some of the other journals. Thus, on the same page in which we find the cubist "portrait" written by James Henry Sullivan, we also find a perfectly traditional poem by Gervaise Butler (cited in part below):

> There never was a train went past
> Below me in the hollow
> But made me want to look my last
> Upon this place, and follow.
> — — — — — —
> Trains puff and pass the livelong day,
> Birds fly, by Spring and Fall,
> While I progress from clay to clay
> Behind a garden wall.
>
> *Trend* 2, 1 (1933), 24

The difference between the two poems—and the aesthetics (or even traditions) each represents—is made quite clear if Butler's poem is compared with Sullivan's (see p. 258). In addition to the obvious typographical difference, which includes Sullivan's interesting use of white space and an almost pictorial pattern of words, "portrait" is extremely self-conscious about the complex question of representation itself. In the end, the idea of a "portrait" is reduced to or exposed as "words" that "carve figurines/ on dreams," a strategy which repeats that of several cubist poems previously discussed and which anticipates current criticism as well.

Trend also reproduced the cubist-influenced "Roofs," a woodcut by Eugene Morley, as well as one of Juan Gris' synthetic compositions. Given its title and the relative paucity of cubist verse it published, *Trend* proves to be an interesting barometer for indicating the changing poetic climate in America, for it is at approximately this historical juncture that the force of cubism appears to have become more the province of individual poets (and usually in more lengthy, sustained works) than that of shared poetic ventures in modern avant-garde journals.

*****

At approximately the same time that Williams was organizing *Contact* or that *Trend* was (rather indecisively) publishing both traditional and cubist poetry, George Oppen began writing *Discrete Series,* a volume of verse that to the eye looks very similar to that of Williams, but which is, Oppen has argued, fundamentally different from that of his contemporary.[7] In fact, almost immediately, Babette Deutsch described Oppen's book as being "reminiscent of Dr. Williams"—and Williams endorsed the volume, while other critics referred to his work as "anti-poems," born of an "isolated, dried-up bladder."[8]

Early on, however, Ezra Pound distinguished the difference between the two writers, as has Marjorie Perloff more recently in "The Shape of the Lines," an essay in which she contrasts the "stability of pattern" in Williams' verse with the "discrete" or fragmented quality of Oppen's work.[9] Yet what may be most important about Perloff's contrast is the extension that, taken together, Williams and Oppen demonstrate succinctly the possibility of analytic and synthetic cubist verse in the domain of the short poem—between the intellectual study of form and the creation of a newly derived form born of fused or interpenetrating fragments. Although the entire volume of *Discrete Series* might be most accurately seen as one long synthetic cubist poem (which at least one critic comes close to articulat-

241

ing),[10] the "discrete" units of Oppen's volume also pose a complex questioning not only of temporality and space, but also of representation itself in a way that is characteristic of synthetic (versus analytic) cubist painting and the longer synthetic cubist poems mentioned above. The last page of this series, reproduced below, testifies to the complexity of each separate poetic grouping (and to their equally complex interrelations as well):[11]

Drawing

Not by growth
   But the
Paper, turned, contains
This entire volume

Deaths everywhere — — —
The world too short for trend is land — — —
   In the mouths,
     Rims

In this place, two geraniums
In your window-box
Are his life's eyes.

Written structure,
Shape of art,
More formal
Than a field would be
(existing in it) — — —
Her pleasure's
Looser;
'O — —'

    'Tomorrow?' — —

Successive
Happenings
(the telephone)

It is almost impossible to decide if the last page is a single poem called "DRAWING," if the word "drawing" is simply a line in a longer poem, or if it is the title for a very short "discrete" poem of only four lines. Such intense ambiguity is certainly not characteristic of the majority of Williams' verse.

Yet such a categorical distinction between Oppen and Williams fails, admittedly, to appreciate and to testify to the latter's poetic range in one significant way. As Williams' "Descent of Winter," published nearly a decade before in *The Exile,* amply demonstrates, Williams was himself capable of producing synthetic cubist verse of great complexity. What is most important as a register of the difference between these two poets is not finally the "analytical" preference of the one and the "synthetic" preference of the other, but rather the continued faith Williams placed in the power of words over the next decades versus Oppen's recoil at participating in the very "written structure" which constitutes and sustains both our socio-political structures and our linguistic structures. The institutionalization of modern poetry as a "right wing tradition" in the 1930s undermined, for Oppen at least, any attempt to fight the "hegemony of the dons, of Eliot, the Church of England, and of agrarianism," while Pound's subsequent political stand reinforced the felt need for a rupture between poetry and politics.[12]

That Oppen did resume writing in the 1960s marks another political stand, and that his recent work is still largely cubist does as well, with possibly even more reverberating possibilities. In his recent verse, such as "Of Hours," white space becomes a space of silence, a place for *conversion* in which what was "unteachable" in words finds a threshold for knowledge defined in its very distance:[13]

Of Hours

. . . as if a nail whose wide head
were time and space . . '

at the nail's point the hammer-blow
undiminished

Holes   pitfalls open
In the cop's accoutrement

Crevasse

The destitute metal

Jail metal

Impoverished   Intimate
As a Father did you know that

Old friend   old poet
Tho you'd walked

Familiar streets
And glittered with change the circle

THE WANING OF CUBISM

Destroyed its content
Persists   the common

Place   image
The initial light   Walk on the walls

The walls of the fortress   the countryside
Broad in the night light the sap rises

Out of obscurities the sap rises
The sap not exhausted   Movement
Of the stone   Music
Of the tenement

Also is this lonely theme   Earth
My sister

Lonely sister my sister but why did I weep
Meeting that poet again what was that rage

Before Leger's art poster
In war time Paris perhaps art

Is one's mother and father   O rage
Of the exile   Fought ice

Fought shifting stones
Beyond the battlement

Crevasse   Fought

No man
But the fragments of metal
Tho there were men there were men   Fought
No man but the fragments of metal
Burying my dogtag with H
For Hebrew in the rubble of Alsace

I must get out of here

Father   he thinks   *father*

Disgrace of dying

Old friend   old poet
If you did not look

What is it you 'loved'
Twisting your voice   your walk

Wet roads

Hot sun on the hills

He walks twig-strewn streets
Of the rain

Walks homeward

Unteachable

If we accept the majority of American cubist verse as being resistant to dominant and dominating political structures both realized and supported by traditional linguistic structures, then Oppen's silence for a quarter of a century must be regarded as a supreme cubist "expression," however ironically we may call it that. For even if prompted by the desire for social action, Oppen's silence exposes the possibility that the ethical stand of a cubist aesthetic (that is, the validation of multiplicity and the questioning of any dogmatic or totalitarian perspective) is itself merely illusory and that continued participation in meaningful linguistic structures simply perpetuates (rather than "resists") the problem. In this way, cubism turns back on itself, admitting that even its "stand" is, itself, "a perspective" potentially open to misuse.

Such a complex, ambiguous state of the relationship between poetics and politics as is indicated by both Williams and Oppen may clarify why, with increasing intensity, some poets would want to divorce aesthetic concerns from political or social issues—to engage in artistic appreciation and production without recourse to political judgment. This remains, I think, one of our most critical cultural issues and one which will have to be conscientiously debated again, not only as a function of our increasing awareness that all language is political (even when unintentionally), but also as a function of increasing revelations about famous artists of this period, including Picasso himself, Pound, and even Stevens.[14]

In this regard, James Laughlin's opening remarks (cited in the previous chapter) in his anthology of *New Directions in Prose and Poetry,* published in 1936, more clearly look backward in time to the self-consciously politicized language of the intended revolutions during and after the Great War and forward to recent historical and theoretical criticism.[15] His contemporaneous evaluation of what he loosely calls "experimental writing" as something intimately involved with "social reform," and therefore implicitly ethical in the deepest sense, is a specific reminder that however consciously "destructive" a faction of the artists during this period may have been, in America at least, with its own Whitmanesque tradition connecting freedom and free verse, the emphasis tended to fall on creative reform and possibility rather than merely on destructive deformation.

Reformation is not, however, without danger. The ambiguity and anxiety inherent in any attempt to "reform" is also clarified in Laughlin's introduction when he says, with what seems to be the growing American sentiment, that "If the community allows one word to mean two things mistakes will be made by its members in their social actions. And if we allow many words to mean, in effect, nothing at all we shall be eligible for the presidency of a large university, a national trust, or a legislative body." And against this state of Babel (his term), Laughlin urges the "word worker" to create new social concepts — since, he says, "language is at once the cause and the cure" of the "world in crisis." In other words, simultaneously with the desire for reform and experimentation, Laughlin expresses what we might accurately call a logocentric desire for surety in meaning that is, itself, necessarily complicated by the very cubist aesthetic which questions all tradition (including the tradition — or perhaps genre — of "meaning" itself).

Laughlin includes Gertrude Stein, Ezra Pound, and Louis Zukofsky in this special volume dedicated to those "who have begun successfully THE REVOLUTION OF THE WORD," as well as Gorham Munson ("New Directions in Economics") and E. E. Cummings. In addition, Jean Cocteau and Eugène Jolas appear among the pages. However, so do Marianne Moore, William Carlos Williams, Elizabeth Bishop, and Wallace Stevens (among others). Some of the pieces appear specifically cubist, such as Cummings' "Three Poems," Williams' "Perpetuum Mobile: The City," and Zukofsky's "'Mantis': An Interpretation," a synthetic cubist poem which self-consciously *represents* the traditionally-lined "'Mantis'" which precedes it in the text. (In fact, among the accessible cubist works that appear in Laughlin's collection, and which are consequently not reprinted in this volume, are Pound's "Canto XLVI" and a number of poems by Cummings.)

Other works either appear to be more traditional or are more difficult to place. In this regard, Bishop provides a very interesting juncture, particularly in her early verse, for combining what were often divergent streams — specifically, a concern with traditional poetic form together with surrealistic themes. As Cocteau says in "The Laic Mystery," which had been printed earlier in *Pagany*, "Picasso. Chirico. Futurists. Expressionists. The newer generation combines them, refines them — but can no more get away from them than from Ducasse or Rimbaud."[16]

In general, this volume of *New Directions* is one of the later and more successful gatherings of the force of cubism in American verse, but a collection already marked by a certain editorial conservatism (despite Laughlin's continued support of modern poetry) that would become increasingly common within the next three or four years.

*****

Of the works reprinted here from *New Directions,* one deserves additional comment. At least in this particular context, and at this particular time, Wallace Stevens' "A Thought Revolved" bears a highly complex relation to cubism that anticipates that of "The Man with the Blue Guitar," written the following year. While the title and sectional numberings are cubist in a way similar to those of the early "Thirteen Ways of Looking at a Blackbird," both the form of "A Thought Revolved," in which each section is composed of regular metrical patterns and regular rhymes, and the content, which is highly problematic, complicate the poem's (and poet's) relation to cubism, especially in the third and fourth sections.

"A Thought Revolved" invites us to compare it with "The Man with the Blue Guitar" published the following year. Although one critic has recently described the latter poem as a surrealist poem,[17] in strategy and theme it seems far more cubist than surrealist. The lines from the fifteenth canto cited above, for example, exhibit the tendency toward collage — not only by referring to Picasso, to his own words (and therefore to another verbal "text"), but also by integrating and then changing the context of words from a popular song, "Good-bye, Good-bye Harvest Moon."[18] Furthermore, as Stevens clarifies in his letters, the various sections of the poem are composed as contrasts, as a shifting of perspective toward the complicated issue of "things as they are." "The Man with the Blue Guitar" is genuinely, in a way that the poem given the title is not, "A Thought Revolved" — and one revolved in a very cubist fashion.

In this poem, however, Stevens also explicitly rejects (again in Canto XV) the very destructive element of cubism that was so exploited in surrealist works and that was becoming increasingly popular at the time. Stevens' specific rejection of surrealism only a few years later is therefore consistent with this poem rather than contradictory.[19] And, I should add, the purely creative aspect of art (rather than its destructive counterpart) that Stevens celebrates in the closing lines of this poem when he writes, "Here is the bread of time to come/ here is its actual stone . . ./ We shall forget by day, except/ The moments when we choose to play/ The imagined pine, the imagined jay," is also celebrated by Williams in his tribute to Charles Sheeler's work only two years later: "It is ourselves we seek to see upon the canvas, as no one ever saw us, before we lost our courage and our love. . . . A picture at its best is pure exchange. . . . I think Sheeler at his best is that, a way of painting powerfully articulate."[20] Although Williams is discussing Sheeler's entire corpus, such a description of one of the more prominent American cubist painters once again reinforces the American interpretation of cubism as something ultimately creative, encouraging community, rather than something destructive and essentially anarchistic.

Yet despite important vestiges of cubism in American poetry, it is also true that by 1939 both American politics and American poetics were immersed in a very different atmosphere—as a look at one more "little magazine" founded at this moment suggests—than in that which had been prevalent when the decade began. And part of the new climate, whether for better or worse, was an essential abandonment of cubist poetics, partially prompted by a specific, political loss of faith in the power and possibilities of change itself.

Initially, at least, *Furioso,* edited by James Angleton and Reed Whittemore, appears to be a direct descendant of the kind of magazine we have considered thus far. The first issue, for example, which appeared in the summer of 1939, includes Ezra Pound's "Introductory Text-Book" (an economics pamphlet of sorts), a poem by E. E. Cummings, and one by Pat Haynes that testifies to the growing influence of Cummings (see p. 274). Something of a major rupture in American poetics—and among American poets—is, however, witnessed between the first and second issues of this journal. Despite the assumption of a "Pound/Williams" tradition, in the second issue of *Furioso* Williams specifically denigrates "Propaganda in Poetry. Poetry that tries to influence people" with the specific examples of Pound (who "says that everything he's written has economic implications"), Genevieve Taggard (whose works say "'better read Marx'"), and an "extreme case," the "concepts that walk around as T. S. Eliot" (*Furioso,* 1, 2 [1940], 21). Williams goes so far as to say that "what men seldom learn is that the end of poetry is a poem," thus sounding much like Wallace Stevens, who two years later says that a poet does not owe "any more as a social obligation than he owes as a moral obligation."[21] Ironically it is Stevens who redefines the appeal to pure aesthetics (if that is possible) as a socially and politically contextualized necessity: "The truth is," Stevens writes, "that the social obligation so closely urged is a phase of the pressure of reality which a poet (in the absence of dramatic poets) is bound to resist or evade today."[22]

It is therefore all the more significant that after publishing three of Cummings' poems in the third issue (one of which is included here), *Furioso* appears to abandon its interest in the more avant-garde work—including cubism in particular—in favor of a different (though not finally traditional) sort of poetry, characterized in part by Stevens' "Poem with

Rhythms" or "The Pastor Caballero." As Frank Lentricchia has recently remarked in a book appropriately entitled *Ariel and the Police*,[23]

> The fundamental hope in Stevens is political — though neither Stevens nor his critics are comfortable with that word: it is conspicuously absent from their discourse — and he is politically hopeful, moreover, in the idealist tradition running from Schiller to Marcuse in which the aesthetic is the antithesis to the totalitarian story Foucault narrates in *Discipline and Punish.*

Although I would add that such a "fundamental hope" (rather than a mere knee-jerk, reactionary defense) defines much of the impetus behind many other "idealist" poets and artists during this period, it is especially important to note, given the immediate historical context of these artists, that Lentricchia continues his remark with a disturbing warning: that the aesthetic as antithesis to totalitarianism "may well be one of the subtlest effects of an incipient totalitarianism and its culture." Here, the irony of Pound's virtually concurrent radio pronouncements in support of a fascist regime proves almost unspeakably bitter and ominous.

In addition to these specifically political divergences in modern American poetics, ultimately the sheer passage of time — which means, among other things, that the editors of the journals being founded at the beginning of World War II were literally of a different generation than the editors of most of the journals discussed thus far — contributed to the widening gap between what had been an historical *intention* in the "revolution of the word" and the received tradition of that very poetry. Reed Whittemore, for instance, one of the founding editors of *Furioso*, remarks — to our surprise — in his pamphlet, "Little Magazines," that he has "never seen a copy of *The Little Review* and so must depend on secondary sources and on *The Little Review Anthology*."[24] Yet, at the same time, the pamphlet gives a very detailed history of Ezra Pound's involvement in the "little magazines" (which he notably defines this way: "a little magazine is a serious magazine or a serious magazine is a little magazine").[25] Despite its rather obvious attempt to be politically involved, then, *Furioso,* and more specifically the people connected to it as editors and contributors, stand at a particular historical moment when what Whittemore himself calls "civilization-saving in literature" had become simultaneously an historical tradition (and therefore counter to its own interest) and challenged by a new, politically removed aestheticism which achieved its own intensely ironic expression in the Bollingen Award of 1949.[26]

Within this very complicated context, two issues of *Furioso* deserve special mention: the summer issue of 1941 and the fall issue of 1947, both of which exhibit the impact of and a simultaneous resistance to cubism in American verse. In the summer of 1941, for example, *Furioso* printed four poems by Wallace Stevens, three of which deviate typographically (in particular, with unexpected white space) from the way in which they are reprinted in his own volumes of poetry. The deviations in "Woman Looking at a Vase of Flowers" and "The Well Dressed Man with a Beard" are quite minor, but in "Les Plus Belles Pages" (reprinted here), Stevens initially appears to have toyed with white space in the text in a characteristically cubist manner. However, close inspection suggests that such "experimentation" here is nonexistent—each unexpected spacing occurs between the end of a sentence and the beginning of the next and, therefore, at a *logical space,* but does not alter meanings between words or function as a part of the meaning itself. And, in fact, the other poem published with this group, "Poem with Rhythms," suggests at least in its title a certain opposition to what had become the reigning "tradition" of experimental poetry. It seems likely, then, that the typographical layout of "Les Plus Belles Pages" is an error of the sort Stevens had complained about only a few months before:[27]

> Often in my manuscript I leave broad space in short lines that follow long lines in order that the short lines will not look so short. This is merely something for the eye. The stenographer usually copies these spaces because she thinks they mean something. But they don't mean a thing except to the eye. Then the printer comes along and repeats these spaces, doing exactly what no printer should do, that is, leaving holes in the lines. . . . I say this because I don't want you to get the idea that I believe in queer punctuation.

Four years earlier, he had written to Ronald Latimer (in response to the printing of *The Man with the Blue Guitar*) that he has "a horror of poetry pretending to be contemporaneous because of typographical queerness."[28] The implication is that he wants to be regarded as genuinely contemporary because of what he has to say (a theme which he explores specifically in "Of Modern Poetry"). Yet surely we can feel some sympathy for the printers' errors here, given the context of the other poetry being published for over two decades, for assuming that deviations from traditional poetic alignment were intentional and (ironically) meaningful.

The other issue of *Furioso* which deserves special attention, the fall issue of 1947, appears to make a certain joke which has bearing on this study. The contents are advertised as "POETRY BEFORE PICASSO" and "POETRY AFTER PICASSO," thus pointing to a self-conscious awareness of the changed aesthetic in poetry as a function of cubist perspective. The joke, however, is that there is no significant difference in this issue between those poems "before" and "after" Picasso. It is merely that four poets' work precedes, in literal pagination, several drawings by Picasso, which are in turn followed by the work of several other poets.

Thus, with *Furioso*, we find a very precise example of the aesthetic battle which was being waged just before and during World War II—a battle in which, to a large degree, the earlier cubist "revolution" was either "resisted" (as indicated above) or replaced (as in *View*, founded in 1940 by the same editor who had earlier begun *Blues*). Nevertheless, the impact of cubism on American verse can still be found in *Furioso* as late as 1952, in Ernest Kroll's "The Problem" and "The Swifts." The first of these is particularly interesting, for it appears to allude to Jeanne D'Orge's "The Problem Is," included in the special issue of *Others*, "for the Mind's eye," thirty-five years before:

> The problem is—
>   but I have forgot—there is no problem.
>   I have only to put my sea
>   into a bottle of thin green glass
>   simple of form, as you suggest;
>   and to enclose my sky
>   in a carven case of pure ivory.
>   The test will be
>   when these stand upon your writing-table.
>   Will my sea fill the room
>   with its salt and its singing,
>   with wine, with vigor and movement?
>   Will my sky escape
>   lean over and give
>   her suns and moons
>   and the lightning of her silence
>   and the manna of rest
>   and musical sleep?
>
>   *Others* (December 1917), 16

Curiously, Stevens' "The Poem that Took the Place of the Mountain," which bears a marked affinity to both D'Orge's and Kroll's poems, would appear about six months after Kroll's poem (in *The Hudson Review* 5, 3 [Autumn 1952]). In turn, it should be noted, Kroll's "The Swifts" seems a cubist conflation (albeit a simplistic one) of Stevens' 1916 "Domination of Black" and the concluding lines of Keats' "To Autumn."

Yet, despite the continued influence of cubism that Kroll's poems might suggest,[29] the changed attitude among American poets, especially after the end of the Second World War, is summarized by another poem published in *Furioso* in 1952, Lora Dunetz' "And on the Other Hand," which dismisses both Pound and language that violates poetic and semantic norms:

And on the Other Hand

"To write a poetry that can be carried as a communication between intelligent men"
                                                                    The Serious Artist — Ezra Pound

You on the one hand
Saying nothing
For many pages
That is not style says Ezra—
And he on the other hand
Communicating in his own private language
(Shall we call it Esperanto). . .
The most effective way
To say nothing
Is
To keep quiet
To which end *io studio quanto posso*
But find it
Very
Difficult.

                                                                    Furioso 7, 3 (1952), 47

The selections which follow from this journal therefore trace a period of transition in American verse in which the specifically "evolutionary" intention of a new verbal aesthetic is either diffused or actually rejected. It is all the more poignant that Whittemore notes that "When we *stopped* publication" (his italics) of the journal (which never had more than four hundred subscribers, despite its relative longevity), "we began to be told what a good and important publication *Furioso* had been."[30]

*****

Finally, though not an intrinsic part of this study, *View* testifies to another important artistic strain in America during World War II — the rise of surrealism, either as a reaction against or as a reflection of the horrors of World War II. Founded by Charles Henri Ford (who had earlier been the founding editor of *Blues*), *View* begins in 1940 with at least a superficial resemblance to his earlier magazine. Parker Tyler appears, for example, in the first issue, as does Wallace Stevens. Very quickly, however, the journal changed in both format and content. Despite the appearance of Tyler, Cummings, and Zukofsky in later issues, the specific aesthetic interest of *View* is dominated almost exclusively by surrealism. (The sixth issue may feature "Anti-Surrealist Dali," by Nicolas Colas, but the next issue, edited by Colas, is billed as the "All-Surrealist Number" and includes André Breton and Max Ernst, among others.)

Yet these issues seem relatively benign compared to those that would follow — such as the April, 1943 issue, which includes the "Children's Page," or many of the subsequent issues which are increasingly obsessed with violence, death, pestilence, and destruction. Curiously, Stevens' "Materia Poetica" (which, itself, bears a resemblance to a verbal collage) appears not once, but twice, in *View,* overtly denouncing surrealism: "The essential fault of surrealism is that it invents without discovering. To make a clam play an accordion is to invent not to discover."[31] Another of the adages printed in "Materia Poetica," however, points backward to the entire period we have been examining and to the aesthetic battle which became heightened just before the Second World War began: *"All poetry is experimental poetry,"* he insists, with something of the same resistance to the "tradition" of modernist poetry that he felt in 1948 when he complained that

> the world in general is not really moving forward. There is no music because the only music tolerated is modern music. There is no painting because the only painting permitted is painting derived from Picasso or Matisse.[32]

Whether the American poets of this period tended to side with the more radical expressions that had already become commonplace in Europe or with something closer to traditional poetry (in the sense suggested by Madison Cawein's "Waste Land"), it is clear from both *Furioso* and *View* that by the middle of the Second World War the poetic climate, as well as the political climate, of America had changed utterly. In fact, when Oscar Williams produced his *New Poems 1944,* an anthology of American and British poets, with, notably, a "Selection of Poems from the Armed Forces," he said quite pointedly that he "omitted a number of fairly well-known modern young poets who are imitating each other to death and to the death of their audiences. In a sense this anthology serves a corrective to such verse, anemophilous from all points of the compass."[33] The dismissal of the new "modern young poets" stands in utter contrast to Sanborn's earlier enthusiasm for the "kindling breath" that had, thirty years before, fueled a new kind of poetry in America. With Oscar Williams' pronouncement, then, I think we can say that this "vital page in literary history" had indeed come to an end — despite the fact that, as numerous critics would argue, the impact of cubism continues to be felt in nearly all the arts today.

But more provocatively, perhaps, something of a *lament* for what may have been lost during this very page in literary history that we have been examining—as well as an explicit criticism of the kind of verse it produced—is expressed by Katinka Loeser in a poem entitled "modern language," also published during World War II:

modern language

this is the time of prose
the lyric sticks in the taut dry throat
the alexandrine will not come again
the sonnet is tacit remote.

the phrase is proper
do not condone the independent clause
there is only time for the tight sparse words
of exigency   and the pause.

do not punctuate
the rules are false and unfit
the monosyllabic message requires
no grammatical guarded permit

for the few
the singing is done   the stanza is gone
we shall relinquish even the paragraph
in staccato communication

Trend 1, 2 (February 1942), 8

Although Loeser's disturbing prophecy of what may be happening to modern language and, therefore, to modern culture, is historically specific, her poem demonstrates the actual impact of an aesthetic she appears to reject (with the two white "pauses" and irregular punctuation) while anticipating a "post-modern" understanding of language—an understanding that has ramifications that extend well into contemporary criticism and theory. It is this critical legacy, rather than the continuance or vestige of cubist poetry in contemporary verse, to which I wish briefly to turn in the conclusion.

CONTACT

Four Poems

1.

"let's start a magazine
to hell with literature
we want something redblooded

lousy with pure
reeking with stark
and fearlessly obscene

but really clean
get what I mean
let's not spoil it
let's make it serious

something authentic and delirious
you know something genuine like a mark
in a toilet

graced with g·ts and g·tted
with grace"

squeeze your n·ts and open your face

4.

ondumonde"
(first than caref
ully ;pois
edN-o wt he
n
,whysprig
       sli
nkil
-Y-
  strol(pre)ling(cise)dy(ly)na(
   mite)
    ;yearnswoons:
    &Isdensekil-
     ling-whipAlert-floatScor
     ruptingly)

          ca-y-est
         droppe5
        qu'es-ce que tu
        Dwrith
       il est trop fort le negre
      esn7othingish8s
     c'est fini
    pRaW,1T;o:
   allons
    9
   &

   .

        (musically-who?
pivoting
SmileS
"ahlbrhoon

E. E. Cummings
(*Contact*, August 1932)

Song 9

In Arizona
   (how many years in the mountains)
The small stumped bark of a tree
Looks up
    in the shape of an adored pup

The indians do not approach it
The round indian tents
     remain where they are
The tanned whites
      are never seen by it
And one can imagine its imploring eyes

The skies
    it seems to look up to
     are always blue
The same sun that warms the desert
Warms what one
    can imagine to be its ears.

        LOUIS ZUKOFSKY
        (*Contact*, Oct. 1932)

TREND

portrait

his voluntary words
carve figurines
on his involuntary dreams

he considers an intrepid mist
where forms plunge
      and lunge
        and fret
      undefined

where continuous stones
          groan
    and form shapes
      that rise uncut
    where eyes stare
    in a misty haze
        of days

and plunge
and lunge
and fret

      as words
    carve figurines
    on dreams

JAMES HENRY SULLIVAN
(*Trend*, 2, 1, 1933)

NEW DIRECTIONS

A Thought Revolved

THE MECHANICAL OPTIMIST

A lady dying of diabetes
Listened to the radio,
Catching the lesser dithyrambs.
So heaven collects its bleating lambs.

Her useless bracelets fondly fluttered,
Paddling the melodic swirls,
The idea of God no longer sputtered
At the roots of her indifferent curls.

The idea of the Alps grew large,
Not yet, however, a thing to die in.
It seemed serener just to die,
To float off on the floweriest barge,

Accompanied by the exegesis
Of familiar things in a cheerful voice,
Like the night before Christmas and all the carols.
Dying lady, rejoice, rejoice!

II

MYSTIC GARDEN & MIDDLING BEAST

The Poet striding among the cigar stores,
Ryan's lunch, hatters, insurance and medicines,
Denies that abstraction is a vice except
To the fatuous. These are his infernal walls,
A space of stone, of inexplicable base
And peaks outsoaring possible adjectives.
One man, the idea of man, that is the space,
The true abstract in which he promenades.
The era of the idea of man, the cloak
And speech of Virgil dropped, that's where he walks,
That's where his hymns come crowding, hero-hymns,

Chorals for mountain voices and the moral chant,
Happy rather than holy but happy-high,
Day hymns instead of constellated rhymes,
Hymns of the struggle of the idea of God
And the idea of man, the mystic garden and
The middling beast, the garden of Paradise
And he that created the garden and peopled it.

III
ROMANESQUE AFFABULATION

He sought an earthly leader who could stand
Without Panache, without cockade,
Son only of man and sun of men,
The outer captain, the inner saint,

The pine, the pillar and the priest,
The voice, the book, the hidden well,
The faster's feast and heavy-fruited star,
The father, the beater of the rigid drums,

He that at midnight touches the guitar,
The solitude, the barrier, the Pole
In Paris, celui qui chante et pleure,
Winter devising summer in its breast,

Summer assaulted, thundering, illumed,
Shelter yet thrower of the summer spear,
With all his attributes no god but man
Of men whose heaven is in themselves,

Or else whose hell, foamed with their blood
And the long echo of their dying cry,
A fate intoned, a death before they die,
The race that sings and weeps and knows not why.

IV
THE LEADER

Behold the moralist hidalgo,
Whose whore is Morning Star
Dressing in metal, silk and stone,
Syringa, cicada, his flea.

In how severe a book he read,

Until his nose grew thin and taut
And knowledge dropped upon his heart
Its pitting poison, half the night.

He liked the nobler works of man,
The gold façade round early squares,
The bronzes liquid through gay light.
He hummed to himself at such a plan.

He sat among beggars wet with dew,
Heard the dogs howl at barren bone,
Sat alone, his great toe like a horn,
The central flaw in the solar morn.

WALLACE STEVENS
(*New Directions in Poetry and Prose*, 1936)

Perpetuum Mobile: The City

      —a dream
we dreamed
      each
separately
      we two
of love
      and of
desire—

that fused
in the night

in the   distance
      over
the meadows—

        by day
impossible—

      The city
disappeared
      when
we arrived—

261

              A dream
a little false
toward which
              now

we stand
              and stare
transfixed—

All at once
              in the east
rising!

              All white!

              small
as a flower —

a locust cluster
a shad bush
              blossoming

Over the swamps
              a wild
magnolia bud—
              greenish
white
a northern
              flower—

And so
              we live
              looking—

At night
              it wakes
On the black
              sky—

a dream
              toward which
we love—

at night
          more
than a little
          false—

We have bred
we have dug
we have figured up
our costs
we have bought
an old rug—

We batter at our
unsatisfactory
          brilliance—

There is no end
          to desire—

Let us break
          through
and go there—
in
                    vain!

—delectable
          amusement:

Milling about—

Money! in
armoured trucks—
Two men
          walking
at two paces from
          each other
their right hands
          at the hip—

on the butt of
an automatic—

till they themselves
hold up the bank

THE WANING OF CUBISM

and themselves
        drive off
for themselves
        the money
in an armoured car—

    For love!

Carefully
    carefully tying
carefully

      selected
wisps of long
dark hair
    wisp
by wisp
upon the stubbs
of his kinky wool —

For two hours
three hours
    they worked—
    until
he coiled
    the thick
knot upon
that whorish head—

Dragged
    insensible
upon his face
by the lines—
—a running horse

    For love!

Their eyes
    blown out—

—for love, for love!

Neither the rain
nor the storm —

can keep them

      for love!

from the daily
accomplishment
      of their
appointed rounds —

Guzzling
the cream foods
      while
out of sight
      in
the sub-cellar —
the waste fat
the old vegetables
      chucked down
a chute
      the foulest
sink in the world—

And go

on the out-tide
ten thousand
      cots
floating to sea
      like weed
that held back
the pristine ships—

And fattened there
      an eel
in the water pipe—

      No end—
There!
      There!

THE WANING OF CUBISM

There!

        —a dream
of lights
        hiding
the iron reason
         and stone
a settled
        cloud—

City
        whose stars
of matchless
        splendor—

        and
in bright-edged
         clouds
        the moon—
        bring
silence
        breathlessly—

Tearful city
        on a summer's day
the hard grey
        dwindling
in a wall of
        rain—

        farewell!

WILLIAM CARLOS WILLIAMS
(*New Directions in Poetry and Prose*, 1936)

"Mantis"

Mantis! praying mantis! since your wings' leaves
And your terrified eyes, pins, bright, black and poor
Beg—"Look, take it up" (thoughts' torsion)! "save it!"

I who can't bear to look, cannot touch — You —
You can — but no one sees you steadying lost
In the cars' drafts on the lit subway stone

Praying mantis, what wind-up brought you, stone
On which you sometimes prop, prey among leaves
(Is it love's food your raised stomach prays?), lost
Here, stone holds only seats on which the poor
Ride, who rising from the news may trample you —
The shops' crowds a jam with no flies in it.

Even the newsboy who now sees knows it
No use, papers make money, makes stone, stone,
Banks, "it is harmless," he says moving on — You?
Where will he put *you?* There are no safe leaves
To put you back in here, here's news! too poor
Like all the separate poor to save the lost.

Don't light on my chest, mantis! do — you're lost,
Let the poor laugh at my fright, then see it:
My shame and theirs, you whom old Europe's poor
Call spectre, strawberry, by turns; a stone —
You point — they say — you lead lost children — leaves
Close in the paths men leave, saved, safe with you.

Killed by thorns (once men), who now will save you
Mantis? what male love bring a fly, be lost
Within your mouth, prophetess, harmless to leaves
And hands, faked flower, — the myth is: dead, bones, it
Was assembled, apes wing in wind: On stone,
Mantis, you will die, touch, beg, of the poor.

Android, loving beggar, dive to the poor
As your love would even without head to you,
Graze like machined wheels, green, from off this stone
And preying on each terrified chest, lost
Say, I am old as the globe, the moon, it
Is my old shoe, yours, be free as the leaves.

Fly, mantis, on the poor, arise like leaves
The armies of the poor, strength: stone on stone
And build the new world in your eyes, Save it!

267

THE WANING OF CUBISM

"MANTIS," AN INTERPRETATION
OR NOMINA SUNT CONSEQUENTIA RERUM
NAMES ARE SEQUENT TO THE THINGS NAMED

Mantis! praying mantis! since your wings' leaves

 Incipit Vita Nova
 le parole...
 almeno la loro sentenzia
the words...
at least their substance

at first were
"The mantis opened its body
It had been lost in the subway
It steadied against the drafts
It looked up—
Begging eyes—
It flew at my chest"

   —The ungainliness
  of the creature needs stating.

No one would be struck merely
By its ungainliness,
Having seen the thing happen.

Having seen the thing happen,
There would be no intention 'to write it up,'

But *all* that was happening,
The mantis itself only an incident, *compelling any writing*
The transitions were perforce omitted.

Thoughts'—two or three or five or
Six thoughts' reflection (pulse's witness) of what was happening
All immediate, not moved by any transition.

Feeling this, what should be the form
Which the ungainliness already suggested
Should take?

   —Description—lightly—ungainliness
  With a grace unrelated to its surroundings.

Grace there is perhaps
In the visual sense, not in the movement of
"eyes, pins, bright, black and poor."

Or considering more than the isolation
Of one wrenched line,

Consider:
"(thoughts' torsion)"
la battaglia delli diversi pensieri . . .
the battle of diverse thoughts—
The actual twisting
Of many and diverse thoughts

What form should *that* take
      —The first words that came into mind
   "The mantis opened its body—"
   Which might deserve the trope:
   the feeling of the original which is a permanence
  ?

Or the feeling accompanying the first 27 words' inception
the original which is a permanence
?),
That this thoughts' torsion
Is really a sestina
Carrying subconsciously
Many intellectual and sensual properties of the forgetting and
                           remembering Head

One human's intuitive Head

           Dante's rubric
             Incipit
          Surréaliste
          Re-collection

A twisted shoe by a pen, an insect, lost,
"To the short day and the great sweep of shadow."

The sestina, then, the repeated end words
Of the lines' winding around themselves,
Since continuous in the Head, whatever has been read,

269

> whatever is heard,
> whatever is seen

Perhaps goes back cropping up again with
Inevitable recurrence again in the blood
Where the spaces of verse are not visual
But a movement,
With vision in the lines merely a movement.

What is most significant
Perhaps is that C — and S — and X — of the 19th century
Used the "form" — not the form but a Victorian
Stuffing like upholstery
For parlor polish,
And our time takes count against them
For their blindness and their   (unintended?)   cruel smugness.

Again: as an experiment, the sestina would be wicker-work —
As a force, one would lie to one's feelings not to use it

One feels in fact inevitably
About the coincidence of the mantis lost in the subway,
About the growing oppression of the poor —
Which is the situation most pertinent to us —
With the fact of the sestina:
Which together fatally now crop up again
To twist themselves anew
To record not a sestina, post Dante,
Nor even a mantis.

Is the poem then, a sestina
Or not a sestina?

The word sestina has been
Taken out of the original title. It is no use (killing oneself?)

> — Our world will not stand it,
> the implications of a too regular form.

Hard to convince even one likely to show interest in the matter
That this regularity to which 'write it up' means not a damn
(Millet in a Dali canvas, Circe in E's Cantos)
Whatever seeming modelling after the event,
649 years, say, after Dante's first canzone,

If it came back immediately as the only
Form that will include the most pertinent subject of our day—
The poor—
Cannot mean surely implied comparison, unreality
Usually interpreted as falsity.

Too much time cannot be saved
Saying:
The mantis might have heaped up upon itself a
Grave of verse,
But the facts are not a symbol.

There is the difference between that
And a fact (the mantis in the subway)
And all the other facts the mantis sets going about it.

No human being wishes to become
An insect for the sake of a symbol.

But the mantis *can start*
History etc.
The mantis situation remains its situation,
Enough worth if the emotions can equate it.

"I think" of the mantis
"I think" of other things—
The quotes set repulsion
Into movement.

Repulsion—
Since one, present, won't touch the mantis,
Will even touch the poor—

but carefully.

The mantis, then
Is a small incident of one's physical vision
Which is the poor's helplessness
The poor's separateness
Bringing self-disgust.

The mantis is less ungainly than that.

There should be today no use for a description of it
Only for a "movement" emphasizing its use, since it's been
around,

271

An accident in the twisting
Of many and diverse "thoughts"
I.e. nerves, glandular facilities, electrical cranial charges

For example—
line 1—entomology
line 9—biology
lines 10 and 11— the even rhythm of riding underground, and
the sudden jolt are also of these nerves,
glandular facilities, brain's charges

line 12—pun, fact, banality
lines 13 to 18— the economics of the very poor—the newsboy
—unable to think beyond "subsistance still
permits competition" banking, *The Wisconsin
Elkhorn Independent*—"Rags make paper,
paper makes money, money makes banks,
banks make loans, loans make poverty,
poverty makes rags."
lines 22 to 24—Provençe myth
lines 25 to 29—Melanesian self-exctinction myth
line 33—airships
lines 35 and 36—creation myth (Melanesia), residue of it in our
emotions no matter if fetched from the moon,
as against l. 25 to 29.
and naturally the coda which is the
only thing that can sum up the
jumble of order in the lines weaving
"thoughts," pulsations, running commentary, one upon the other,
itself a jumble of order
as far as poetic
sequence is concerned:
                              the mantis
                              the poor's strength
                              the new world.

29—"in your eyes"
                              the original shock still persisting—

So that the invoked collective
Does not subdue the senses' awareness,
The longing for touch to an idea, or

272

To a use function of the material:
The original emotion remaining,
    like the collective,
Unprompted, real, as propaganda.

The voice exhorting, trusting what one hears
Will exhort others, is the imposed sensuality of an age
When both propaganda and sensuality are necessary against—
"—we have been left with nothing
just a few little unimportant ships
and barges" (British Admiralty even in 1920)

or jelly for the Pope

la mia nemica, madonna la pietà
my enemy, my lady pity,

36—"like leaves"
The Head remembering these words exactly in the way it
remembers
la calcina pietra
the calcined stone.

But it remembers even more constantly
the poor
than
com' huom pietra sott' erba
as one should hide a stone in grass.

Nor is the coincidence
Of the last four lines
Symbolism,
But the simultaneous,
The diaphanous, historical
In one head.

November 4, 1934,
New York.

Louis Zukofsky
(*New Directions in Poetry and Prose*, 1936)

FURIOSO

Reg. Imp

eugenia
is some
gal she
is
 queen
   bee
     of
bronksb
urg (pal

PAT HAYNES
(*Furioso*, Summer 1939)

!blac
k
agains
t

(whi)

te sky
?t
rees whic
h fr

om droppe

d

,
le
af

274

a:;go

e
s wh
IrlI
n

·g

E. E. Cummings
(*Furioso*, Spring 1940)

Les Plus Belles Pages

The milkman came in the moonlight and the moonlight
Was less than moonlight.   Nothing exists by itself.
The moonlight seemed to.

             Two people, three horses, an ox
And the sun, the waves together in the sea.

The moonlight and Aquinas seemed to.   He spoke
Kept speaking, of God.   I changed the word to man.
The automaton, in logic self-contained,
Existed by itself.   Or did the saint survive?
Did several spirits assume a single shape?

Theology after breakfast sticks to the eye.

WALLACE STEVENS
(*Furioso*, Summer 1941)

The Problem

*"Given the sky, pines, rocks,
the sea — to make a poem"*

So boulder-fastened, so pine-tree-packed a shore,

Cold-sea-surrounded, sun-crossed and
Bird-crossed, even in sunlight sometimes
Lost in vapor—

        so offshore-island-guarded who knows
Whence the sweet sound of the bell,
             behind one island,

Comes, or in the channel whither,
Dazzling clean, the trawler, cross-trees moving slowly
Out from the green shore seaward,
            goes. . . .

The Swifts

I watch the ceremony round the orifice
Of chimney swifts in flight,
      compelled
To act this rite like leaves
Whirled by the wind
      and
Littering the air—
Until the last one
      audibly
Wheeling in the deeper gloom
Drops
Into the birdpacked room
And draws the
Darkness
In.

ERNEST KROLL
(*Furioso*, Spring 1952)

VIEW

Materia Poetica

The essential fault of surrealism is that it invents without discovering. To make a clam play an accordion is to invent not to discover. The observation of the unconscious, so far as it can be observed, should reveal things of which we have previously been unconscious, not the familiar things of which we have been conscious plus imagination.

★

The imagination does not add to reality.

★

The great well of poetry is not other poetry but prose: reality. However it requires a poet to perceive the poetry in reality.

★

At the moments when one's terror of life should be greatest (when one is young or old) one is usually insensible to it. Some such thing is true of the most profoundly poetic moments. This is the origin of sentimentality, which is a failure of feeling.

★

Poetry is reality and thought or feeling.

★

If one believes in poetry then questions of principle become vital questions. In any case, if there is nothing except re-

ality and art, the mere statement of that fact discloses the significance of art.

★

The dichotomy is not between realists and artists. There must be few pure realists and few pure artists. We are hybrids absorbed in hybrid literature.

★

All poetry is experimental poetry.

★

Each of us has a sensibility range beyond which nothing exists. In each this is different.

★

In poetry, you must love the words, the ideas, the images and the rhythms with all your capacity, to love anything at all.

★

A journey in space equals a journey in time.

★

Poetry must be irrational.

★

The purpose of poetry is to make life complete in itself.

★

Poetry increases the feeling for reality.

★

Consider:
   a. That the whole world is material for poetry;
   b. That there is not a specifically poetic material.

★

One reads poetry with one's nerves.

★

The poet is the intermediary between people and the world in which they live and, also, between people as between themselves; but not between people and some other world.

WALLACE STEVENS
(*View*, Oct. 1942)

Conclusion

Every time we approach a period of transition someone cries out: This is the last! the last of Christianity, of the publishing business, freedom for the author, the individual!

So William Carlos Williams wrote in 1951.[1] While both Marxist and deconstructionist criticism encourage us to examine at length the unconscious assumptions behind the conflation (if not equation) of Christianity, business (especially the publishing of words), authorial freedom (and authority), and the largely Western concept of the individual itself, what interests me here is Williams' description of the anxiety that informs any "period of transition." As he goes on to note in this review of Ford Maddox Ford's *Parade's End*, the period "just prior to the beginning of the First World War" was a "noteworthy transition period." If the anxious feared during this period, however, that social revolution and linguistic revolution would ultimately lead to anarchy, unintelligibility, and generalized social collapse, that anxiety seems to have been equally prevalent during World War II (as Katinka Loeser's "modern language" so succinctly suggests), and to be equally — probably neither more nor less — prevalent today. It is an anxiety that I have elsewhere called the "anxiety of differance," in particular the anxiety among some critics of being abandoned in some expanding well of infinite regress should the deconstruction of the "logocentric" prove successful.[2]

Perhaps because, at least in America, we still retain the "New Critical" tradition of the aesthetic neutrality of the arts, the political ramifications of linguistic revolution have largely shifted from the domain of poets to the domain of critics. Here, with increasing frequency in the second half of this century, the underlying political structures that are informed by and supported by particular verbal structures are being challenged or defended with great vigor—and sometimes with great hostility—in a nature similar to that which marked the rivalry between particular factions of the little magazines in the first part of this century. We are therefore now, as much as in 1914 or 1944, in a "period of transition," faced with similar challenges and risks.

Given the particular influence Gertrude Stein had over the period we have examined in this volume, and given the seminal place she had in transplanting and translating a new aesthetic from France to the United States, it is almost an historical frisson that it may have been she who first coined the term "deconstruction"—by which, Carolyn Burke argues, "she meant dismantling both the structural principles of the object and *traditional habits of perception*"[3] (italics mine). However much it may now seem that for Picasso, such "deconstruction" was motivated by destruction, it was as true then as now that we still have both the power of interpreting the possible space opened by the deconstructing or dismantling of existing structures as a space for ethical and communal transformation, as well as the power of exploiting this space as one of mere destruction.

At least in 1915, one critic chose to see the poetic "deconstruction"—and experimentation—in Alfred Kreymborg's *Others* as a "democracy of feeling rebelling against an aristocracy of form," rather than "mere diabolic . . . stammering."[4] The possibility for a "democracy of feeling" in modern poetry continues as the "kindling breath" behind William Carlos Williams' "The Poem as a Field of Action" (1948), his particular concern with "what pitch the battle is today and what may come of it," and his proposal for "sweeping changes from top to bottom of the poetic structure. I said structure."[5] (As he also says, "A whole semester of studies is implicit here. Perhaps a whole course of post-graduate studies—with theses—extending into a life's work! !") Such a desire is explored with more ambivalence toward the immediate poetic predecessors we have examined here in such works as Robert Duncan's 1960 volume, *The Opening of the Field.*[6] And while long withheld by critics from participating in either this purpose or this particular poetic climate, Wallace Stevens specifically describes the possibility of (and even urgency for) creative transformation rather than nihilistic deformation in his 1951 paper entitled, significantly, "The Relations between Poetry and Painting."[7]

The historical context and specificity of Stevens' essay cannot be dismissed, for it addresses precisely the poets, the painters, and finally the larger political and ethical concerns which inform the works included in this volume. It is not without significance that in this paper, Stevens cites

Leo Stein, Gertrude Stein's brother; that he dismisses "exploitation of form" in some modern poetry (such as "small letters for capitals, eccentric line-endings, too little or too much punctuation and similar aberrations"); or that he somewhat contemptuously marks the beginning or the "definition" of modern art as being focused in Cézanne and essentially interpreted by Picasso. As he makes clear in the essay, however, his complaint about modern art is its ironically inverted elitism, a certain exclusivity against which modern art initially had set itself, and (even more ironically, given that of all these poets, it is Stevens who is most consistently accused of being an aesthete) the "modern" prohibition against meaning:

> A really modern definition of modern art, instead of making concessions, fixes limits which grow smaller and smaller as time passes and more often than not come to include one man alone, just as if there should be scrawled across the façade of the building in which we now are [the New York Museum of Modern Art], the words *Cézanne delineavit*. Another characteristic of modern art is that it is plausible. It has a reason for everything. Even the lack of a reason becomes a reason. Picasso expresses surprise that people should ask what a picture means and says that pictures are not intended to have meanings. This explains everything. Still another characteristic of modern art is that it is bigoted.

Such complaints could accurately be made against certain facets of modern criticism as well.

It is therefore all the more significant that in this essay Stevens quite specifically defines the possibility of "decreation."[8] Rather than using the term "deconstruction," which he may or may not have known from Gertrude Stein, he borrows the term "decreation" from Simone Weil, who places it in opposition to "destruction":

> She says that decreation is making pass from the created to the uncreated, but that destruction is making pass from the created to nothingness. Modern reality is a reality of decreation, in which our revelations are not the revelations of belief, but the precious portents of our own powers. . . . I am elevating this a little, because I am trying to generalize and because it is incredible that one should speak of the aspirations of the last two or three generations without a degree of elevation. Sometimes it seems the other way.

Though critics who cannot see Ezra Pound and Wallace Stevens as part of the same climate, and as responding to it in oddly similar ways, may disagree, such "decreation" seems precisely the painful movement, if not discovery, of the "Pisan Cantos" in which the very questioning of "ego scriptor," "spiritus questi," leads to the broken but resounding affirmation that "What thou lovest well remains." And despite the controversies involved, it is fitting that both poets were awarded the Bollingen Prize at approximately the same time (Pound in 1949, Stevens in 1950).

Stevens begins his essay with the remark that "The truth is that there seems to exist a corpus of remarks in respect to painting. . . which are as significant to poets as to painters" and concludes that "It is enough to have brought poetry and painting into relation as sources of our present conception of reality." The degree to which the first remark is true has, I hope, been amply demonstrated in this volume. The degree to which the second is true — even now — is perhaps most amply demonstrated by our current critical, rather than poetic, controversies.

In this regard, it is quite fitting that Jacques Derrida, easily the best-known and most influential proponent of the deconstructive enterprise, begins one of his most recent books, *The Truth in Painting* (which is, obviously, an exploration of the verbal medium as well), with a 1905 remark from none other than Cézanne: "I OWE YOU THE TRUTH IN PAINTING AND I WILL TELL IT TO YOU."[9] Given the problematics of representation and presentation faced by both pictorial and verbal texts, self-consciously explored by cubism, and fully exposed by recent criticism, this remark of the prominent precursor of cubism itself fittingly provokes in Derrida a sustained textual meditation that reenacts the same series of problematics.

Derrida, however — and this is what many modern critics, who simply run any text (whether poetic or critical) through the deconstructive mill, reducing it (predictably) to meaningless fragments, seem to miss — is not himself content to reduce all texts and structures to reiterating the empty abyss. *The Truth in Painting* concludes with the necessarily ambiguous possibility of "reliability," of witnessing, of community, possibly achieved in the sharing of perceptions.[10] This important aspect of his work is, I think, the most critical (in all senses of the word) aspect of deconstruction which we, as participants in this modern reality, must attend, repeating as it does the possibility for a "democracy of feeling" against the "totalitarianism of form" which characterized the first of American cubist verse. In this sense, it seems fair to say that Derrida may now be our most prolific cubist writer, whose deconstruction of linguistic, social, and political structures could conceivably open the space for global community (rather than Western dominance) — a community dependent upon our ability to accept multiple perspectives, upon our ability to put into action lessons learned from a cubist aesthetic.[11]

"If one concedes a right to manipulate language, a concession has already been made to the manipulation of human beings," writes Jed Rasula in "The Politics of, the Politics in."[12] Conversely, if one recognizes the strictures of language, a recognition has been made of the constriction (and conscription) of human beings. Whether in critical discourse, political activity, or artistic creation, the difficulty of manipulating in order to relieve unfair constructions remains a difficulty ripe for abuse in either the form of totalitarian dominance or anarchistic destruction. The personal lives of some of the poets included in this volume—and now, it seems, the personal lives of some of our best-known critics as well—testify to the dangers of believing too much or too little. And it is a difficulty which we, who will eventually contribute to a future understanding of textuality and contextuality, cannot afford to dismiss from our climate. At the very least, recognition and recovery of the political urgency and political misunderstandings that surrounded the most innovative aesthetic development of this century should encourage us not only to revise our perhaps naive and narrow notions of modernism itself, but to reenvision our critical enterprise itself as a part of a context, the contradictory presumptions of which we have not escaped, but of which we must be aware if we are to take responsibility not for the will to power, but for our irrepressible will to interpret.

Appendix

Editorial

THIS number of CAMERA WORK contains two articles written by Miss Gertrude Stein, an American resident in Paris.

But while it so happens that one of these articles treats of Henri Matisse and the other of Pablo Picasso; and while the text is accompanied by fourteen reproductions of representative paintings and sculptures by these artists; the fact is that these articles themselves, and not either the subjects with which they deal or the illustrations that accompany them, are the true *raison d'être* of this special issue.

A considerable number of the exhibitions that have been held by the Photo-Secession during the past five years have been devoted to phases of a general art movement that originated in France and which, with a merely chronological appropriateness, has been christened Post-Impressionism.

The development of this movement is the outward and visible sign of an intellectual and esthetic attitude at once at odds with our familiar traditions and undreamed of by most of our generation. So that its attempts at self-expression are more or less puzzling, if not wholly unintelligible, to the average observer who approaches them for the first time. And while this is especially true when the attempted expression is made through an art like painting (in the interpretation of which the average observer is only sufficiently trained to be able to recognize, when he meets it, that which habit has taught him to look for); it happens that the movement found its first expression in the field of painting and that in that field have appeared its most striking, and therefore its most discussed manifestations.

It must, however, be apparent that if the expression came through an art with the raw materials and rough practice of which we were ourselves familiar—let us say through the art of literature, whose raw material is words—even an unpiloted navigator of the unknown might feel his way into the harbor of comprehension.

And it is precisely because, in these articles by Miss Stein, the Post-Impressionist spirit is found expressing itself in literary form that we thus lay them before the readers of CAMERA WORK in a specially prepared and supplemental number.

These articles bear, to current interpretative criticism, a relation exactly analogous to that born by the work of the men of whom they treat to the painting and sculpture of the older schools.

So close, indeed, is this analogy that they will doubtless be regarded by many as no less absurd, unintelligible, radical or revolutionary than the so-called vagaries of the painters whom they seek to interpret.

Yet—they employ a medium in the technical manipulation of which we are all at least tyros.

They are expressed in words.

And hence they offer—to all who choose to examine them with an inquiring mind—a common denominator of comprehension; a Rosetta stone of comparison; a decipherable clew to that intellectual and esthetic attitude which underlies and inspires the movement upon one phase of which they are comments and of the extending development of which they are themselves an integral part.

We wish you the pleasure of a hearty laugh at them upon a first reading. Yet we confidently commend them to your subsequent and critical attention.

ALFRED STIEGLITZ

(*Camera Work*, Special No. 1912)

American Art

THERE is an American Art. Young, robust, energetic, naive, immature, daring and big spirited. Active in every conceivable field.

The Panama Canal, the Sky-scraper and Colonial Architecture. The East River, the Battery and the "Fish Theatre." The Tug Boat and the Steam-shovel. The Steam Lighter. The Steel Plants, the Washing Plants and the Electrical Shops. The Bridges, the Docks, the Cutouts, the Viaducts, the "Matt M. Shay" and the "3000." Gary. The Polarine and the Portland Cement Works. Wright's and Curtiss's Aeroplanes and the Aeronauts. The Sail Boats, the Ore Cars. Indian Beadwork, Sculptures, Decorations, Music and Dances. Jack Johnson, Charlie Chaplin, and "Spike" in "The Girl in the Game." Annette Kellermann, "Neptune's Daughter." Bert. Williams, Rag-time, the Buck and Wing and the Clog. Syncopation and the Cake-walk. The Crazy Quilt and the Rag-mat. The Minstrels. The Cigar-store Indians. The Hatters, the Shoe-makers, the Haberdashers and the Clothiers. The Window Dressers. Helene the Seamstress. The Motor Boat and the Automobile. The Fife and Drum Corps. The Fiddlers. Christy Mathewson, Ty Cobb. Robert and Alfred Taylor, Prunnetta Henderson, Greatorex. Football. Mayor Gaynor's Letters. Chin Yin, Frank Tinney. The Clowns, the Jugglers, the Bareback and the Rough Riders. The Bull-doggers, the Ropers and the Hoolahanners. The Motorcycle. Coney Island, the Shooting Galleries, Steeplechase Park, the Beaches. Mount Washington Church and the Church of All Souls. "Others," "Poetry," "Boxing Record," "The Police Gazette," the Sporting Pages, Krazy Kat, Tom Powers. Old John Brown. Nick Carter, Deadwood Dick, Old King Brady, Tom Teaser, Walt Whitman and Poe. William Dean Howells, Artemus Ward and Gertrude Stein. Alfred McCann. "Dixie," "Nobody" and the "By Heck Foxtrot." The Toy Soldiers in the Hippodrome. Slivers. The Zoo. Staten Island Warehouses, Parkhurst's Church and the Woolworth Building. The Metropolitan Tower. Prospect Park. The City Hall. Jim Duncan. The Pennsylvania Station, The Pullman, the Centipedes and the Camelbacks. The Electric Signs and the Railroad Signals. Colt's Revolvers, Savage Rifles. Willie Hoppe. Hans Wagner, Home-Run Baker. The Giant on Rogers Peet's. Stauch's. The Roller Coasters. The Gas House. Madison Square Garden on a fight night. The Runners, the Jumpers, the Swimmers, the Boxers, the Battle Ships and the Gunners. Shepard and Meredith. Kiviat. Thompson and Thorpe. Kahanamoku. Levinsky, Ahearn, McFarland. Dundee and Richie. The Movie Posters. The Factories and Mills. The Jack Pot. Dialects and Slang. Type. Jack Dillon, Leo Johnson. The Gowanus Canal and the Bush Terminal. The Batteries. Hooper, Duffy, Speaker. The Jockeys. The Carpenters, the Masons, the Bricklayers, the Chimney Builders, the Iron Workers. The Cement Mixers, the Uneeda Biscuit Building. The Pulleys and Hoists. The Buckets and Pumps and the Keyseaters. The Cranes, the Plows, the Drills, the Motors, the Thrashers, the Derricks, Steam Hammers, Stone Crushers, Steam Rollers, Grain Elevators, Trench Excavators, Blast Furnaces — This is American Art.

It is not a refined granulation nor a delicate disease—it is not an ism. It is not an illustration to a theory, it is an expression of life—a complicated life—American life.

The isms have crowded it out of "the art world" and it has grown naturally, healthfully, beautifully. It has grown out of the soil and through the race and will continue to grow. It will grow and mature and add a new unit to Art.

(To be continued.)

R. J. COADY
(*Soil*, Dec. 1916)

On The Right, Ladies and Gentlemen . . .

Tulips and Chimneys, by E. E. Cummings. Seltzer.

It is disconcerting to be compelled to revise one's opinions, and I owe Mr. E. E. Cummings at least two grudges on that score.

When I first read a poem of his—it was *Orientale* in the present volume—we were in college together, with a bare bowing acquaintance across the Yard, and I immediately went out and voted for him for Class Poet, and urged everyone I met to do the same. *Orientale* was published in the *Harvard Monthly*, that fertile organ which has given birth successively to the *New Republic* and *The Dial*, and the poem was printed like any other poem, reading from left to right, from the top of the page to the bottom, and with scansion, spelling, punctuation, and grammar quite according to the rules of the English Department.

A war and a few other things intervened, and Mr. Cummings was no more heard of, until one day he broke out like a new kind of typographical measles in *The Dial*.

This time not only did all his lines begin with small letters, but even the word "i" was not capitalized, whole stanzas consisted of nothing but commas, and the words were spattered over the page in a manner irregular in the extreme. The effect, of course, was to set everyone talking of the new poet—those who disliked eccentricity for its own sake with irritation, and the Others with admiration and delight.

Now in this we were unjust to Mr. Cummings, as the present volume abundantly makes clear. The usual thing to say of *Tulips and Chimneys* is that it contains a great deal of good poetry, in spite of the extraordinary character of its style. Some old bellwether—I believe it was *Vanity Fair* a year or so ago—led off with this declaration; Mr. Gorman in the *Times* followed, and one after another the critical sheep were gone, bobbing over the fences in their rear.

A simple experiment is enough to test the validity of this issue. Persons who have heard Carl Sandburg read his poems must agree that his medium is not the printed page at all—he should circulate only on phonograph records. But a reading of Mr. Cummings at once demonstrates that his medium is solely and exclusively the printed page. In speech, half his qualities vanish—some of his pieces fall flat altogether, others, like the luscious and delicate *Puella Mea*, retain their major charm; most of them become melodious and slightly conventional poems in the style of pre-Elizabethan verse. Return to type, and an impish delight peers out from behind each syllable, every comma twists its tail and scurries away down amusing vistas, solemn semicolons join hands and waltz off with the imagination. The poems read themselves—or perhaps skim rather than read, with extreme nimbleness, and in a sort of mental undertone. Every eccentricity fits into its place—small i's strut with their tongues in their cheeks and their hands in their pockets, snaky sibilants uncoil and hiss for a second at the intruder. A peculiar line swing that does not consist in pauses, really, nor in oral stress, but in a kind of minor, delicate, ocular accentuation, dips in and out and expresses itself in most quaint and exquisite harmony by the unusual placing of these words on the page.

In producing these effects, to be sure, Mr. Cummings is not perhaps merely a poet—he has invented a new form of entertainment—he is a linotype-sketcher, possibly, or a draughtsman in printer's ink. His art is more akin to that of the drum-major than to that of the drummer—he has succeeded, and for the first time in history, in freezing the gesture onto the printed page. Gifted in the plastic arts as well as in literature, he abandons the voice, with its single dimension, for the surface, which has length and breadth.

The new resources unfolded by this method are astonishing. If Mr. Cummings is describing a celebration, for example, he can say

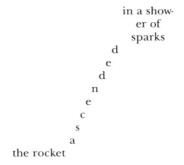

APPENDIX

— if a river,

```
           the w    a
                 t
               e
                 r
                 f
               a
               l  u h    ov        rocks
               l r  s  ed    er the
```

But these are crude and insulting parodies, related to Mr. Cummings' poetry somewhat as the work of a sign-painter is to that of an etcher.

What he really does do is this in a portrait of a prostitute:

. . . opening the hard great
eyes to noone in particular she
gasped almost
loudly
i'm

so
drunG

k, dear

or this exquisite little poem about a star:

i was considering how
within night's loose
sack a star's
nibbling in-

fin
-i-
tes-
i
-mal-
ly devours

darkness the
hungry star
which
will e

-ven
tu-
al
-ly jiggle
the bait of
dawn and be jerked

into

eternity when over my head a
shooting
star
Bur   s

    (t
       into a stale shriek
like an alarm-clock)

The "translation" of either of these poems into ordinary copy would be an obvious sacrilege, in which nobody but those reviewers who were silly enough to try it, could possibly wish to share. No other method ever used would produce such a vivid and exciting result as the one Mr. Cummings has invented.

But the selection of certain passages to illustrate his more obvious effects, does a great injustice to the subtlety and whimsicality of the entire volume, as well as to certain of Mr. Cummings' qualities by no means dependent on his printer's care. There are parts of *Puella Mea* that are among the loveliest and most delicate erotic verse in the language, and if there is anywhere in modern poetry a more charming passage than the beginning of this lyric, I do not know it:

Songs

II

Always before your voice my soul
half-beautiful and wholly droll
is as some smooth and awkward foal
whereof young moons begin
the newness of his skin,

Sweetness and limpidity, a certain delicious whimsicality, and a delight in rich and elaborate metaphor, are Mr. Cummings' chief qualities, underneath all his cloak of sophistication. Indeed I think the cloak of sophistication has been donated chiefly by his critics. His material is impartially phantasies of fine ladies, or swift miniatures of prostitutes — though he writes occasional poems about spring and fall and moonlight, he belongs with the poets of personal emotion, rather than with the Topographical or Climatic schools of verse. He is, in fact, the only poet I know, living or dead, who writes of prostitutes at once with tenderness and realism, and with hardly a grain of sentimentality, and I can do no better than close by quoting Sonnet VI in the first group, one of the finest poems of the book:

when thou has taken thy last applause, and when
the final curtain strikes the world away,
leaving to shadowy silence and dismay
that stage which shall not know thy smile again,
lingering a little while i see thee then
ponder the tinsel part they let thee play;
i see the large lips livid, the face grey,
and silent smileless eyes of Magdalen.
The lights have laughed their last; without, the street
darkling awaiteth her whose feet have trod
the silly souls of men to golden dust:
she pauses on the lintel of defeat,
her heart breaks in a smile — and she is Lust. . . .

mine also, little painted poem of god

ROBERT L. WOLF

Syrinx.

A complete study of Cummings should take penetrating account of his painting and drawing, and no estimate of his literary work can begin without noting the important fact that Cummings is a painter. It has bearing, as we shall later see, on his written words. Cummings creates perfect LYRICS, and a perfect lyric is indefinable and unanalyzable. The nearest we can come to it beyond a subjective recognition and feeling is to say, as Cummings wrote of the Mountain by Gaston Lachaise and of the personality of Jean Le Nègre, that the perfect lyric is a verb: it is an IS. But to admit the impregnability of the lyric is not necessarily to proclaim it as the highest manifestation of art. If we say that the lyric equals IS, we can still say that the full development of art equals a SENTENCE, and thereby indicate roughly the relation of the lyric to more ideological forms. Nor does every sentence requires an IS. The verb-quality of the lyric, however, throws criticism back upon the attributes of the IS that Cummings creates. The most distinguishing attribute of Cummings' lyricism is its GRACE. And grace again is unanalyzable and indefinable. Even Poe could not crystallize it. Of grace, he wrote, "perhaps the elements are a vivid fancy and a quick sense of the proportionate. Grace, however, may be most satisfactorily defined as 'a term applied, in despair, to that class of the impressions of Beauty which admit of no analysis.'"

When we attack Cummings' ORIGINALITY, we can, however, proceed further by quoting from Poe again "My first object (as usual) was originality. The extent to which this has been neglected in versification, is one of the most unaccountable things in the world. Admitting that there is little possibility of variety in mere *rhythm*, it is still clear that the possible varieties of metre and stanza are absolutely infinite — and yet, *for centuries, no man, in verse, has ever done, or ever seemed to think of doing, an original thing.* The fact is, that originality (unless in minds of very unusual force) is by no means a matter, as some suppose, of impulse or intuition. In general, to be found, it must be elaborately sought, and although a positive merit of the highest class, demands in its attainment less of invention than negation." Today, this statement still covers with all its primal pertinence the majority of poets. A minority has found in *vers libre* great possibility of variety in rhythm and of this minority, Cummings has probably accomplished more original things in rhythm, metre and stanza than any three other poets combined. And it is precisely by negation that he has attained originality. He has simply cancelled out his Education (the dignified name for an unquestioning acceptance of custom).

The result is, he sees freshly. Cummings *sees* words. As Dr. J. S. Watson noted, his words stand "erect on the page with a clean violence."

The originality of Cummings resolves into two elements. The first is the accurate choice of words. The second is the pains taken to display his accuracy unmistakably. The latter is, of course, much more uncommon in literature than the first. It is an adaptation of advertising technic to literary intentions.

To display and force upon the reader his accuracy, Cummings has been obliged to reorganize punctuation and typography. *Cummings makes punctuation and typography active instruments for literary expression.* Here his painter's skill in composition aids him. Yet, in no case, does he leave the frontiers of literature for the plastic arts as did Apollinaire in *Calligrammes.* His typographical design in every example reinforces his literary content. He has perceived that the printing-press has made poetry something to be seen as well as heard: he has realized that visual notations of auditory rhythms stimulates the ears of silent readers. He is the first successful creator of calligrams. Most writers could profitably take lessons in arresting attention from American advertising experts. American advertising experts can take lessons from Cummings.

I catalog below some of the means employed by Cummings to display his accuracy and to indicate tempo.

1. Capitals are used principally for emphasis. This abolishes immediately the academic nonsense about the capitalization of the first letter in every line of poetry and the capitalization of the pronoun, I. It is then a simplification for the sake of pointing an unmistakable finger at emphatic words. E.g., —

> *to enjoy the composed sudden body atop which always*
> *quivers the electric Distinct face haughtily vital clinched*
> *in a swoon of synopsis.*

2. Commas are used to indicate pauses wherever the poet decides that cadence requires them, even if it involves the separation of words never previously divided in that manner. E.g., —

> *(if you toss him a coin he will pick it cleverly from, the*
> *air and stuff it seriously in, his minute pocket).*

3. Blank space is often used to isolate a word or words in a naked exactitude and emphasis from the rest of the poem. E.g., —

> *whistles   far   and wee.*

4. In order to indicate slow tempo, words are spread apart by hyphens or spaces or have extra letters added. E.g., —

> *gen*
> *teel-ly*
> *lugu-*
> *bri ous.*

5. In order to indicate quick tempo, several words are often run together as one word. E.g., —

> *and break onetwothreefourfive pigeonsjustlikethat.*

6. Stanzaic divisions, line breakage and space relationships are freely varied for the display of accuracy and the indication of auditory rhythm. The cadences are emphatically not disjointed by such methods. On the contrary, Cummings' sentences often being their meaning in one stanza and jump to the next before completing it. The parts of his poem do not run down, but continue their operation until the final line. That is why, I conceive, Dr. Watson likened them to a roller coaster on a scenic railway. *Three United States Sonnets* (*Broom*, May, 1922).

To illustrate how expressive punctuation can become in Cummings' hands, I cite from *Caritas* (*Broom*, July, 1922) a complete stanza made up solely of punctuation marks. A splendidly average citizen listening to a Salvation Army meeting is asked to increase the collection by twenty-five cents in order to make an even dollar. His mental processes are precisely and economically recorded as follows:

```
?
??
???
!
```

This, if one likes, also makes notation of a crescendo banged on the evangelical drum and reaching its final Boom ! Boom ! in the next stanza which is

Nix, kid.

Accuracy in itself has esthetic quality. Although it is not necessarily elegant, but Cummings has an exquisite ear. His neat successes in hitting the bullseye are always accompanied by a crisp sense of verse-music. I am absolved from dilation on this by the simple expedient of quoting a stanza from *Puella Mea*. (*The Dial*, January, 1921):

In her perfectest array
my lady, moving in the day,
is a little stranger thing
in the morning wandering.

And to double-clinch conviction, this concluding stanza 8 of a poem from *The Dial*, October, 1921:

The flute of morning stilled in noon —
noon the implacable bassoon —
now Twilight seeks the thrill of moon,
washed with a wild and thin
despair of violin.

Cummings avoids the pictorial excesses of Apollinaire with sureness. With equal certainty, he escapes the "musicality of literature" esthetic. His care for the word in its ideational meanings hold him to the moorings that Swinburne disastrously cut. For he remembers that if ideas are lost in pictorial, or musical qualities, then writing ceases to be literature and becomes weakly something else.

One of the essences of the pure lyric is simplicity, and simplicity requires (a) that it present an isolated idea as its base or (b) that it present a brief summary of an ideational research. As (b), it is the incomplete and uncomplicated reduction to a song of huge documents of ratiocination. As his idea-base, Cummings seems to prefer the lyrical summary.

His topics are the again-and-again-and-again handled themes of all lyricists: and what he says about these enigmas does not differ in substance from what has been reiterated. The difference lies rather in the freshness with which they are apprehended, in the novelty with which they are presented. The old result stated in new terms regains its former glamor.

Thus, the concept that life is a brevity composed of pleasure and pain emerges in an appealing new coat of varnish as

> *(Do you think?) the*
> *i do, world*
> *is probably made*
> *of roses & hello:*
> *(of solongs and, ashes).*

On another occasion the concept that spring is a quickening revivifying season is conveyed by re-creating that season as a fetching sloppy ragtime mistress. Again, the statement that war is a horror which cannot drown out the magnetic life of young men and women, cannot submerge the inexorable uprush of human tides, is equally freshly conveyed. Death is seen as a faultless gentleman: death is approached in a jaunty American fashion.

> *he was a handsome man*
> *and what i want to know is*
> *how do you like your blueeyed boy*
> *Mister Death.*

A particular triumph in the recreation of an old concept — that of Pan — occurs in an untitled poem. Cummings wisely places the poem in undefiled childhood. The season is "Just-spring," the world is "mud-luscious" and "puddle-wonderful," the children are playing marbles, piracies, hop-scotch and jump-rope, when a balloonman whistles, and off they run in quick response to his magical personality. The data of our childhoods immediately informs us that the balloon vendor was our authentic Pan, that his whistle blew the pure strains of the joyous god.

And now to render amends for these partial reductions of Cummings' lyrics, I quote one of his poems entire (*Sunset, Broom,* July, 1922). Note the vowel and consonantal relationships, the color unity of the first stanza, the bell unity of the second, the dragging tempo of the last, the live transitions, the enhancing typographical display, the consummate magic. Cummings is right in declaring that Swinburne did not exhaust the lyric.

Sunset.

stinging
gold swarms

upon the spires
silver
        chante the litanies the
great bells are ringing with rose
the lewd fat bells
                        and a tall
wind
is dragging
the sea
with
dream
-s

Neither of Cummings pieces of criticism, one devoted to the sculptor, Gaston Lachaise, the other to T. S. Eliot, strikes me as achieved. The critique on Eliot is unpardonably out of key with its subject. For positive criticisms, both are overmuch concerned with the stupidities of other critics and inferior artists. Both are stalled short of developed crystallizations by a foolish disrespect for criticism, a disrespect that belongs peculiarly to the last century. To write of the Mountain by Lachaise: "Merely to contemplate its perfectly knit enormousness was to admit that analysis of, or conscious thinking on our part about, a supreme aesthetic triumph, is a very pitiful substitute for that sensation which is impossibly the equivalent of what the work itself thinks of us": is merely to exhibit an amazing confusion. For surely it is not a question of substituting analysis for the original impact, but a matter of adding a term to that impact, a business of still more enhancing our first pleasure by conscious thought about it. I do not wish to imply that Cummings cannot or does not analyze his esthetic impressions: he does and would do so publicly, doubtless, if he did not strangely regard that act as unseemly. Consequently, the contour of his criticism is impressionistic and therefore incomplete.

Cummings' criticism focuses flashlights upon his own work. He states admirably the approach which should be taken towards himself in particular and indeed towards all primitive (technical sense) art. This art "cannot be grasped until we have accomplished the thorough destruction of the world". He notes certain accomplishments which "require of us an intelligent process of the highest order, namely the negation on our part, by thinking, of thinking." That is to say, our first process is the inducing of a relaxed sensitiveness, the opening of all our receptive pores, the complete surrender to what is before us. Afterwards, we can stiffen, we can call in our education, we can fight back. If our reception-data survive this recovery, then we have what we must admit is a personal validity.

Coming closer, we find Cummings turning on the intention of Eliot a passage from Eliot on Marlowe. We may take the same passage and turn it back on Cummings' poetry and forward on his prose. The statement is:

". . . this style which secures its emphasis by always hesitating on the edge of caricature at the right moment. . . .

. . . this intense and serious and indubitably great poetry, which, like some great painting and sculpture, attains its effects by something not unlike caricature."

Closer still, we discover statements on the personality of Lachaise which seem to me to encompass in a large degree the temperament of Cummings. Lachaise, he says, is "inherently naif, fearlessly intelligent, utterly sincere. It is accurate to say that his two greatest hates are the hate of insincerity and the hate of superficiality." He desires "to negate the myriad with the single, to annihilate the complicatednesses and prettinesses and trivialities of Southern civilizations with the enormous, the solitary, the fundamental." He achieves superlative esthetic victories by a "complete intelligence, or the intelligence functioning at intuitional velocity." Let us, I suggest, read the name, Cummings, for the name, Lachaise. And let us add this note on Cézanne by way of understanding why Cummings can be called naif and primitive. "Cézanne became truly naif—not by superficially contemplating and admiring the art of primitive peoples, but by carefully misbelieving and violently disunderstanding a second hand world."

(Evidently), we are now entangled in Cummings' temperament as a condition for his work. In order to define it sufficiently, we must examine the part it acts in *The Enormous Room*. (Boni and Liverright).

The subject-matter of this book consists of a brutal environment, an ignoble set of circumstances, *and* an artist countering against them. Cummings was an ambulance driver in the Norton Harjes unit during the recent bloody squabble for markets. His friend, B., in the same unit wrote some letters evincing an intelligent outlook on this mean scramble which were intercepted by the censor. Thereupon, both B. and Cummings were speedily propelled into a horrible detention camp, Ferte de la Macé, and with some three score comrades ill-treated for several months. After which edification, Cummings was released through the intervention of American authorities, and B. went on to a "regular prison" for further outrage before the incredibly brilliant U.S. Government secured his release likewise. Circumstance and environment were therefore abnormal, bizarre, filthy, degrading, and wounding. Against them Cummings countered with everything he had, and that was much more than the single blind rage of Dos Passos. For besides rage, Cummings had scorn, irony, sarcasm, courage, and a love for simple men. Especially, he had a drama-tizing sense, a childlike faculty for personification and play-building. More especially, he had an undefeatable sense of humor. Most especially, he was tuned up to record in detail the slightest quiver contained in the slightest split-second of the slightest jar upon his being: that is, he was intensely and every instant *alive*. What came to him came vividly and indelibly. His triumph — the triumph of artist over hostility — is *The Enor-mous Room*.

On page 249 of this brilliant work, its basis is stated. « for an educated gent or lady, to create is first of all to destroy — that there is and can be no such thing as authentic art art until the *bons trucs* (whereby we are taught to see and imitate on canvass and by words this so-called world) are entirely and thoroughly and perfectly annihilated by that vast and painful process of Unthinking which may result in a minute bit of purely personal Feeling. Which minute bit is Art » .

It took a high amount of Unthinking to produce such accuracies as for instance, these: « a room about sixteen feet short and four feet nar-row » ; « a hunk of bread and a piece of water. » But the unusual quality of Cummings' feeling resides, in two things: his painter's eye and his writer's ear. That eye is keen in noting planes, angles, textures, colors, the essential determining features: that ear is expert in reducing the visual booty to cadences. Take these as instances of their cooperation.

(1) « I had taken automatically some six or eight steps in pursuit of
« the fleeing spectre when, right over my head, the grey stone curdled
« with a female darkness ; the hard and the angular softening in a
« putrescent explosion of thick wriggling laughter. I started, looked up,
« and encountered a window stuffed with four savage fragments of crowd-
« ing Face ; four livid, shaggy disks focussing hungrily ; four pair of
« uncouth eyes rapidly smouldering; eight lips shaking in a toothless and
« viscous titter. Suddenly above and behind these terrors rose a single
« horror — a crisp vital head, a young ivory actual face, a night of firm,
« alive, icy hair, a white large frightful smile ».

(2) « Card table : 4 stares play banque with 2 cigarettes
« (1 dead) & A pipe the clashing faces yanked by a
« leanness of one candle bottle-stuck (Birth of X)
« where sits The Clever Man who pyramids, sings
« (mornings) 'Meet Me . . . »

« which specimen of telegraphic technique being interpreted, means :
« Judas, Garibaldi, and The Holland Skipper (whom the reader will meet
« *de suite*)—Garibaldi's cigarette having gone out, so greatly is he ab-
« sorbed—play *banque* with four intent and highly focussed individuals
« who may or may not be The Schoolmaster, Monsieur Auguste, The
« Barker, and Même ; with The Clever Man (as nearly always) acting as
« banker. The candle by whose somewhat uncorpulent illumination the
« various physiognomies are yanked into a ferocious unity is stuck into
« the mouth of a bottle. The lighting of the whole, the rhythmic disposi-
« tion of the figures, construct a sensuous integration suggestive of The
« Birth of Christ by one of the Old Masters. The Clever Man, having had
« his usual morning warble, is extremely quiet. He will win, he pyramids
« —and he pyramids because he has the cash and can afford to make
« every play a big one. All he needs is the rake of a *croupier* to complete his
« disinterested and wholly nerveless poise ».

There is another duality in Cummings' feeling that increases its special quality. He is both realistic and fanciful. Without a wince, he can describe a fresh smoking turd or a brutal mauling with stove-pipes and on the next page evoke the most charming gnomes or fairies or fantastic attic toys. This combination of hardness and fancy is not often encountered.

But to get back to the passage on the minute bit of purely personal feeling which is art, does this not mean, in bald esthetic terms, that Commings [*sic*] is a partisan of content-first, form-second, writing ? Does it not mean that his first stimulus comes from the emotional and perceptive materials of his experiences ? And afterwards, he crystallizes them into formal beauties ? Certainly, that was the proceedure [*sic*] in *The Enormous Room*. Here Cummings had a huge mass of experience whose energy demanded expression. This experience, this dynamic reality, held his major interest. It dictated word by word the problems of its presentation. Whereas a form-first, content-second, writer, although he started with this initial experience, would very soon shift his major interest to his presentation problems, would play loose and fast with his initial bits of pure feeling for the sake of his non-representative design. His pure feelings would be but helpless pawns in the grip of his intellect, whereas in *The Enormous Room* we have an intellect performing an efficient servitude to feeling. In Cummings case, neither content nor form, neither the representative nor the non-representative, overbalance one another. There is a unique marriage there between form and content, that marriage—which we are told denotes successful art.

Let us examine this union in *The Enormous Room*. No, first let us point out several additional interesting details of that book. One is fresh adjectival juxtapositions. Again and again by a simple transposition ancient couplings are revivified. Another is a hand at word coinage, a game largely discontinud by the English speaking since the days of Queen Elizabeth. Another is a repercussion from the American detective story, with its speed of narration, its exaggerated villain and hero types, its piling-up of exciting situations, all marvellously sublimated in Cummings' mind. A fourth is the awareness of the knockabout vitality, vigor, raciness, authenticity, humor, poetry and vividness of the American language. After reading Sandburg and Cummings, one believes in the possibilities of this new tongue as one does not believe in it after reading John V. A. Weaver. Fifth, there is splendid caricature. But back to the larger successes of The Enormous Room!

One of its large successes is its minor organisms. Sentences, paragraphs, incidents, chapters are all carefully built up. (Unlike most of his contemporaries, Cummings can still swing a long sentence. His verbs have a remarkable kick: enough to keep a dozen adjectives on the move.) As a minute specimen of minor organization, take this:

« It must have been five o'clock. Steps. A vast cluttering of the
« exterior of the door — by whom? Whang opens the door. Turnkey-
« creature extending a piece of chocolate with extreme and surly caution.
« I say « Merci » and seize chocolate. Klang shuts the door ».

It is a miniature, but note that its introduction creates imminence, its progression rises in a crescendo, and its final sentence closes neatly the incident.

As a more extended minor organism, consider the portrait of the little doll-like Belgian Machine-Fixer which rises to this lyrical invocation — an indirect reproach a hundred times more effective, it seems to me, than the direct, well-chewed anger of the usual protestant against inhumanity.

« And his ghastly and toylike wizened and minute arm would try to
« make a pass at their lofty lives. O *gouvernement français*, I think it was not
« very clever of you to put this terrible doll in La Ferté ; I should have left
« him in Belgium with his little doll-wife if I had been You ; for when
« Governments are found dead there is always a little doll on top of them,
« pulling and tweaking with his little hands to get back the microscopic
« knife which sticks firmly in the quiet meat of their hearts ».

In the final chapter there is a magnificent arrangement of surprize and contrast. In an abbreviated Joycian manner, the cupboards of the disagreeable are spilled all over the page and THEN as the ship enters New York harbor comes this:

« My God what an ugly island. Hope we don't stay here long. All the
« redbloods first class much excited about land, Damned ugly, I think.
« Hullo.
« The tall, impossibly tall, incomparably tall, city shoulderingly
« upward into hard sunlight leaned a little through the octaves of its
« parallel edges, leaningly strode upward into firm hard snowy sunlight ;
« the noises of America nearingly throbbed with smokes and hurrying
« dots which are men and which are women and which are things new
« and curious and hard and strange and vibrant and immense, lifting
« with a great ondulous stride firmly into immortal sunlight. . . . »

Each chapter mounts on its own crescendo, and each crescendo
relates to all the others. There is then a major organization. This major,
roughly modelled upon Bunyan's *Pilgrim's Progress*, must have presented
great resistances to Cummings, as a glance at his plan will immediately
corroborate. The first third of his book is a chronological narrative, the
following half is a timeless series of descriptions, the final sixth is again
chronological narrative, yet he has actually shifted from a narrative and
time technic into a timeless and descriptive technic and back again
without the slightest loss of movement. Indeed, the curve of his central
crescendo keeps ascending from portrait to portrait until it seems as
though its climax is certainly reached in an unforgettable eulogy of Jean
Le Nègre, but even after that it moves up higher as the book changes to
narrative. B. is sent by the investigating committee to Precigne. After he
leaves, Cummings records:

« I went to my bed and lay down quietly in my great *pelisse*. The
« clamor and filth of the room brightened and became distant and faded.
« I heard the voice of the jolly Alsatian saying :
« ' *Courage, mon ami,* your comrade is not dead; you will see him later '
« and after that, nothing. In front of and within my eyes lived suddenly
« a violent and gentle and dark silence ».

In that silence the arc of *The Enormous Room* halts its upward prog-
ress runs level a few seconds, and then drops rapidly down for the
concluding chapters.

Each page of this book is a rewarding study in mechanics; over-
whelming as Cummings' subject matter was it has all been crystallized in a
way to give the last jerk and whirret that inhered therein. Cummings has

---

[In reproducing this manuscript, I have incorporated the handwritten
corrections Munson made on the original published versions. His own copy,
with his corrections, is held at the HRHRC, Austin, Texas.]

jabbed his pen into life, but he has also twisted it in the wound, and it is this twist of the pen that makes literature.

GORHAM B. MUNSON

(Secession, July 1923)

Table of Contents

304

G<small>LOSSARY</small>

[*transition*, June 1929]

Scheme for Physical Improvement of Writers' Medium

spaces, capitals, stops, margins, signs *and* pace have their significance in the make-up of a writer's medium.

Now that the value of each letter no less than each word is beginning to be gauged the real sway of scribbler's signs out to be accurately shaped

with the coming of the incoherent technique of modern reading matter this is especially necessary

too long have we been the slaves of atavistic printers & public publishers & readers

CONSPUEZ les CONVENANCES

WRITERS why don't you revolt?

(mais que ça soit non seulement une révolte mais une veritable revolution)

consider   each letter   how it is to stand high or sit low or lie prostrate   how each word is to hang aloft   lonely as a star   or attached   (courante as a piece of BACH'S) prominent or spectral   a counterblast   a prognostic or an aftermath = fragrance left over the sound of them   their taste their look. Their feel   how they feel to the paper may be a new method of printing will have to be invented so as to give the letters *and* the words (different psychics with uncountable different origins tempers reactions the word reacting *to* the letter or *against* them   subservient or masterful   spurning them   chasing them holding them in check their own individual inbeing liberating one confining another letting them play or carouse or abstain or have fits or wail or adore or break themselves on the wheel   or just drift for the medium as well as the craftsman the MAXIM is "REBEL"

rebel

REBEL REBEL ᴸ R ꞓ ꟼ ꟼ LEBER

REBEL

SPACES: I want e d   tosay
I w   ant ed to   s   a   y
Iw   an   te   dto   sa   y
I   wa   n   te   dt   o   say
(the illustration is perfect)

are you awake?   **NO**
A r r r R e you a w ake?   no
ar   ey   oua wa a ake?   **no**
(whispered)   a a are y o   ua w a a a ke?   no

SNORE !!!
(3 snores are here clearly shown   they can be heard on the
page)

CAPITALS: the hurts we get from unimaginative publishers and their
crew is shattering. in connection with these majestic letters
in England it is the mode to use them for:
a)   days of the week
b)   months
c)   adj. of nationalities (other than english even)
d)   names of places, people, titles, 1st letter in sentence,
pronouns complementary to divinity, abstract terms
and I daresay in many other thoughtless ways
where capitals are aesthetically theoretically scientifically
psychologically dynamically moodily humouristically satis-
fying they are austerely ignored
(Extract from my last work)

How the place STank!   pavements DUST   passers-
BY   REfuse   HEAPED on the OUTskirts of the
LITtle town a RAnk world motors HONKing and
whirrinG FEET on the pavEment WHeels of drAYs
Factory wHistleS Steam lOrries VoiceS dOgs
YAPPing YAp YaPPing: hurting SoundS
so many SeS = esses

RYTHM as well as EMPhasis is trapped by means
of this simple technique.

soon (it can't be long) capitals of every size or shape . . . .
romanesque baroque gothic rococo chinese indian will
be as overflowing as the people of every nation   as various
then the page will have its own character   saucy aloof
winning   cruel.

STOPS: joyce has successfully experimented with their abolition
for the moment spaces can be used

MARGINS: a clause relating to some SPecial perSonality or SUbject or
ideA is aesthetically emphaSized or STimulated by widen-
ing the margin   take the wiFE   whenever She comeS in
the margins might be widened from ½ to 1 in.   for the
child especially if it is a diSaSter   to 2 ins.   for the dog
leave only 1 in. of printing.
or again:
the man gets ½ in.   his houSe 1 ½ in.   his ideas 3 in. in a
4 ¾ in. wide page this SCheme gives a motif quite as
effective as the muSical ones in opera

SIGNS: they can be produced ad. infin. with immenSe effect   out-
Side the mathmatical signs for character or SCenic de-
Scription there are the peculiar ones invented by the writer
which will inStantly SuggeSt themSelves to any live
imagination
Ex: Smells heavy narcotic = Smudged black printing
eluSive Scents = wild roSe would be indicated by a faint
italic type
vigorouS activity such aS a whipping   boy with top   brawl
in Street would be made offenSive by irregular rather dirty
printing in very heavy 𝖌𝖔𝖙𝖍𝖎𝖈 𝖙𝖞𝖕𝖊

(PACE:)   i have suggested the tempo in my latest but one by means
of musical signs let into the margin   *MAESTOSO ACelᵒ cres*
e ⏴ app. dim morendo & so on   the entire meaning of a
work may be misconstrued if read too fast or too slow.
it is not necessary i imagine to hint to the intelligentsia of
"Transition" how trenchantly we can uSe musical terms
when dealing with PERSONS GENDERS ORGANS . . . . .

MUSICAL
SIGNS: a LIVER may be *accelᵒ   presto largo*   a WIfe *fff* or hysterically
tremolando   a BABY *pizzᵒ* or *Sfᵒ   piano sfp sfz.p.*
the MOTHER *ad lib. allargᵒ*

the entire DRAMA could exist by nothing but musical signs
The dram. pers. being explained for the enlightment of
𝄪 ♮ s in the same way as playwrights indicate on fly leaf

EX:
♭	=	husband i.e. flat
×	=	wife i.e. double sharp
#	=	former mistress i.e. natural.
animato	=	aero pilotin chief character in plot) i.e. with soul
pizzicato	=	babe
8va.	=	daughter i.e. ottava
ppp	=	wife's pretended lover i.e. very very dim or soft

Mus¹ SIGNS :S: = cellarat or nearest american bar (the excursions
 con^d as   to or from which would naturally be: Al Segno
DRAMA: dal segno)
7ᵗʰ = the joint production of ♭ and × i.e. septet
6ᵗʰ = ,,   ,,   ,,   ,, ♭ and *an°* or # (query?) best
         expressed by Schumann's WARUM?
A tempo = dinner hour or bedtime ff in italics = rate of
              motion
▭ = staff i.e. remainder of servants not immedi-
      ately concerned in plot.
      the logic takes place as follows:
MAESTOSO: 𝄪 on lower *G* ＜ *fff* (the ＜ means not only
                              increasing volume of
                              tone but also size of
                              paunch also advancing
                              years and general un
                              buttonedness)

breves   semibreves   minums   gs & g flats = his outraged dignity
adagio = his senility i.e. brain & motions speech & up-take SLOW
mez? Sop? = dull flat uninterested populace
white notes = mob
black notes = individuals
cresc? = upward flight of aeroplane
dim. = brakes of motor
affret? = years ,,   ,,
tremolando = stars
DA CAPO = planets i.e. from the beginning
all play their role in the drama

the *PAUSE* is used extensively

repetitions   spaces   refrains *||* the flight of the aero is indicated by these 3. the tonic chord denoting the start the dominant the flight. the 7th. a turn over in mid air the 11th a crash the 13th annihilation.

VIVACE: .X on uppermost FX *tremolo aecel♭*   *||pizz♭:* from next room *animato ad lib.* Shoots in from crashing airplane through window crying: *Coco* (indicating to return to proper pitch) *A tem* = she arrives in time.

Ottava Bassa falls through ceiling onto her head (*bassa* is added when she displeases *alla* when she is agreeable)

\# restores a note which has been raised by the sharp to its original pitch (peculiarly applicable to ♭ & ×

animato on *F* ♮ *G* ♮ hums *TASTO SOLO* i.e. a direction to play a part in unison.

DIM♭

PIAN♭   *AL SEGNO*

DA   *CAPO:* means of course ♮'s return to majestic ineptitudes.

FINE

nobody listens

Marius Lyle
(*transition*, March 1932)

Notes

Preface

1. Edward F. Fry, *Cubism* (New York: Oxford University Press, 1978), 35. In addition, Wylie Sypher has suggested that cubism best describes our twentieth-century perspective; see *Rococo to Cubism in Art and Literature* (New York: Random House, 1960).

2. Henry M. Sayre, *The Visual Text of William Carlos Williams* (Chicago: University of Illinois Press, 1983), 12.

3. A. Hyatt Mayor, "Picasso's Method," *Hound & Horn* 3, 2 (Jan.–Mar., 1930): 177.

4. Stephen Kern, *The Culture of Time and Space* (Cambridge: Harvard University Press, 1983), 303.

5. Ibid., 302.

6. Wallace Stevens, "The Relations between Poetry and Painting" (1951), reprinted in *The Necessary Angel* (New York: Viking, 1951), 167–68.

7. For example, Stevens wrote "Two Versions of the Same Poem" (subtitled "That Which Cannot Be Fixed") in 1946, "Someone Puts a Pineapple Together" in 1947, and "Two Illustrations That the World is What You Make of It" and "Prologues to What Is Possible" in 1952 — all of which reflect the influence of cubism; all reprinted in *The Palm at the End of the Mind*, ed. Holly Stevens (New York: Vintage, 1972).

8. Sayre, 29.

9. See Marjorie Perloff, *The dance of the intellect* (Cambridge: Cambridge University Press, 1985), 12, 16. Note also that Ezra Pound originally intended the *Cantos* to follow a pattern very similar to that of the *Divine Comedy* with the hope of suggesting a regenerative movement for the Western world — and America in particular.

10. Compare the following lines from Ezra Pound's "Hugh Selwyn Mauberly," in *Personae* (New York: New Directions, 1971), 188; and Wallace Stevens' "Of Modern Poetry," in *The Collected Poems of Wallace Stevens* (New York: Knopf, 1975), 240:

    The age demanded an image
    Of its accelerated grimace,

> Something for the modern stage,
> Not, at any rate, an Attic grace. . . .
> ("Hugh Selwyn Mauberly")

> It has to face the men of the time and to meet
> The women of the time. It has to think about war
> And it has to find what will suffice. It has
> To construct a new stage.
> ("Of Modern Poetry")

11. Dorothy Norman, "Introducing *291*," *291*, 1–12 (1915–1916), reprint New York: Arno Press, 1972.

Introduction

1. See among others Henry M. Sayre, *The Visual Text of William Carlos Williams* (Urbana: University of Illinois Press, 1983); William Marling, *William Carlos Williams and the Painters, 1909–1923* (Athens: Ohio University Press, 1982); Marjorie Perloff, *The dance of the intellect* (Cambridge: Cambridge University Press, 1985) and *The Futurist Moment* (Chicago: University of Chicago Press, 1986); and Glen MacLeod, *Wallace Stevens and Company: The Harmonium Years, 1913–1923* (Ann Arbor: UMI Research Press, 1983). In addition, see Christopher J. MacGowan, *William Carlos Williams' Early Poetry: The Visual Arts Background* (Ann Arbor: UMI Research Press, 1984); Andrew M. Clearfield, *These Fragments I Have Shored: Collage and Montage in Early Modernist Poetry* (Ann Arbor: UMI Research Press, 1984); and Joan Richardson, *Wallace Stevens: The Early Years, 1879–1923* (New York: Morrow, 1986).

2. Apollinaire's work is translated and reprinted in George Wittenborn's edition of *The Cubist Painters* (New York, 1949). For a discussion of whether or not cubism in literature is possible, see *Cubisme et littérature*, Special Issue of *Europe: Revue littéraire mensuelle* 638–39 (1982), especially Michel Decaudin, "Petite histoire d'une appellation: 'Cubisme littéraire,'" 7–25.

3. Pablo Picasso, "Picasso Speaks," *The Arts*, May 1923, 316–26, reprinted in Edward F. Fry, *Cubism* (New York: Oxford University Press, 1978), 168.

4. See *transition*, 16–17 (June 1929). Subtitled "The Revolution of the Word," this special issue moves, significantly, from literary texts to visual texts, including some of Picasso's cubist paintings. Jerome Rothenberg chose this phrase as the title for *Revolution of the Word: A New Gathering of American Avant Garde Poetry, 1914–1945* (New York: Seabury Press, 1974), an anthology more diverse in purpose than this work, but which provides a significant supplement to the understanding of the American poetic climate during this period.

5. Picasso, in Fry, 166–67.

6. A. Hyatt Mayor, "Picasso's Method," *Hound & Horn*, 3, 2 (Jan.–Mar., 1930), 177.

7. Dorothy Sayers, *Lord Peter Views the Body*, first published in 1928; reprinted by Avon, 1969, 7. It is also somewhat humorous that, at least according to Marsden Hartley, "young cubists" were to be found "over-dressing. . . à la Londres, with white spats on all occasions" in contradistinction to the

rather decadent "Empire Style" of the earlier period; see "Farewell, Charles" [Demuth], in *The New Caravan of 1936*, ed. Alfred Kreymborg, Lewis Mumford, and Paul Rosenfeld (New York: Norton, 1936), 553. That the term has continued to have validity among writers is evinced by a 1966 issue of the *Chicago Review* (18:207), in which Max Jacob is described as a "French cubist poet."

8. Kenneth Rexroth, "The Influence of French Poetry on American," cited in the introduction to *William Carlos Williams: Selected Poems,* ed. Charles Tomlinson (New York: New Directions, 1985), xi.

9. See Richard L. Admussen, *"Nord-Sud* and Cubist Poetry," *JAAC* 27 (1968); Paul Hadermann, "De quelques procédés 'cubistes' en poésie," *Actes du VIIIe Congrès de l'Association Internationale de Littérature Comparée* (1980); and Wendy Steiner, *The Colors of Rhetoric* (Chicago: University of Chicago Press, 1982), respectively.

10. F. Carmody offers a narrow, temporal interpretation of cubist poetry in "L'esthétique de l'esprit nouveau," *Le flaneur des deux rives*, 2 (December 1955); Admussen defines cubist poetry strictly in terms of *Nord-Sud.*

11. Fry, 10.

12. Marling, 95.

13. Glen MacLeod sees Stevens' "The Man with a Blue Guitar" as a surrealist (rather than a cubist) poem in "Stevens and Surrealism: The Genesis of 'The Man with the Blue Guitar,'" *American Literature* 59, 3 (October 1987): 359–77. MacLeod's insistence that the particular influence of Picasso on Stevens was in his surrealist mode, however, dismisses Picasso's cubist influence on Stevens somewhat peremptorily.

14. The difference between Ezra Pound's imagistic poem, "In a Station of the Metro," and Williams' more cubist "Red Wheelbarrow" is that in the former, the interest lies almost exclusively in the mental perception created by the images, whereas in the latter the mental perception involved is complicated to mental perceptions while, simultaneously, equal interest is focused on the material construction of the poem itself. A heightened concern with the materiality of the printed page also distinguishes between what we may now call free verse and cubist verse. While the former may explore the possible "freedom" from fixed metrical feet and regular rhyme, it lacks an interest in the actual typographical elements (including different typographical fonts, unusual line and word spacing, and unexpected irregularities in punctuation and capitalization) that mark the cubist-inspired experimentation of the earliest verse in this volume. (A similar distinction, it should be noted, is readily found in French verse as well.) For further discussion of these terms, see Timothy Materer's "Imagism," Donald Wesling's "Free Verse," and my "Cubism" in *The Princeton Encyclopedia of Poetry and Poetics*, 3d ed., ed. Alex Preminger and T. V. F. Brogan (Princeton: Princeton University Press, 1992).

15. Robert Sanborn, "A Champion in the Wilderness," *Broom* 3, 3 (October 1922): 175.

16. Carolyn Burke, "The New Poetry and the New Woman," in *Coming to Light,* ed. Diane Wood Middlebrook and Marilyn Yalom (Ann Arbor: University of Michigan Press, 1985), 38.

17. Francis Ferguson, "Caravansary," review of *The Second American Caravan,* ed. Alfred Kreymborg, Paul Rosenfeld, and Lewis Mumford (New York: Macaulay, 1928), in *Hound & Horn* 2, 2 (Jan.–Mar., 1929): 174–77. The special women's number of *Others* 3, 3 (September 1916), edited by Helen Hoyt, includes Harriet Monroe, H. D., Marguerite Wilkinson, Muna Lee, Jeanne D'Orge, Marjorie Allen Seiffert, and Jean Davis, among others.

18. Marling notes that "Moore's style seemed to him [Williams] sometimes cubist, but mainly futurist" (43). Also, as Alan Filreis has recently pointed out, the contemporary perception of the literary domains during this time, at least in terms of gender, was that there was "'N.Y. criticism' on the one hand (predominantly male)" and a movement of women writers who "took native American [Indian] traditions seriously" and who "often went West"; see "Voicing the Desert of Silence: Stevens' Letters to Alice Corbin Henderson," *The Wallace Stevens Journal* 12 (1988): 6.

19. For example, in his famous "Les Demoiselles d'Avignon" (1907), Picasso violates not only traditional linear perspective but also what Edward Fry calls "the classical norm for the human figure" (Fry, 13), as he did in his many other cubist paintings. As has recently been suggested, however, the artistic "revolution" which Picasso achieved in his cubist paintings may be, disturbingly, something closer to deliberate "deformity" prompted by a specific hatred of women and by a life-long "starkly divided vision of women as madonnas or whores"; see Arianna Stassinopoulos Huffington, "Creator and Destroyer," *The Atlantic Monthly* 261, 6 (June 1988): 37–78. Although not directly concerned with my point here, this article supports my speculation about the possible psychological repugnance of cubism to a majority of women writers. See Huffington's *Picasso: Creator and Destroyer* (New York: Simon and Schuster, 1988), especially chapters 7 through 9, for a more extensive discussion of the personal violence underlying Picasso's artistic temperament.

20. In addition to the numerous contemporary articles on Stein that will be mentioned in this volume, see Marianne DeKoven, "Gertrude Stein and Modern Painting: Beyond Literary Cubism," *Contemporary Literature* 22, 1 (1981): 81–95; Randa Dubnick, *The Structure of Obscurity: Gertrude Stein, Language, and Cubism* (Urbana: University of Illinois Press, 1984); Claude Grimal, "Stein, cubiste intégrale," *Europe: Revue littéraire mensuelle* 638–39 (1982): 162–71; Eleanor Robinson, "Gertrude Stein, Cubist Teacher," *Lost Generation Journal* 2, 1 (1974): 12–14; Marilyn Gaddis Rose, "Gertrude Stein and the Cubist Narrative," *Modern Fiction Studies* 22, (1976–1977): 543–55; and Wendy Steiner, *Exact Resemblance to Exact Resemblance: The Literary Portraiture of Gertrude Stein* (New Haven: Yale University Press, 1978).

21. Steiner, *The Colors of Rhetoric;* and Willard Bohn, *The aesthetics of visual poetry, 1914–1928* (Cambridge: Cambridge University Press, 1986).

22. Sayre, 4. It is interesting to note that a special issue of *Others* (December 1917) was subtitled "A Number for the Mind's Eye / Not to Be Read Aloud."

Chapter 1: The "Kindling Breath" of the 1910s

1. Although cubism may have been superseded by other avant-garde movements since World War II, several poets discussed intermittently throughout this volume demonstrate the continued influence of this aesthetic in contemporary verse. In terms of the visual arts, Patrick De Long, who served in the military during World War II, and who most frequently paints in the cubist manner when recreating his war experience, offers an especially interesting bridge. I find it especially salient, given the idealistic impulse behind many of the poets here, that De Long uses cubist technique to express the "'life-enhancing' phase of flying" more successfully (in his opinion) than the "barbaric and 'life-negating' aspects of serial combat." See "Freedom and the Artist," M.A. Thesis, Kent State University, 1959 (iii), which includes reproductions of his paintings, as well as discussion.

2. For excellent discussions of these and other similar poets, see Marjorie Perloff, *The dance of the intellect* (Cambridge: Cambridge University Press, 1985), especially chapters 9 and 10; and Stephen Fredman, *Poet's Prose* (New York: Cambridge University Press, 1983; 2d ed., 1990), especially chapter 4. John Matthias' *Poem in Three Parts* originally appeared in his *Bucyrus* (Chicago: Swallow Press, 1970) and is being reissued, with an introduction by Michael Anania (Aquila Press, forthcoming).

3. As early as 1913, for example, Joseph Stella (among others) contrasted these two aesthetic movements by saying that "Cubism is static. Futurism is dynamic. Cubism tries to find and finds its descendance in the work of some of the old masters. Futurism strives to be absolutely free of any tradition" ("The New Art," *The Trend* 5, 3 [June 1913]: 394). However, Marius de Zayas' analysis of cubism (cited above) seems to me much more faithful to the spirit of cubist painting. In this regard, see William Marling's discussion of the confusion between the terms in his *William Carlos Williams and the Painters, 1909–1923* (Athens: Ohio University Press, 1982), 43.

4. All of the quotations which follow in this discussion are taken from *Camera Work* 36 (October 1911): 48–54.

5. I find it quite amusing that in the first issue of *291*, the journal which followed *Camera Work*, Agnes Ernst Meyer would write in reference to Huneker that "The best one can say of American art criticism is that its CLEVERNESS OFTEN CONCEALS ITS LACK OF PENETRATION" (*291*, 1 [March 1915]). The recent article on Picasso, however, "Creator and Destroyer," exposes a personal urge to destroy that either prompted or informed Picasso's work that now makes it difficult to dismiss Huneker with such amused ease; see Arianna Stassinopoulos Huffington, in *The Atlantic Monthly* 261, 6 (June 1988): 37–78, as well as *Picasso: Creator and Destroyer* (New York: Simon and Schuster, 1988).

6. See Benjamin De Casseres, "Insincerity: A New Vice," *Camera Work*, 42–43 (November 1913): 15–17; and John Weichsel, "Cosmism or Amorphism?" *Camera Work*, 42–43 (November 1913): 69–82.

7. See the entire issue of *Camera Work*, Special Number (June 1913). In

reference to Picasso's portrait of Stein, Huffington writes that with its mask-like quality, it was "a harbinger of a new direction in Picasso's art" (*Picasso*, 89).

8. See, for example, Marling, who says that Loy was "the foremost proponent of Futurist poetry in the United States" (38); in referring to Duchamp, Marling (43) is following Patrick L. Stewart, "The European Invasion of American Art and the Arensberg Circle, 1914–1918," *Arts Magazine*, 51, 9 (May 1977): 109.

9. In his discussion of Loy, Marling notes that "The white space between the lines or verses, as in Cézanne's painting, was intended to connect the parts, even to stand as a metaphor for the newly freed space" (39). More recently, however, Carolyn Burke has described Loy's visual strategies as recreating "the inner spaces of the female body"; see "The New Poetry and the New Woman," in *Coming to Light,* ed. Diane Wood Middlebrook and Marilyn Yalom (Ann Arbor: University of Michigan Press, 1985), 53.

10. John Golding, *Cubism: A History and an Analysis, 1907–1914* (New York: Harper & Row, 1959; rev. 1968), 84.

11. The series of responses to "What *291* Means to Me" is printed in *Camera Work* 47 (January 1915). Also, note that when Stieglitz advertised the new *291,* he specifically announced the intention to produce "experiments . . . based upon work which had been done with type and printers' ink, and paper, by Apollinaire in Paris, and by the Futurists in Italy" (*Camera Work* 48 [October 1916]: 62).

12. The phrase is taken from Rosalind E. Krauss, *Passages in Modern Sculpture* (New York: Viking Press, 1977).

13. Marling, 36.

14. Both poems are reprinted in Jerome Rothenberg, *The Revolution of the Word* (New York: Seabury Press, 1974), 4–7. In addition, he cites Arensberg's statement that he has "the urge to say a little about Cubism, being one of those who was expecting something from that *geometric word*" [italics mine], but who now with ironic disillusionment contemplates DADA" (4).

15. See Willard Bohn, *The aesthetics of visual poetry, 1914–1928* (Cambridge: Cambridge University Press, 1986), chapter 10.

16. Dorothy Norman, "Introducing *291.*" *291*, 1–12 (1915–1916), reprinted New York: Arno Press, 1972.

17. Burke, 48.

18. See, for example, Daniel Mark Fogel, "Imaginative Origins: 'Peter Quince at the Clavier' and Henry James," *Wallace Stevens Journal* 8, 1 (1984): 22–27; Mary Nyquist, "Musing on Susanna's Music," in *Lyric Poetry: Beyond New Criticism,* ed. Chaviva Hosek and Patricia Parker (Ithaca: Cornell University Press, 1985), 310–27; and Kinereth Meyer and Sharon Baris, "Reading the Score of 'Peter Quince at the Clavier': Stevens, Music, and the Visual Arts," *Wallace Stevens Journal* 12, 1 (1988), 56–67.

19. Marling, 61.

20. Stevens concludes this seminal poem with the lines that "the theory of description matters most" because

> everything we say
> Of the past is description without place, a cast
> Of the imagination, made in sound;
> And because what we say of the future must portend,
> Be alive with its own seemings, seeming to be
> Like rubies reddened by rubies reddening.

(*The Collected Poems of Wallace Stevens* [New York: Knopf, 1975], 345–46). The final image, which is not a physical presence but rather an intellectual presence, corresponds to many cubist paintings in strategy.

21. In this regard, consider Juan Gris' later remark in "On the Possibilities of Painting" that "all architecture is construction, but not every construction is architecture," by which he includes those constructions "intellectual, material, visual, or acoustic," in Daniel-Henry Kahnweiler, *Juan Gris: His Life and Work*, tr. Douglas Cooper (1947; rev. ed., New York: Abrams, 1969), 197; cited in Henry M. Sayre, *The Visual Text of William Carlos Williams* (Urbana: University of Illinois Press, 1983), 8.

22. Filreis, 7. In addition to a number of short articles on metrics which appeared in *Poetry*, see "The Free-verse Movement in America," *English Journal* 13 (1924): 691–705, reprinted in her *Poets & Their Art* (New York: Macmillan, 1926).

23. See the special Sonnet Number of *Poetry* 22, 6 (September 1923) for Kreymborg's sonnet series "Madonna di Campagna," which he wrote in 1922 in the village of that name; and Zukofsky's "Of Dying Beauty," *Poetry* 23, 4 (January 1924): 197.

24. Reed Whittemore, *Little Magazines*, University of Minnesota Pamphlets on American Writers, no. 32 (Minneapolis: University of Minnesota Press, 1963), 8.

25. It is critical here to remember that Pound's famous injunction to "MAKE IT NEW" describes a desire to continue tradition into a modern form which would keep tradition alive, rather than a desire to be divorced from the past.

Chapter 2: The "Revolution" of the Early 1920s

1. Sanborn, cited in Foreword above.

2. Although Reed Whittemore lists two magazines called *Contact* in his *Little Magazines*, one edited by Williams and Robert McAlmon between 1920 and 1923, the other edited by Robert Ryan, begun in 1959, there was actually an intermediate *Contact*, published in 1932, that was edited by Williams with the assistance of McAlmon and Nathanael West. (Through its brief run, this second *Contact* printed parts of what would be West's well-known novel, *Miss Lonelyhearts*.)

3. The history of the magazine(s) called *The Dial* is extremely complex. Briefly, the first one was edited by Margaret Fuller and Emerson in Boston from 1840 to 1844; the second one, begun in Chicago by Francis Brown in 1880, was primarily a critical magazine, featuring articles and reviews; the third is described by Whittemore as a "belligerent political and social

weekly"; and the fourth, the one with which we are most concerned here, became, under the leadership of such editors and writers as J. S. Watson, Scofield Thayer, Kenneth Burke, and Marianne Moore, the famous literary magazine of this period, featuring creative work (including that of Cummings, Williams, Eliot, and Sherwood Anderson, as well as Picasso, Matisse, Yeats, and Joyce); see Whittemore, *Little Magazines* (Minneapolis: University of Minnesota Press, 1963), 44–45.

4. Williams' choice of the term "free verse" (or *vers libre*) here appears to be an anomaly since, as Marjorie Perloff has pointed out, he rejected the term as early as 1913 when he declared *vers libre* a "contradiction in terms," adding that it is merely prose. See Perloff, *The dance of the intellect* (Cambridge: Cambridge University Press, 1985), 89–90, and especially note 2 (114), for a discussion of and extended references to this complex topic. However, as Carolyn Burke has recently pointed out, at this particular time the term "free verse" was being associated with "free feet" (not just a "free" metrical foot, but the freed feet of Isadora Duncan), with "free love" (especially as advocated in the free-verse poetry written by women such as Mina Loy), and—most threateningly—freed women. The impact of the female "revolution" at this time on the terminology should not be dismissed, encouraging, as it did, the use of the word "free" in several interrelated contexts. Yet, as Burke clarifies, both Gertrude Stein and Mina Loy could approach writing in this typically modernist spirit, in part because of their familiarity with contemporary art movements, *especially cubism* (emphasis added). See "The New Poetry and the New Woman: Mina Loy," in *Coming to Light*, ed. Diane Wood Middlebrook and Marilyn Yalom (Ann Arbor: University of Michigan Press, 1985), 37–57.

5. Frank Lentricchia, *Criticism and Social Change* (Chicago: University of Chicago Press, 1983), 140.

6. In the same year, Baker Brownell published an interesting article in *Others* entitled "Irrational Verse" in which he specifically calls attention to contemporary experiments with words "as sensory stuff"—a phrase which is quite applicable to both Stevens' and Williams' poems mentioned above; *Others* 5, 1 (1918): 22–25.

7. Even among his own contemporaries, Stevens was often criticized (as in the well-known instance of Stanley Burnshaw) for his lack of social awareness. For recent discussions of this topic, see Perloff, *The dance of the intellect*, especially the first chapter, "Pound/Stevens: whose era?", 1–32; and her recent indictment of Stevens' political irresponsibility in "Revolving in Crystal: The Supreme Fiction and the Impasse of Modernist Lyric," in *Wallace Stevens: The Poetics of Modernism*, ed. Albert Gelpi (Cambridge: Cambridge University Press, 1985), 41–64.

8. While I find myself sympathetic to both Pound and Stevens, Perloff correctly argues that (with the exception of Denis Donoghue) critics have felt almost forced to side with one of these poets against the other: "This is neither an idle quarrel nor a narrow sectarian war between rival academics," for the "split goes deep, and its very existence raises . . . central questions about the meaning of Modernism" (*The dance*, 2, 18).

9. See my "Wallace Stevens: Poems Against His Climate," in which I argue

that Stevens' resistance to contemporary "objectivism" as instantiated in the verse of Williams and his resistance to verbal realism in the form of political propaganda converge to produce the great poetry of his middle period, *Wallace Stevens Journal*, 11 (Fall 1987): 75–93.

10. This point is discussed by Alan Filreis in "Voicing the Desert of Silence," *Wallace Stevens Journal* 12 (Spring 1988): 6.

11. Filreis, 4.

12. See, for example, Jo-Anna Isaak, "James Joyce and the Cubist Esthetic," *Mosaic* 14, 1 (Winter 1981): 61–90; and Jessica Prinz Pecorino, "Resurgent Icons: Pound's First Pisan Canto and the Visual Arts," *Journal of Modern Literature* 9 (1982): 159–74. Andrew M. Clearfield argues, however, for a distinction between the cubist use of collage and a non-cubist use of montage: within this distinction, he sees *Ulysses* and *The Waste Land* as collages, but Pound's *Cantos* as a montage; *These Fragments I have Shored: Collage and Montage in Early Modernist Poetry* (Ann Arbor: UMI Research Press, 1984), especially 9–16.

13. Jerome Rothenberg, *The Revolution of the Word* (New York: Seabury Press, 1974), 57.

14. As Burke succinctly puts it, Loy's "writing confirmed the popular view that free verse probably led to free love" 43. For a history of the liberation of feminine sexuality in this century, see Linda Gordon, *Woman's Body, Woman's Right: A Social History of Birth Control in America* (London: Penguin, 1977).

15. Maxwell Anderson not only says that he has "read all her books on verse save one without taking whole-hearted pleasure in a solitary poem or a solitary passage," but goes on to conclude that Amy Lowell is a lifeless "cutter of gems" (which "go nicely with evening gowns and formal affairs"); "A Prejudiced Word," *The Measure*, 6 (August 1921): 17–18. The prejudice to which Anderson admits seems blatantly a sexist one. Similarly, Rolfe Humphries begins his review of Moore by stating that "Women who sit in houses, watching, develop that air of pride and bleak finality," before referring to Emily Dickinson and Moore contemptuously as "these girls" (neither of which, he feels, has much of life or passion); "Precieuse," *The Measure*, 53 (July 1925): 15–17.

16. Filreis, 15, 3.

17. The most notable differences between the version of this poem printed in *Broom* and that printed in Stevens' *Collected Poems* are that the lines "Politic man ordained/ Imagination as the fateful sin" are completely set off in the *Broom* version; and the fourth section of the poem, which has no quasi-stanza divisions in the *Collected*, has three divisions in the earlier version.

18. Picasso, cited in André Breton's "Conversation avec Picasso," ed. Christian Zervos, *Cahiers d'Art*, 10 (1935): 173; cited in Susan B. Weston, "The Artist as Guitarist, Stevens and Picasso," *Criticism* 17 (1975): 115. The phrase "hoard of destructions" and "horde of destructions" appears, variously, in Stevens' "The Man with the Blue Guitar" (Canto XV) and his essay, "The Relations between Poetry and Painting" (with specific reference to Picasso both times); for a discussion of this, see Weston, 114–15.

19. The Harry Ransom Humanities Research Center at Austin, Texas, holds

what appears to be Munson's own copies of this journal, with (notably) his own handwritten corrections of typographical errors and facts. No. 5, in particular, which was incorrectly printed as No. 6 (and corrected in Munson's hand), includes the review of Cummings discussed in the text and bears the marks of several original corrections.

20. Henry M. Sayre, *The Visual Text of William Carlos Williams* (Chicago: University of Illinois Press, 1983), 49.

21. In contradistinction to Williams' own autobiographical account of the relative spontaneity of this poem, William Marling has offered a persuasive aesthetic connection between "Klange" and "The Great Figure"; see his *William Carlos Williams and the Painters, 1909–1923* (Athens: Ohio University Press, 1982), 174.

22. Sayre, 35.

23. Stevens, to Alice Corbin Henderson (November 17, 1922); cited in Filreis, 19.

Chapter 3: The "Predominant Force" of the Late 1920s to Early 1930s

1. Edward F. Fry, *Cubism* (New York: Oxford University Press, 1966), 11.

2. With both humor and understatement, Barry Ahearn notes that "The creation of Louis Zukofsky's lone poem 'A' took almost fifty years. It will probably be another fifty before we have a good idea of what it all amounts to," *Zukofsky's "A": An Introduction* (Berkeley, Los Angeles, London: University of California Press, 1982), xi. In terms of the end of cubism in the visual arts, it is worth noting that both Juan Gris' "Dish of Pears" and Charles Demuth's "I Saw the Figure 5 in Gold" were painted after 1925.

3. As Charles Russel has pointed out, the revolutionary aspect of the modern artistic movements weighed upon the consciousness of all writers in the "modern" era—both the "possibilities—and responsibilities," regardless of the particular aesthetic movement with which they might be aligned; see *Poets, Prophets, & Revolutionaries* (New York: Oxford University Press, 1985), 62.

4. See Marjorie Perloff, *The dance of the intellect* (Cambridge: Cambridge University Press, 1985), especially "The portrait of the artist as collage-text: Pound's *Gaudier-Brzeska* and the 'italic' texts of John Cage," 33–73.

5. Richard L. Admussen, "*Nord-Sud* and Cubist Poetry," *Journal of Aesthetics and Art Criticism* 27 (1968): 21–25.

6. As actually printed in *The Exile,* Hemingway's poem bears the misspelled title of "NOTHOEMIST POEM." One of the original issues held at the Newberry Library in Chicago, however, has the helpful emendation "Neothomist" penciled in the margin.

7. Perloff, 35.

8. As Henry Sayre has pointed out, this 1926 painting, which appeared untitled in this particular issue of *transition,* probably had a specific influence on the poetry of Williams; see *The Visual Text of William Carlos Williams* (Urbana: University of Illinois Press, 1983), 27–28.

9. Stevens, "Study of Two Pears," in his *Collected Poems* (New York: Knopf, 1975), 196–97. While this poem bears an obvious relation to the work of Cézanne in some of its sections, the entire poem — as well as the last section quoted above — presents the kind of cubist change in perspective that borders on abstraction (such as Gris' painting is intended to evoke).

10. Notably, Winters distinguishes experimental poetry from "pseudo-experimental" poetry (the latter of which he derides, giving Cummings as an example) in his *In Defense of Reason: A Study of American Experimental Poetry* (Chicago: Swallow Press, n.d.), 86; for further discussion, see Sayre, 17–18.

11. *New Directions in Prose and Poetry*, ed. James Laughlin (Norfolk, Conn.: New Directions, 1936).

12. See Sayre, 16–18.

13. Ibid., 16.

14. In addition to Spector's poem mentioned above, consider his "I'll Be Goddamned," Alfred Kreymborg's "Black Chant, 1917," Spector's "These Are Those Back-Again, Once-Before, Home-Again Blues," and William Closson Emory's "Theme for a Blues Song," published in subsequent issues of this journal.

15. Williams, "The Poem as a Field of Action" (1948); reprinted in *Selected Essays of William Carlos Williams* (New York: Random House, 1954), 290.

16. See Charles Tomlinson's discussion of Rexroth's remark in *William Carlos Williams: Selected Poems*, ed. C. Tomlinson (New York: New Directions, 1985), xi.

17. Neil Baldwin, "The Letters of William Carlos Williams to Louis Zukofsky: A Chronicle of Trust and Difficulty," in *WCW & Others*, ed. Dave Oliphant and Thomas Zigal (Austin: HRHRC, 1985), 122.

18. Stevens, *The Necessary Angel* (New York: Vintage, 1951), 168.

19. Stevens, letter to José Rodriguez Feo, December 19, 1946; in his *Letters* (New York: Knopf, 1972), 544. These facts have been discussed, though with a somewhat different interpretation, in Perloff, "Pound/Stevens: whose era?" in *The dance*, 8 ff. See also my "Wallace Stevens: Poems Against His Climate," *Wallace Stevens Journal* 11, 2 (1987): 75–93, for a discussion of Stevens' particular misunderstanding of Williams and of the political ramifications of that misunderstanding which were realized in the poetry he wrote during World War II.

20. Laughlin, xi.

Chapter 4: The Waning of Cubism in the Late 1930s to Early 1940s

1. Dated January 21, 1931 by H. D.; reprinted in *The New Republic Anthology: 1915–1935*, ed. Groff Conklin (New York: Dodge, 1936), 370.

2. As Arianna Stassinopoulos Huffington has recently pointed out, both of these pictures are informed by personal violence and abuse; see "Creator and Destroyer," *The Atlantic Monthly* 261, 6 (June 1988), especially 59–61, as well as her recent book by the same name. Huffington's detailing of

Picasso's life makes Stevens' remark in "Effects of Analogy" (*The Necessary Angel* [New York: Viking 1951], 120), not merely prescient but precise:

> Now, the poet manifests his personality, first of all, by his choice of subject. . . . What is true of poets in this respect is equally true of painters, as the existence of schools of painters all doing more or less the same thing at the same time demonstrates. The leader of the school has a subject. But his followers merely have his subject. Thus Picasso has a subject, a subject that devours him and devastates his region.

For further discussion of the source of the phrase "horde of destructions," see chapter 2, note 18, above.

3. James Laughlin, "Preface: New Directions," in *New Directions in Prose and Poetry* (Norfolk, Conn.: New Directions, 1936), vii.

4. Gerald L. Bruns, "Law as Hermeneutics," in *The Politics of Interpretation*, ed. Robert von Hallberg (Chicago: University of Chicago Press, 1983), 319.

5. For a lengthy discussion of the place of poetry in our own political climate, see Terrence Des Pres, *Praises & Dispraises: Poetry and Politics, the 20th Century* (New York: Viking, 1988), in particular chapter 2 and the very moving "Conclusion."

6. See the discussion of this 1912 issue of *Camera Work* in chapter 1 above.

7. In 1968 Oppen humorously defended himself against the charge that his poetry resembled Williams' by saying that "the opposite is true"; interview with L. S. Dembo, first printed as "George Oppen," *Contemporary Literature,* 10 (Spring 1969): 159–77; cited in Marjorie Perloff, "'The Shape of the Lines': Oppen and the Metric of Difference," in *George Oppen: Man and Poet,* ed. Burton Hatlen (Orono, Maine: National Poetry Foundation, 1981), 215.

8. See Babette Deutsch's review of *Discrete Series* in *New York Herald Tribune Books* (1 April 1934): 16; cited in part in *George Oppen* (previous note), 464. Williams' "The New Poetical Economy," *Poetry* 44, 4 (July 1934): 220–225 is reprinted in its entirety in *George Oppen,* 267–70.

9. Pound's distinction between the two poets first appeared in the "Preface" to *Discrete Series* (New York: Objectivist Press, 1934), v; cited in Perloff, 216. For her lengthy discussion of the metrical difference between Oppen and Williams, see all of "'The Shape of the Lines,'" 216–229.

10. See Abby Shapiro, "Building a Phenomenological World: Cubist Technique in the Poetry of George Oppen," in *George Oppen,* 243–256.

11. Oppen, from *Discrete Series,* reprinted in *The Collected Poems of George Oppen* (New York: New Directions, 1975), 14.

12. Cited in Burton Hatlen and Tom Mandel, "Poetry and Politics: A Conversation with George and Mary Oppen" [interview, June, 1980], in *George Oppen,* 26.

13. "Of Hours," from *Seascape: Needle's Eye* (1972); reprinted in *Collected Poems,* 210–12.

14. The basic tenet of much of the finest contemporary criticism and theory is that all language is unavoidably and inextricably bound to political situations, so that quite literally verbal texts and the texture of life are

inseparable. If we accept this premise, then the new revelations about Picasso (in "Creator and Destroyer"), further evidence of Pound's anti-Semitism (see Robert Casillo, *The Genealogy of Demons: Anti-Semitism, Fascism, and the Myths of Ezra Pound* [Evanston, Ill.: Northwestern University Press, 1988]), and certain troubling facts about Stevens' relation to his wife (see Joan Richardson, *Wallace Stevens: The Early Years, 1879–1923* [New York: Morrow, 1986]) may present serious challenges to the previously reigning critical interpretations of their work.

15. Laughlin, xi; subsequent quotation, viii.

16. Jean Cocteau, "The Laic Mystery," tr. Olga Rudge; in *New Directions*, 22.

17. See Glen MacLeod, "Stevens and Surrealism: The Genesis of 'The Man with the Blue Guitar,'" *American Literature* 59, 3 (1987): 359–77.

18. See the series of letters Stevens wrote to Renato Poggioli in 1953 about this poem in *Letters of Wallace Stevens*, ed. Holly Stevens (New York: Knopf, 1972), especially 25 June 1953, 783; and the earlier letters to Hi Simons in 1940, especially 8 August 1940, 360.

19. Stevens' rejection of surrealism is discussed later in this chapter; however, the rejection of surrealism, at least on Stevens' part, is the flip side of the concurrent attraction to abstraction in art (as in the paintings of Paul Klee, one of Stevens' favorite painters by the mid-1940s).

20. See Williams' "Charles Sheeler—Paintings—Drawings—Photography" (1939); reprinted in *Selected Essays of William Carlos Williams* (New York: Random House, 1954), 234.

21. Wallace Stevens, "The Noble Rider and the Sound of Words," first read at Princeton University, 1941; reprinted in *The Necessary Angel*, 27.

22. Ibid., 28.

23. Frank Lentricchia, *Ariel and the Police* (Madison: University of Wisconsin Press, 1988), 217.

24. Reed Whittemore, *Little Magazines*, University of Minnesota Pamphlets on American Writers, no. 32 (Minneapolis: University of Minnesota Press, 1963), 40.

25. Ibid., 5.

26. Ibid., 33.

27. *Letters*, 387.

28. Ibid., 326.

29. In a telephone conversation (16 February 1990) and subsequently in correspondence (letter to author; 17 February 1990), Ernest Kroll traces his sense of his own aesthetics through a collage-like conflation of influences, including Imagism, early twentieth-century poets (Stevens, Williams, Cummings, Frost, and Robinson), and the desire for "concision, speed, wit, and music." He goes on to add, "But my influences go back to the Roman and Greek classics, as well as to the haiku masters of Japan and the Chinese poets Po Chu I and Tu Fu in the Arthur Waley versions."

30. Whittemore, 42.

31. "Materia Poetica" appeared in *View* 1, 1 (September 1940): 3; and again in *View*, 2d series, 3 (October 1942): 28.

32. *Letters,* 622.
33. Oscar Williams, *New Poems 1944* (New York: Howell, Soskin, 1944), vi.

Conclusion

1. William Carlos Williams, review of Ford Maddox Ford's *Parade's End* (New York: Knopf, 1950), in *Sewanee Review* (1951). Reprinted in *Selected Essays of William Carlos Williams* (New York: Random House, 1954), 315.

2. *Stevens and Simile: A Theory of Language* (Princeton: Princeton University Press, 1986), 24.

3. See Carolyn Burke, "The New Poetry and the New Woman," in *Coming to Light,* ed. Diane Wood Middlebrook and Marilyn Yalom (Ann Arbor: University of Michigan Press, 1985), n. 39.

4. J. B. Kerfoot's remark, first printed in *Life,* is reprinted as the foreword page to *Others* 1, 5 (1915); the second quotation, taken from James Huneker, is reprinted in *Camera Work* 36 (October 1911) and discussed in chapter 1 above.

5. "The Poem as a Field of Action," reprinted in *Selected Essays,* 281; subsequent quotation, 291.

6. Robert Duncan, *The Opening of the Field* (New York: Grove Press, 1960). This volume manipulates both the legacy of the cubist tradition and the more modern rejection of this tradition, especially in the scattered series of poems entitled "The Structure of Rime" (I–XIII).

7. Stevens' essay, first read at the New York Museum of Modern Art in 1951 and subsequently published by the Museum as a pamphlet, is reprinted in *The Necessary Angel* (New York: Vintage), 159–76. I would like to credit Linda Taylor with calling to my attention the critical context, particularly in terms of cubism, of this important essay.

8. Roy Harvey Pearce has long maintained that understanding the "de-creative" mode in Stevens is critical to understanding nearly all his major works, though without the particular background of the possibility of cubist "destruction" I am describing here; see "Toward Decreation: Stevens and the 'Theory of Poetry,'" in *Wallace Stevens: A Celebration,* ed. Frank Doggett and Robert Buttell (Princeton: Princeton University Press, 1980), 286–307.

9. Jacques Derrida, *The Truth in Painting,* tr. Geoff Bennington and Ian McLeod (Chicago: University of Chicago Press, 1987); the quotation from Cézanne (2) is taken from a letter to Emile Bernard, 23 October 1905.

10. Although, as any reader of Derrida well knows, any single quotation is suspect when taken out of context, we should take seriously the import of this part of his discussion of "The Arnolfini Marriage": "The notion of reliability is here anterior to the opposition between the useful and the sacred. Without reliability there would be no usable product, but nor would there be any symbolic object," 351.

11. In calling Derrida a "cubist writer," I am appealing to the conception of cubism developed in this volume, one which concentrates on the implicit ethics of multiplicity, rather than to the stereotyped assertion that visual

324

cubism was a movement trying to recapture (rather than subvert) form. While possibly true of the earliest of cubist works, such motivation does not account for the majority of paintings termed cubist, much less the body of literature and poetry influenced by cubism.

12. Jed Rasula, "The Politics of, the Politics in," in *Politics and Poetic Value,* ed. Robert von Hallberg (Chicago: University of Chicago Press, 1987), 320. See also Robert Pinsky's "Responsibilities of the Poet" (von Hallberg, 18), in which he argues that

> The poet's first social responsibility, to continue the art, can be filled only through the second, opposed responsibility to change the terms of the art as given—and it is given socially, which is to say politically.

Select Bibliography for Further Reading

ADMUSSEN, RICHARD L. "*Nord-Sud* and Cubist Poetry." *Jornal of Aesthetics and Art Criticism* 27 (1968): 21–25.

ALTIERI, CHARLES. "Picasso's Collages and the Force of Cubism." *Kenyon Review* 6 (1984): 8–33.

BENNETT, BENJAMIN K. "Strindberg and Ibsen: Toward a Cubism of Time in Drama." *Modern Drama* 26 (1983): 262–81.

BEVERIDGE, NANCY. "Mayakovsky and Cubism." *Rackham Literary Studies* 2 (1972): 89–96.

BLUMENKRANZ-ONIMUS, NEOMI. "Cubisme et futurisme italien." *Europe: Revue littéraire mensuelle* 638–39 (June–July 1982): 150–61.

BOHN, WILLARD. *The aesthetics of visual poetry, 1914–1928.* Cambridge: Cambridge University Press, 1986.

———. "Joan Salvat-Papasseit and Visual Form." *Kentucky Romance Quarterly* 30 (1983): 29–43.

———. "Landscaping the Visual Sign: Apollinaire's 'Paysage.'" *Philological Quarterly* 65 (1986): 347–69.

BORDAT, DENIS, AND BERNARD VECK. *Apollinaire.* Paris: Hachette, 1983.

BREUNIG, LEROY C. "From Dada to Cubism: Apollinaire's 'Arbre.'" *About French Poetry from Dada to "Tel quel": Text and Theory.* Ed. Mary Ann Caws. Detroit: Wayne State University Press, 1974. Pp. 25–41.

BREUNIG, L. C., AND J.-C. CHEVALIER. *Les peintres cubistes.* Paris: Hermann, 1965.

BROUGHTON, PANTHEA REID. "The Cubist Novel: Toward Defining the Genre." '*A Cosmos of My Own': Faulkner and Yoknapatawpha, 1980.* Ed. Doreen Fowler and Ann J. Abadie. Jackson: University of Mississippi Press, 1981. Pp. 36–58.

———. "Faulkner's Cubist Novels." '*A Cosmos of My Own': Faulkner and Yoknapatawpha, 1980.* Ed. Doreen Fowler and Ann J. Abadie. Jackson: University of Mississippi Press, 1981. Pp. 59–94.

BURKE, CAROLYN. "The New Poetry and the New Woman: Mina Loy." *Coming to Light: American Women Poets in the Twentieth Century.* Ed. Diane Wood Middlebrook and Marilyn Yalom. Ann Arbor: University of Michigan Press, 1985. Pp. 37–57.

BUSH, ANN MARIE, AND LOUIS D. MITCHELL. "Jean Toomer: A Cubist Poet." *Black American Literature Forum* 17 (1983): 106–8.

CHAPON, FRANÇOIS. "De quelques livres de poètes et de peintres." *Europe: Revue littéraire mensuelle* 638-39 (1982): 32-44.

CHEVALIER, J.-C., AND L.C. BREUNIG. "Apollinaire et 'Les Peintres cubistes.'" *Revue des lettres modernes* 104-7 (1964): 89-112.

CLEARFIELD, ANDREW. *These Fragments I Have Shored: Collage and Montage in Early Modernism.* Ann Arbor: UMI Research Press, 1984.

CUTLER, ANTHONY. "Acrobats and Angels: Art and Poetry in the Cubist Period." *Emory University Quarterly* 20 (1964): 52-56.

DEBON, CLAUDE. "'L'Ecriture cubiste' d'Apollinaire." *Europe: Revue littéraire mensuelle* 638-39 (1982): 118-27.

DECAUDIN, MICHEL. "Cubisme littéraire: Le cas fermée." *Europe: Revue littéraire mensuelle* 638-39 (1982): 133-37.

———. "Petite histoire d'une appelation: 'Cubisme littéraire.'" *Europe: Revue littéraire mensuelle* 638-39 (1982): 7-25.

DEKOVEN, MARIANNE. "Gertrude Stein and Modern Painting: Beyond Literary Cubism." *Contemporary Literature* 22 (1982): 81-95.

DES PRES, TERRENCE. *Praises & Dispraises: Poetry and Politics, the 20th Century.* New York: Viking Press, 1988.

DIJKSTRA, BRAM. *The Hieroglyphics of a New Speech.* Princeton: Princeton University Press, 1969.

DUBNICK, RANDA. *The Structure of Obscurity: Gertrude Stein, Language, and Cubism.* Urbana: University of Illinois Press, 1984.

FRY, EDWARD F. *Cubism.* New York: Oxford University Press, 1978.

GOLDING, JOHN. *Cubism: A History and an Analysis, 1907-1914.* New York: Harper & Row, 1959. Rev. ed. 1968.

GREEN, ROBERT. "The Good Soldier: Ford's Cubist Novel." *Modernist Studies: Literature and Culture 1920-1940* 3 (1979): 49-59.

GRIMAL, CLAUDE. "Stein, cubiste intégrale." *Europe: Revue littéraire mensuelle* 638-39 (1982): 162-71.

HADERMANN, PAUL. "De quelques procédés 'cubistes' en poésie." *Actes du VIIIe Congrès de l'Association Internationale de Littérature Comparée.* Ed. Bela Kopeczi and Gyorgy M. Vajda. Stuttgart: Bieber, 1980. Vol. 1, pp. 901-5.

HELLERSTEIN, NINA. "The Position of Georges Braque in 'Quelques réflexions sur la peinture cubiste' of Paul Claudel." *Claudel Studies* 10 (1983): 24-31.

HOMER, WILLIAM INNES. *Alfred Stieglitz and the American Avant-Garde.* Boston: New York Graphic Society, 1977.

HUBERT, ETIENNE-ALAIN. "Pierre Reverdy et le 'poésie plastique' de son temps." *Europe: Revue littéraire mensuelle* 638-39 (1982): 109-18.

IGLY, FRANCE. *Apollinaire, poète ami et défenseur des peintres cubistes: Choix de poèmes.* Sherbrooke: Naaman, 1982.

ISAAK, JO-ANNA. "James Joyce and the Cubist Esthetic." *Mosaic* 14 (1981): 61-90.

KAMBER, G. *Max Jacob and the Poetics of Cubism.* Baltimore: Johns Hopkins University Press, 1971.

KENNER, HUGH. "The Cubist Portrait." *Approaches to Joyce's Ulysses: Ten Essays.* Ed. Thomas F. Staley and Bernard Benstock. Pittsburgh: Pittsburgh University Press, 1976. Pp. 171-84.

KERN, STEPHEN. *The Culture of Time and Space.* Cambridge: Harvard University Press, 1983.

KIDDER, RUSHWORTH M. "Cummings and Cubism: The Influence of the Visual Arts on Cummings' Early Poetry." *Journal of Modern Literature* 7 (1979): 255–91.

KLEIN, MICHAEL. "John Covert and the Arensberg Circle: Symbolism, Cubism and Protosurrealism." *Arts Magazine* 51, 9 (1977): 113–15.

KOUIDIS, VIRGINIA M. *Mina Loy, American Modernist Poet.* Baton Rouge: Louisiana State University Press, 1980.

KRAUSS, ROSALIND. *Passages in Modern Sculpture.* New York: Viking Press, 1977.

KRONHAUSER, JULIAN. "Kubisticni prostor v poeziji Radeta Drainca." *Slavisticna Revija* 34 (1986): 273–78.

LEAVENS, ILEANA B. *From "291" to Zürich: The Birth of Dada.* Ann Arbor: UMI Research Press, 1983.

LEROY, CLAUDE. "Braque écrivain ou la signature du peintre." *Europe: Revue littéraire mensuelle* 638–39 (1982): 59–67.

———. Foreword to "Cubisme et littérature." *Europe: Revue littéraire mensuelle* 638–39 (1982): 3–5.

LEVESON, MARCIA. "*The Love Song of J. Alfred Prufrock* as a Cubist Poem." *English Studies in Africa* 26 (1983): 129–39.

MACGOWAN, CHRISTOPHER. *William Carlos Williams' Early Poetry: The Visual Arts Background.* Ann Arbor: UMI Research Press, 1984.

MACLEOD, GLEN. *Wallace Stevens and Company: The Harmonium Years, 1913–1923.* Ann Arbor: UMI Research Press, 1983.

MARCEILLAC, LAURENCE. "Cubisme et théâtre: Les Réalisations de Valmier pour art et action." *Revue d'histoire du théâtre* 35 (1983): 338–47.

MARCH-MARTUL, KATHLEEN. "Cubist Fluctuant Representation in the Creacionista Poetry of Gerardo Diego." *Romance Notes* 22 (1981): 155–60.

MARCUS, SUSAN. "The Typographic Element in Cubism, 1911–1915: Its Formal and Semantic Implications." *Visible Language* 6 (1972): 32–40.

MARLING, WILLIAM. "Tense, Inquisitive Clash: William Carlos Williams and Marcel Duchamp." *Southwest Review* 66 (1981): 361–75.

———. *William Carlos Williams and the Painters, 1909–1923.* Athens: University of Ohio Press, 1982.

MESSLER, NORBERT. "Kunst und Literatur des Kubismus: Pablo Picasso und Gertrude Stein." *Universitas* 40 (1985): 557–68.

MILHAU, DENIS. "Lecture du cubisme par deux poètes: Apollinaire et Reverdy." *Europe: Revue littéraire mensuelle* 638–39 (1982): 44–55.

MITCHELL, W. J. T. *Iconology: Image, Text, Ideology.* Chicago: University of Chicago Press, 1988.

MOORE, PATRICK. "Cubist Prosody: William Carlos Williams and the Conventions of Verse Lineation." *Philological Quarterly* 65 (1986): 515–36.

MORSE, RICHARD M. "Triangulating Two Cubists: William Carlos Williams and Oswald de Andrade." *Latin American Literary Review* 14 (1986): 175–83.

NAUMANN, FRANCIS. "Cryptography and the Arensberg Circle." *Arts Magazine* 51, 9 (1977): 127–33.

———. "Walter Conrad Arensberg: Poet, Patron, and Participant in the New York Avant-Garde, 1915–1920." *Philadelphia Museum of Art Bulletin* 76, 238 (1980).

PECORINO, JESSICA PRINZ. "Resurgent Icons: Pound's First Pisan Canto and the Visual Arts." *Journal of Modern Literature* 9 (1982): 159–74.

PERLOFF, MARJORIE. *The dance of the intellect.* Cambridge: Cambridge University Press, 1985.

————. *The Futurist Moment*. Chicago: University of Chicago Press, 1986.

————. "Revolving in Crystal: The Supreme Fiction and the Impasse of Modernism." *Wallace Stevens: The Poetics of Modernism.* Ed. Albert Gelpi. Cambridge: Cambridge University Press, 1985. Pp. 41-64.

PLACELLA SOMMELLA, PAOLA. *Marcel Proust e i movimenti pittorici d'avanguardia.* Rome: Bulzoni, 1982.

ROBINSON, ELEANOR. "Gertrude Stein, Cubist Teacher." *Lost Generation Journal* 2 (1974): 12-14.

ROSE, MARILYN GADDIS. "Gertrude Stein and the Cubist Narrative." *Modern Fiction Studies* 22 (1976-1977): 543-55.

————. "The Impasse of Cubist Literature: Picasso, Stein, Jacob." *Actes du VIIIe Congrès de l'Association Internationale de Littérature Comparée.* Ed. Bela Kopeczi and Gyorgy M. Vajda. Stuttgart: Bieber, 1980. Vol. 1, pp. 685-92.

ROTHENBERG, JEROME. *The Revolution of the Word.* New York: Seabury Press, 1974.

SAYRE, HENRY M. "Ready-Mades and Other Measures: The Poetics of Marcel Duchamp and William Carlos Williams." *Journal of Modern Literature* 8 (1980): 3-22.

————. *The Visual Text of William Carlos Williams.* Urbana: University of Illinois Press, 1983.

Schlumberger, E. "*Camera Work.*" *Connaissance des arts* 26 (1982): 88-93.

SCOBIE, STEPHEN. "Apollinaire and the Naming of Cubism." *Canadian Review of Comparative Literature* 5 (1978): 53-71.

SHAPIRO, ABBY. "Building a Phenomenological World: Cubist Technique in the Poetry of George Oppen." *George Oppen: Man and Poet.* Ed. Burton Hatlen. Orono: National Poetry Foundation, University of Maine at Orono, 1981. Pp. 243-56.

SOLA, AGNES. "Cubisme et futurisme russe." *Europe: Revue littéraire mensuelle* 638-39 (1982): 144-50.

STEINER, WENDY. *The Colors of Rhetoric.* Chicago: University of Chicago Press, 1982.

————. "A Cubist Historiography." *The Structure of the Literary Process: Studies Dedicated to the Memory of Felix Vodicka.* Ed. Peter Steiner et al. Amsterdam: Benjamins, 1982. Pp. 521-45.

————. *Exact Resemblance to Exact Resemblance: The Literary Portraiture of Gertrude Stein.* New Haven: Yale University Press, 1978.

STEWART, JACK F. "Cubist Elements in *Between the Acts.*" *Mosaic* 18 (1985): 65-89.

STEWART, PATRICK L. "The European Art Invasion: American Art and the Arensberg Circle, 1914-1918." *Arts Magazine* 51, 9 (1977): 108-12.

SYPHER, WYLIE. *Rococo to Cubism in Art and Literature.* New York: Random House, 1960.

TASHJIAN, DICKRAN. *William Carlos Williams and the American Scene, 1920-1940.* New York: Whitney Museum of American Art, 1978.

THAU, ANNETTE. "Max Jacob and Cubism." *La revue des lettres modernes* 474-78 (1976): 145-72.

THOMAS, F. RICHARD. *Literary Admirers of Alfred Stieglitz.* Carbondale: Southern Illinois University Press, 1983.

TOMLINSON, DAVID. "T. S. Eliot and the Cubists." *Twentieth Century Literature* 26 (1980): 64-81.

TUCKER, JOHN. "William Faulkner's *As I Lay Dying:* Working Out the Cubistic Bugs." *Texas Studies in Literature and Language: A Journal of the Humanities* 26 (1984): 388–404.

VANOYE, FRANCIS. "Ciné-cubisme." *Europe: Revue littéraire mensuelle* 638–39 (1982): 81–87.

WHITTEMORE, REED. *Little Magazines.* University of Minnesota Pamphlets on American Writers, no. 32. Minneapolis: University of Minnesota Press, 1963.

ZILCZO, JUDITH. "Robert J. Coady, Man of *The Soil.*" *Dada/Surrealism* 14 (1985): 31–43.

ZINNES, HARRIET, ed. *Ezra Pound and the Visual Arts.* New York: New Directions, 1980.

Index

Abstraction, 116, 321 n. 9, 323 n. 19

Admussen, Richard L., 313 n. 9

Aesthetic autonomy, 124–125

Aesthetics: and cultural binding, 236–238; divisiveness of in poetry, theory, and canon formation, 124–125; and politics, relationship of, 123–125, 127, 245, 280–284; relation to war(s), 237; vs. economics, 237–238

Ahearn, Barry, *Zukofsky's "A": An Introduction,* 320 n. 2

Aiken, Conrad, "The Function of Criticism," 70–71

Aisen, Maurice, "The Latest in Art and Picabia," 14

"Anamyths, Psychographs and Other Prose-Texts," 177

Anderson, Margaret, 8, 32; "A Deeper Music," 62; "Toward Revolution," 61–62

Anderson, Maxwell, "A Prejudiced Word on Amy Lowell," 70

Anderson, Sherwood, 66, 318 n. 3

Angleton, James, 248

Apollinaire, Guillaume, 4, 64, 71, 316 n. 11: "Aesthetic Meditations," 65; *Calligrammes,* 22; "Ideogramme," 21; *Les peintres cubistes,* 4

Arensberg, Walter, 7, 19, 27, 316 n. 14; "An Old Game," 20; "Arithmetical Progression of the Verb 'To Be'," 20, 121; "Human," 19; "Ing," 20, 121

Armory Show, 11, 12, 14, 20

Arnold, Matthew, "Dover Beach," 18

Atkin, David, 11

Baldwin, Neil, 123

Baris, Sharon. *See* Meyer, Kinereth

Barnes, Djuna, 16, 65, 66

Barzun (Henri Martin), "Fragment de l'universel poème," 118

Becher, Johannes R. *See* Benn, Gottfried

Benn, Gottfried and Johannes R. Becher, "Can the Poet Change the World?", 123–124

Bible, as allusion, 23

Bishop, Elizabeth, 246

Blast, 114

Blues [musical], 120–121

Blues, x, 7, 61, 113, 118, 126, 238, 239, 250, 252; discussion of, 119–125

Bohn Willard, 9, 21

Bollingen Prize, 124, 249, 282

Botticelli, Sandro, 69

Brancusi, Constantin, 64

Braque, Georges, 11, 15, 21, 22, 64; "Hommage à J. S. Bach," 116; "Woman with a Guitar," 116, 126

Breen, Stella, "My Five Husbands," 114

Breton, André, 253; "Conversation avec Picasso," 319 n. 18

Brogan, Jacqueline Vaught, 280; "Cubism," 313 n. 14; "Wallace Stevens: Poems Against His

333

Designer: Linda M. Robertson
Compositor: Harrison Typesetting, Inc.
Text: 10/12 Baskerville
Display: Franklin Gothic Demi
Printer: Braun-Brumfield, Inc.
Binder: Braun-Brumfield, Inc.